Countermodernism

and

Francophone Literary Culture

NEW AMERICANISTS *A Series Edited by Donald E. Pease*

Countermodernism and Francophone Literary Culture

THE GAME OF SLIPKNOT

Keith L. Walker

Duke University Press Durham & London
1999

Printed in the United States of America on acid-free paper ∞
Designed by C. H. Westmoreland
Typeset in Plantin Light with Futura Bold display by Tseng Information Systems, Inc.
Library of Congress Cataloging-in-Publication Data appear on the last printed page of this book.

An abbreviated earlier version of chapter 2 appeared as "Le rire chez Damas," in *Rencontres littéraires francophones Léon Gontran Damas,* ed. Jacqueline Leiner (Paris, 1988). A version of chapter 5 appeared in *Postcolonial Subjects: Francophone Women Writers,* ed. Mary Jean Green et al. (Minnesota: University of Minnesota Press, 1996).

To DJ, Alma, my father, William E. Walker, and

my mother, the most passionate and luminous

Gwendolyn Valora Walker

Contents

Acknowledgments

Interactions with so many friends, teachers, and colleagues and their work have constituted a major part of the pleasure of the realization of this book. I wish to thank Michael Riffaterre, whose thinking on the work that rhetorical figures, signs, and texts do has sharpened my understanding of the power exerted by words, images, and theories in the way we perceive ourselves; Edward Said, the most Césairian of postcolonial scholars, whose incomparable eloquence on the subjects of colonialism, imperialism, and culture during a seminar at the School of Criticism and Theory has profoundly inspired my work; Homi Bhabha, who read the first draft of chapter 7 and offered much appreciated organizational suggestions; Léon François Hoffman, always my professor, and whose study *Le Nègre romantique,* as will become evident, is for me personally a haunting work of research into the French literary imagination; Sylvia Wynter, whose committed and rigorously intellectual scholarship is a model of thinking and engagement in the tradition of C. L. R. James and Aimé Césaire; Donald Pease, whose excitement about this project remains for me a galvanizing force; John A. Rassias, whose philosophy of language teaching and study since the 1960s has always embraced the universals —what makes us human—as well as the defining particulars of francophone literary culture; Raymond Hall, a sociologist who appreciates literature and who invited me to present an early version of chapter 6 at his University Seminar on Social Domination and Subordination; Elaine Jahner, colleague and team teacher who is always working at the borders of cultural exchange; Raoul Bueno-Chavez, who has shared with me the comparatist's enthusiasm for the study of the multilingual realities of Latin American and Caribbean cultures; Graziella Parati, who has broadened my understanding of women's autobiography and of the eventual intersections of the francophone with the cultural and linguistic complexities of italophone literary culture; Gérard Etienne and Natania Fuerbacher, who have supported my research and provided me with texts, background materials, and no small amount of encouragement; Euzhan Palcy, who has been an inspiring example of artistry and intellectual commitment to francophone literary culture; and finally, Aimé Césaire, with whom it all began and who gave me "La force de regarder demain."

Introduction

In the Denunciatory Tradition

There are many successful ways of thinking about francophone literature. Most approaches, and university presses, group literature strictly according to region: French West Africa, the Caribbean, North Africa, or Southeast Asia, as in Jack Yaeger's important study *The Vietnamese Novel.*[1] There is the thematic approach, which traces a theme such as the journey in a set of texts from a particular region of the francophone world, as in Mildred Mortimer's *Journeys through the French African Novel* or Eileen Julien's suggestive work *African Novels and the Question of Orality.*[2] Notions of race often separate, artificially, North African literature from Black African literature. Gender studies and cultural studies have produced collections and analyses that focus uniquely on texts by women from varying cultural backgrounds; the contributors to these studies are, for the most part, women, as in *Postcolonial Subjects: Francophone Women Writers,*[3] by Mary Jean Green et al. *Countermodernism and Francophone Literary Culture: The Game of Slipknot* seeks to move across the traditionally imposed boundaries of geography and race by studying six representative francophone writers and the interrelated preoccupations of their works. This study is not intended to be a panorama of francophone literature but rather, first of all, a close reading of the works of Aimé Césaire, Léon Gontran Damas, Mariama Bâ, Tahar ben Jelloun, Ken Bugul, and Gérard Etienne. Second, this study considers the rich and instructive relationships between the works of these six authors. Finally, it traces the literary legacy of Aimé Césaire, charting in particular the extent to which the authors and texts selected develop aspects of the agenda his works established. It is Césaire's work that is studied in counterpoint to certain modernist principles of Charles Baudelaire and that serves as the primary source for the notion of the *countermodern.* One of my objectives is to write of this literary culture in terms that are accessible to nonspecialists. From the immanence of the experience of six different writers to the transcendence of the francophone experience, what emerges is a study that bridges the present-day divisions in the study of francophone literature, for colonialism and neocolonialism are global projects of domination, exploitation, and consequence.

This study is driven by a notion of culture, of francophone culture in particular, and the sociogenetic formation of the colonialized and postcolonial subject. As Fanon points out, "Besides ontogeny, there is sociogeny."[4] A Fanonian notion of culture, characterized by a fluctuating and creative instability, requires one to consider culture in its multifacetedness in order to grasp, to some extent, the complexity of the whole. Francophone culture is that all-embracing reality in which questions of language, economics, politics, gender, religion, and the consequences of the moral relativism and false ethnography of the colonial project are intertwined. What it means to be White or Black, to be the colonizer or the colonialized, to be a man or a woman—and, ultimately, what it means to be human—constitutes an intricate slipknot of relations. Thus, in the same vein as the critical stance of Black American feminist critic Valerie Smith, this study will attempt to hold in balance the cultural variables of race, language, history, gender, class, and so on, in order to "destabilize" the "centrality of any one" of them, and to move toward what Sylvia Wynter would designate "a unified theory of culture."[5] Finally, if there is an overarching theme in *Countermodernism,* it is, as the prefix *counter* suggests, what I shall call the denunciatory tradition. It was neither the hard sciences nor theology nor the social sciences that questioned the pseudoscientific claims and the false ethnography used to rationalize expansionist, economic, commercial, and human exploitations. Rather, literature and literary figures first effectively expressed the counterhegemonic position and the counterdiscourse that undertook the task of historiographical repair, analyzed the racist philosophical underpinnings of the policy of assimilation, exposed the lie of the civilizing mission, denounced the moral relativism of colonial policy, championed decolonization, posited the dream of a new enlightenment characterized by an all-inclusive counterhumanism, and denounced the postindependence ethnic leaders who betrayed the people's trust.

From its inception in 1921 with René Maran's publication of *Batouala,* which included a preface critical of French colonial practices, francophone literary culture has been marked by a denunciatory tradition. Most exciting are the writers who take up their pens to break through silence and solitude in order to resist and to denounce publicly through literature the oppressive ideologies that mark the lives of colonialized and postcolonial subjects. Mariama Bâ, whose work epitomizes this tradition, has declared the necessity of the denunciatory stance and the writer's responsibility:

> Dans l'œuvre d'édification d'une société africaine démocratique libérée de toute contrainte, l'écrivain a un rôle important d'éveilleur de conscience et de guide. Il se doit de répercuter les aspirations de toutes les couches sociales, surtout des couches sociales les plus défavorisées. Dénoncer les maux et fléaux qui gangrènent notre société et retardent son plein épanouissement, fustiger les pratiques, coutumes et mœurs archaïques qui n'ont rien à voir avec notre précieux patrimoine culturel, lui reviennent, comme une mission sacrée à accomplir, contre vents et marées, avec foi, avec ténacité.[6]

> [In the task of building up a democratic African society freed from all forms of constraint, the writer has an important role as awakener of consciousness and guide, with the duty of reflecting the aspirations of all social classes, especially the most disadvantaged. *To denounce* the ills that plague our society and delay its full development, to *assail* archaic practices, customs, and mores that have nothing to do with our precious cultural heritage, this is the sacred mission that the writer must carry out, come hell or high water, with faith and perseverance.] (emphasis added)

From this denunciatory tradition of francophone literature, I have chosen to study six representative writers from Martinique, French Guiana, Senegal, Morocco, and Haiti. Aimé Césaire denounces French colonialism and studies its lingering effects upon both the colonizer and the colonized. Léon Gontran Damas rejects the alienating effects of French politics and French socialization processes of assimilation. Ken Bugul warns of the disillusionment that can follow overidealization of the European Promised Land as well as the disillusionment among the pitfalls of postcolonialism. Mariama Bâ criticizes man's excesses, his abuses, and his distortion of the Islamic ideal of polygamy, which is based on equal sharing; and she laments women's complicity in perpetuating polygamy for reasons of egoism, vanity, and material gain. Tahar ben Jelloun exposes the layerings of French, Islamic, royal, and clan patriarchy in Moroccan society and elaborates the condition of Moroccan women in postindependence Morocco as well as the condition of Moroccan men as guest workers in France. Gérard Etienne bears witness to the paradoxes of the history of the "First Black Republic" and the immiserization of the Haitian people. Etienne dreams of a future of democracy in Haiti while documenting the atrocities of Haitian life under a Black totalitarian kleptocracy.

Some readers might associate the title and subject matter of this book, *Countermodernism and Francophone Literary Culture: The Game of Slipknot,* with the work of James Arnold and Françoise Lionnet, two scholars in francophone studies. Arnold is the author of the insightful intertextual study *Modernism and Negritude* (1981) and Lionnet of, among other essays, "Métissage, Emancipation, and Female Textuality in Two Francophone Writers."[7] In her essay, Lionnet advances a concept of transcultural, linguistic, and literary hybridity (*métissage*) related to a "braiding" of the paternal and the maternal that gives rise to a created *métis,* or hybrid, through a rewriting of the past and an annihilation of dichotomies.[8] At best, the association between my work and theirs is a free one, for my readings of francophone literature are not opposed to theirs but rather are modulated by a very different voice, perspective, and goal. Some scholars proceed by accepting and rejecting the work of others, inevitably making value judgments and thereby establishing their intellectual position, territory, or, worst of all, their turf. To my mind, this procedure is neither very sophisticated nor helpful in establishing a collaborative community of scholars. At the same time that I greatly appreciate the work of these scholars, it is my goal to contribute my own view on the question. My reading could be characterized neither as a Euro-American perspective that views Negritude as an outgrowth of modernism nor as the particularly French and feminist perspective of Lionnet, who aptly and eloquently uses the image of the braid, which is formed by intertwining three strands of hair. It occurs to me that the braid suggests tightness; a three-part harmony of order, symmetry, and unity; and reconciliation. As an image, the braid provides a limited idea of the dynamics of francophone culture. For example, in *Eloge de la créolité/In Praise of Creoleness,* Bernabé, Chamoiseau, and Confiant, in attempting to define Creoleness, move very quickly from using the braid ("our history is a braid of histories") to using images of "original soup," "primitive chaos," and the "mangrove swamp of virtualities."[9] Alongside Lionnet, the French philosophical writer Michel Serres offers a complementary analysis of "métissage culturel" that functions incisively in the analysis of the francophone condition.

My perspective is that of a Black American who sees something in addition to the tension between the maternal and paternal traces.[10] In most of the texts I deal with, the characters "wrestle with truth," as James Olney would suggest.[11] Things come undone, and the braid does not hold! There is much awe, anguish, conflict, resistance, death, and survival in the francophone texts I read. Instead of cultural braids, one might be tempted to speak of cultural "dreads," not only in terms of defiant Rastafarian politics and aesthetics, but also in the affective, psychological, and existential senses of the word. The profuse disarray of the knotty Rasta dreadlocks embodies a protest against and poignant counterstatement to the colonial structures of physical, political, moral, psychological, and spiritual containment fostered by the military, police, economic, pedagogical, and religious institutions. Rastafarian dreads represent the calibanesque unraveling and reconceptualization of the order. On the other hand, the braid evokes the seductive golden Rapunzel rope inviting one to climb into the tower of Western beauty, assimilation, and control. In Ken Bugul's *The Abandoned Baobab,* the narrator does not describe the colonial and postcolonial world in terms of reconciliation but rather in terms of teeming yet potentially productive contestation:

> Les formules se choquent. Perdu, l'être cavale dans la réflexion, la méditation. Les notions initient, les idées foisonnent, les projections s'éparpillent, les comparaisons comparent. Chacun essaie un chemin dans le vide, mais la fuite incite à la création et créer c'est combler le vide, le seul vrai adversaire de l'homme.

> [Formulas collide. Lost, human beings roam around inside thoughts, meditations. Notions introduce themselves, ideas are born, plans grow

profuse, comparisons compare. Each one tries a new path in emptiness, but flight inspires creations, and to create is to fill the void, humankind's only true enemy.] [12]

The poetry of Léon Damas inspired the title of this study: the term *countermodernism* emerges from the poems "Contre notre amour qui ne voulait rien d'autre," "Pour sûr," and particularly "Black-Label," in which the poet declares unambiguously his counterposition *contre*/against the conspiracy of silence all around him and against Western morality with its procession of precepts, preoccupations, presumptions, preconceived notions, and prejudices. I characterize as countermodernist much of the production of francophone literary culture since the Negritude poets. Arnold focuses on the poet Aimé Césaire, as I did in my book *La Cohésion poétique de l'œuvre césairienne*. In this text, however, the work and thinking of Aimé Césaire serve as the starting point, as does the concept of Negritude, in order to proceed to an embrace of francophone literary culture in its complexity as well as its unifying issues. This constitutes a very different, broader project than a one-author or one-genre study. I wish to discuss modernism by focusing on the resistance, critiques, and countermoves not only of Césaire but also of six other writers, including Anténor Firmin, the Haitian intellectual and author of *De l'égalité des races humaines* (1885).

Francophone literary culture is neither modernist nor antimodernist: refusing and slipping the knot of binary oppositions, it asserts itself as countermodernist. The imperative for francophone literary culture was to reconceptualize, restage, and redescribe the themes of modernism. This was not an outright rejection of modernism but rather a desire to recapture black subjectivity by salvaging, qualifying, and above all modulating through a systematic readjustment and fine-tuning of the themes and techniques of European aesthetic modernism so as to bring them into harmony with the realities of the colonialized subject's experience. Modulation is perhaps the key maneuver, for it suggests the counterpoint of the differing voice, rhetoric, affect, pitch, and melody of a counterpoetics. The counterimage of the Martinican Narcissus gazing into the mirror framed by the specificity of Antillean culture makes this point:

> Nous cherchons notre vrai visage. Nous avons suffisamment condamné la littérature artificielle qui prétend nous en donner l'image: poètes attardés, héros du poncif, superstitieux faiseurs d'alexandrins, très lâches diseurs de rien. Narcisse martiniquais où donc te reconnaîtras-tu? Plonge tes regards dans le miroir du merveilleux: tes contes, tes légendes, tes chants. Tu y verras s'inscrire, lumineuse, l'image sûre de toi-même.[13]

> [We are searching for our true visage. We have sufficiently condemned fake literature which claims to give us a reflection of ourselves: behind-the-times poets, heroes of hackneyed convention, overly scrupulous crafters of alexandrines, quite cowardly sayers of nothing. Martinican Narcissus, where then will you recognize yourself? Plunge your gazes into the mirror of the marvelous: your short stories, your legends, your songs. You will see inscribed therein, luminous, the unfailing image of yourself.]

The short stories, legends, and songs refer to a Creole tradition and cultural wellspring that has given rise to today's discussions of *créolité,* or Creoleness. Creoleness is not so much new as it is a part of a cyclical process of redefinition and unifying cultural affirmation. Creoleness is a renewal, a reinvention, and, in many ways, an avatar of the identity politics of Negritude. Unfortunately, its exponents do not see it as an elaboration of Negritude but rather as its displacement. Nonetheless, the authors of *Eloge de la créolité* are inspired by a counterdiscourse and agree that Aimé Césaire did not simply "appropriate" European modernism or one of its avatars, surrealism:

> With Césaire and Negritude we were steeped in Surrealism. It was obviously unfair to consider Césaire's handling of the "Miraculous Weapons" of Surrealism as a resurgence of literary bovarism. Indeed, Surrealism blew to pieces ethnocentrist cocoons, and was in its very foundations the first reevaluation of Africa by Western consciousness. But, that the eyes of Europe should in the final analysis serve as a means for the rising of the buried continent of Africa, such was the reason for fearing risks of reinforced alienation which left few chances to escape from it except by a miracle: Césaire, thanks to his immense genius, soaked in the fire of a volcanic idiom, never paid tribute to Surrealism. On the contrary, he became one of the most burning figures of this movement, one of these

> figures we cannot understand without referring to the African substrate resuscitated by the operating powers of the verb. Yet African tropism did not prevent Césaire from very deeply embedding himself in the Caribbean ecology and referential space. And if he did not sing in Creole, the language he uses remains, as revealed namely by a recent reading of *Et les chiens se taisaient,* nonetheless more open than generally thought to the Creole emanations of these native depths.[14]

According to the authors of the "Eloge," resistance to colonial discourse and politics, countermoves against European aesthetics, and a system of countervalues of Caribbean discourse are to be discovered in the oral tradition of the French West Indies: "Creole orality, even repressed in its aesthetic expression, contains a whole system of countervalues, a counterculture; it witnesses ordinary genius applied to resistance, devoted to survival."[15]

As Aimé Césaire perseveres, after more than fifty years of public service as mayor of Fort-de-France in Martinique, it is instructive to assess some of the salient issues of his writing. Césaire is no stranger to us here in the United States. For the last forty years, with increasing interest and intensity, Americans have been reading, teaching, and translating the seminal work of this Afro-French thinker, writer, statesman, and visionary. He has been such a compelling figure for us because, more effectively than anyone else in the francophone world, he has dreamed of, articulated, and defended on the world stage the decolonization and liberation of Africa, redefined what it means to be human, and developed new concepts of Black self-esteem, solidarity, cultural affirmation, and human rights.

Many have sought to answer the question, "Who is Aimé Césaire?" Perhaps no one has answered it better than the eighty-five-year-old poet, playwright, historian, mayor, national assemblyman, statesman, and awakener of consciousness, Aimé Césaire himself. After studying in Paris he wrote:

> I would go to this land of mine and I would say, "Embrace me without fear. . . . And if all I can do is speak, it is for you I shall speak. . . . My mouth shall be the mouth of those calamities that have no mouth, my voice, the freedom of those who break down in the solitary confinement of despair." And above all, my body as well as my soul, beware of as-

suming the sterile attitude of a spectator, for life is not a proscenium, a sea of miseries is not a stage, a man screaming is not a dancing bear.[16]

Since these utterances in his inaugural work, *Notebook of a Return to My Native Land* (1939), Aimé Césaire has consistently addressed in his writings and active political life the economic, social, cultural, psychological, and moral consequences of European colonialism on the destiny of Black people in the modern world. Césaire's lifework has been to rouse the modern world from its indifference to human suffering and to expose the lie of the European civilizing mission in Africa, as, for example, in his "Discourse on Colonialism" (1950). Césaire's position as a man of culture has always been that the artist has moral and social responsibilities and should be the most useful citizen of his "tribe." Throughout the 1950s, the artist's duty was not only to hasten the decolonization of the old French colonies but also to promote the decolonization of the mind of the formerly colonized subject, who had internalized the systematic ideological devaluation of Black humanity and culture. Césaire's agenda has been the reconstruction of Black nations after independence and the development of new concepts of the self. In the postindependence moment, artists become inventors of being, propagators of a new spirit, engineers of souls, multipliers of new men and women.[17]

Aimé Césaire has a profound intellectual and cultural connection to the United States and to Black America. For his thesis at the Ecole Normale Supérieure, Césaire wrote on the South in Black American literature. Although Negritude is associated with the Guyanese poet Léon Gontran Damas, the Senegalese poet and statesman Léopold Sédar Senghor, and Césaire, who coined the term, for Césaire Negritude is an American concept in that, as a cultural affirmation, it emerges from the research and artistry of W. E. B. DuBois, Langston Hughes, Claude McKay, Countee Cullen, and Zora Neale Hurston. Not an essentialism nor an antiracist racism, Césaire's Negritude involves three simple affirmations: Black identity; solidarity through time and space with all people of African descent; and identification with cultural values of African origin. Césaire's emphasis is on the culture and the cultural heritage. For Césaire, biology is only truly interesting if considered and transmuted in the specific cultural context. He is interested in the "plasma" of the accumulated, inherited experiences of people of African descent, the plasma of Black cultural memory. Césaire has asserted, "Chromosomes are of little importance to me. . . . I believe in the value of all that is buried in the collective memory and even that which is buried in the collective unconscious. . . . I do not believe that one arrives in this world with the brain empty as in arriving with empty hands."[18]

Césaire's Negritude would lead to a counterhumanism. Césaire is a humanistic critic of European imperial practices, a critic of the European imperial will to power, and a critic of its corollary will to describe, define, represent, interpret, translate, and textualize colonized peoples and places through the Western gaze. He would thrust an alternative all-inclusive universal humanism back at Europe:

> Qu'on le sache: en articulant notre effort de libération des peuples colonisés, en combattant pour la dignité de nos peuples c'est en définitive pour le monde tout entier que nous combattons et pour le libérer de la tyrannie, de la haine et du fanatisme. . . . Alors et alors seulement nous aurons vaincu et notre victoire finale marquera l'avènement d'une ère nouvelle. . . . nous aurons aidé à fonder l'humanisme universel.[19]

> [Let it be known: while articulating our effort of liberation of colonized peoples, while fighting for the dignity of our people, it is definitely for the whole world that we are fighting and to liberate it from tyranny, hatred and fanaticism. . . . Then and only then shall we have been victorious, and our final victory will mark the coming of a new era. . . . we shall have assisted in founding universal "humanisme."]

Césaire's poetry, theater, and his writings on history, and politics form an extraordinary lens through which to ponder the sense of francophone literary culture. Césaire privileges the vegetal as the tortured ontological expression of the history of uprootings, re-enracinations, and survival of Black culture. The laminaria is a form of algae that can extend for many miles into the open sea and yet remain attached to its natal rock or land formation. This algae is one of the many vegetal forms in which Césaire sees mirrored the dramas of the existence, particularly the wandering, of colonized and postcolonial subjects. Typically, the Césairian vision grasps in a poetic instant the complexity, anxiety, hybridity, and liminal quality that mark the legacy of the transcultural contacts between the Euro-American societies and the nations they have colonized. The preface to *Moi laminaire* is a good example:

> Dans toute vie il y a un nord et un sud, et l'orient et l'occident . . . au carrefour . . . l'inégale lutte de la vie et de la mort, de la ferveur et de la lucidité, fut-ce celle du désespoir et de la retombée, la force aussi toujours de regarder demain. Ainsi va toute vie. Ainsi va ce livre, entre soleil et ombre, entre montagne et mangrove, entre chien et loup, claudiquant et binaire.[20]

> [In every life there is a north and a south, and the east and the west . . . at the crossroads . . . the uneven struggle of life and of death, of fervor and of lucidity, be it that of despair and of repercussions, the strength also and always to look toward tomorrow. Thus goes every life. Thus goes this book, between sun and shadow, between mountain and mangrove, at the twilight hour of the dog and the wolf, limping and binary.]

Elsewhere, as in his poem "Dit d'errance" (Tale of Wandering), Aimé Césaire speaks of lost bodies, mutilations, fragmentations, dismemberment, tearings away, the split self, the unresolved, unexploited spaces, and the invention of the self. These images and topics all converge in the image of the most beautiful awaited night sun with its attendant phoenicism and suicidal gestures of immolation for rebirth. The poem maps the issues that haunt the pages, images, and metaphors of francophone literary production, such as the poetics of the uprooted, shipwrecked, and wandering self; cultural schizophrenia; the violent dark days of decolonization; and the sunlight of independence.

As mentioned earlier, francophone literary culture, being neither modernist nor antimodernist, refuses and slips the knot of binary oppositions, thereby asserting itself as countermodernist. Césaire makes the point in his *Discourse on Colonialism* that the colonized masses are not an "either-or" people:

> Once again, I systematically defend our old Negro civilizations: they were courteous civilizations.
>
> So the real problem, you say, is to return to them. No, I repeat. We are not men for whom it is a question of "either-or." For us, the problem is not to make a utopian and sterile attempt to repeat the past, but to

> go beyond. It is not a dead society that we want to revive. We leave that to those who go in for exoticism. Nor is it the present colonial society that we wish to prolong, the most putrid carrion that ever rotted under the sun. It is a new society that we must create, with the help of all our brother slaves, a society rich with all the productive power of modern times, warm with all the fraternity of olden days.[21]

Francophone literary culture is neither a shortsighted solipsistic identity politics nor lyricism. Strictly speaking, it is not antiurbanism, anticommodification, or antiprogress. Rather, it seeks to confront, to contest, and to counter the dehumanizing excesses and legacies of colonial domination. The affix *counter* is crucial in describing francophone literary culture's inflection of modernist aesthetic practices and vision. As a prefix, *counter* posits a relationship of proximity between one action and another, and it declares an oppositional stance within that relationship. *Counter* suggests the substitution of an action *as a reply* to that other action, condition, narrative, or discourse already in existence and considered inimical. The reply is a critique, at times a denunciation, whose purpose is checking or frustrating, correcting or redefining, rivaling or outdoing the inimical Western/colonial discourse by working in particular within the realm of the unacknowledged, the unrecognized, and the unrealized.

Such counterexertions of the denunciatory tradition as countermodernism, counterhumanism, counterstorytelling, countermemory, counterstories, and counterconfessions define the productions of francophone literary culture and contribute to the elaboration of a discourse of *counter* that organizes this study. Part 1 lays the groundwork for highlighting certain enduring characteristics of francophone literary culture in general, certain francophone women writers, and some francophone literary production dating from as early as 1885 to as recently as 1991.

The discussion of countermodernism in Part 1 prepares the way for discussing in Part 2 the fundamental narrative force in francophone literary culture that is counterstorytelling, along with its related dependent genre, the counterconfession. As detailed in Part 3, for the subjugated the counterconfession represents a form of survival effected through a linguistic project and productivity occurring outside the confessional scenes of the prescribed and coercive spaces of the courtroom, the torture chamber, or the church confessional. Colonialism entailed not only the power to annex and exploit other races, but also to textualize the racial Other (see Part 2, chap. 4). It is this textualization against which francophone narratives must always work. Thus, Part 2 further defines the formalist qualities of counter-storytelling by examining samples of early French colonial discourse, politics, and narrative depiction of the subjugated Other.

Finally, there are topical organizing principles in this study, such as the consideration of slavery and colonialism, which informs the entire text. Colonial narrative depictions that reveal obsessions with the body of color constitute another major focus, as does that of the inscribed body in the francophone text. I undertake an analysis of the colonized person's body experience as it relates to the colonial experience in chapter 2, which is devoted to the neglected Guyanese poet Léon Gontran Damas and his distinctive "body talk."[22] This examination of the inscribed body continues with a discussion of Mariama Bâ and the shared rhetoric of menopause and decolonization (chap. 5), Tahar ben Jelloun and his tale of contrasexuality (chap. 6), Ken Bugul and her search for cultural moorings and an anchored identity (chap. 7), and, finally, Gérard Etienne and his witness to tortured flesh of the political detainee (chap. 8).

The themes of exile and return provide another organizing principle for this study. The texts studied reveal that in francophone literary culture the fundamental modernist preoccupation with exile and return is elaborated into a meditation on transitional social realities, migrancy, internal exile and imprisonment, role reversal, status inconsistency, and, ultimately, cultural schizophrenia.

The notion of community and connectedness is yet another thread that binds the diverse texts from varied regions and cultures of the francophone world. Humor, trauma, and books form the core of collective consciousness and contribute to the building of local communities, nations, and transnational communities. Léon Gontran Damas demonstrates how the secret codes of the in-group's humor act as a sociocultural glue for individuals sharing a given community or collective experience. Gérard Etienne reveals that trauma and the unspeakable unite people in their experience of those awesome and awe-ful experiences that can never be contained in words. Since books establish communities as well, Mariama Bâ's assertion that "books knit generations together" is especially poignant for students of literature and in relation to this study, which moves back and forth between centuries and generations of francophone writers.

Cultural braiding is not the only notion that the subtitle of this study, *The Game of Slipknot,* is meant to suggest. In fact, my subtitle has much more to do with the lifelines motif in *Life Lines: Theorizing Women's Autobiography.* Germaine Brée explains the sense of that title:

> Life/Lines: the metaphor is ambiguous and invites us to ponder its relation to the subtitle. Lifelines, ropes thrown to ships or persons floundering in deep waters nearby; lifelines, ropes that link the deep-sea diver to the mother-ship; lifelines, more metaphorically, essential routes of communication between mutually dependent communities, but again, and differently, lifelines, those lines in the palm of the hand that in palmistry, dictionaries tell us, supposedly reveal facts about a person's life to the person who can decode the meaning. More than a metaphor, it defines a space or scene and suggests a purpose.[23]

The inspiration for my subtitle comes from "le jeu du nœud coulant," the concluding line of the poem "Pour toi et moi," by Léon Gontran Damas. The slipknot is also a recurring image in the writings of the Césaire-Damas generation, as we shall see. Like the lifelines metaphor, the slipknot has much to do with the sea and survival. It is polyvalent in its signifying power and multilayered in its richness and aptness to the history and experience of new world Blacks, evoking a string of verbal associations that plot the legacy of the middle passage, colonial domination, plantation experience, and postcolonialism: capture, bound hands, nautical voyage, bondage, suicide, lynching, strangulation, triangulation, struggle, ties, knots, prestidigitation, escape, freedom, and survival. The colonial or the postcolonial subject is always challenged to negotiate between two worldviews, two cultures, and often two competing sets of values. The game of slipknot defines, on an existential level, the challenges, difficulties, fascination, exhilaration, dangers, and snares of the inevitable circulation of the individual between two cultures. In Damas's poem "Pour toi et moi" the words slip and coil around one another in a process that creates new meanings. The collision, reversal, and mirroring of the elements of the poem threaten, destabilize, and undo the original assertion. The images speak directly of the tying, binding, knotting, and unbinding of a "self" with an "O/other."

The game of slipknot imagizes and evokes the psycho- and sociocultural snares involved in the dramas and traumas of colonization, decolonization, and postcolonialism. These snares include the challenges for francophone subjects inherent in negotiating their identity in the in-between zone of cultures where conceptual frameworks collide, and the challenge of residing in a liminal present between an obliterated past and the imagining of a fulfilling democratic future. The slipknot suggests the figure eight, a circuit of journeying, questing, and returning, and a cycle of contesting emotional and intellectual states: triangulated African American–European destinies; the enchantment and disenchantment with the native land; displacements; the enchantment and disenchantment with a Euro-American Promised Land; infinity and the circular trap of self-aversion and mimetic desire. The slipknot concretizes the life challenge for the colonial and postcolonial subject: strangulation or liberation—to tighten the noose the more one struggles to free oneself or to slip the knot. The authors and texts dealt with in this study bear witness to the fact that marginality, oppression, and great pain can lead to extraordinary creativity and achievement. Such are the snares, such are the stakes, and such are the challenges with which francophone literary culture grapples in its game of slipknot.

I

Countermodernism

1

The Game of Slipknot

Poetry was for me the only way
to break the *stranglehold* the accepted French form had on me.

Martinique . . . around its neck the *slipknot* of assimilation.
—Letter to Maurice Thorez (emphases added)

. . . "Odd how the climate has changed. Cold on this island . . .
Have to think about making a fire . . . Well, Caliban, old fellow, it's
just us two now, here on the island, only you and me.
You and me. You-me . . . me-you!"—Aimé Césaire, *A Tempest*

For you and for me who one and the other
were yesterday but one still caught in the game of slipknot
—Léon Gontran Damas, "Pour toi et moi"

You know that before leaving I had undone the noose
around my neck—Gérard Etienne, *Cri pour ne pas crever de honte*

Perspectives: Anténor Firmin and René Maran

Francophone literary culture begins with a denunciation. In 1921 the prestigious French literary Goncourt Prize was awarded to René Maran, a Guyanese French colonial administrator in the Central African district of Oubangui-Chari, for his work *Batouala,*[1] considered the first novel to be written about Africa in French by a Black. In the preface to *Batouala,* the author condemned French colonial practices in Central Africa and appealed to his "brothers of France" to recall France to her revolutionary, egalitarian, and fraternal dignity. The preface and the novel itself were banned in the colonies, and the Goncourt committee was severely criticized for bestowing the prize upon such "dangerous," inflammatory literature. It was not until 1987 that the Goncourt Prize would be awarded to another francophone writer, Tahar ben Jelloun, for *La Nuit sacrée,* the sequel to *L'Enfant de sable* (*The Sand Child*).[2]

Prior to Maran, however, away from Paris in the relative obscurity of Port-au-Prince circa 1885, the Haitian intellectual Anténor Firmin published *De l'égalité des races humaines* (*On the Equality of the Human Races*).[3] In 1855, seven years after the 1848 abolition of slavery in the French colonies, Comte Joseph-Arthur de Gobineau's *L'Essai sur l'inégalité des races humaines* (*Essay on the Inequality of the Human Races*) had been published.[4] Gobineau's essay was not only an a posteriori "scientific" justification of slavery but also an a priori justification for modernity's continuation of colonialist practices of exploitation, which in the postslavery period took the form of oppressive debt systems and the forced labor, servitude, and indenture of Africans, Asians, and Amerindians. Firmin wrote his essay as a counter and a reply to, as well as a denunciation of, the physical, medical, intellectual, and moral anthropology of the period, a discourse considered inimical, or in his terms "iniquitous." Firmin was addressing not only the rhetoric of Gobineau but also that of others, including Ernest Renan in *Philosophical Dialogues:*

> Les hommes ne sont pas égaux, les races ne sont pas égales. Le Nègre, par exemple, est fait pour servir aux grandes choses voulues et conçues par le blanc.
>
> [Men are not equal. The Negro, for example, is made to serve the great things conceived and desired by the White man.] [5]

Firmin's 662-page project has three major organizing goals. First, with an overabundance of evidence, Firmin eloquently defends Egyptian, Ethiopian, and sub-Saharan civilizations, enumerating their contributions to human progress. Firmin thus anticipated the twentieth-century research of Jean Price-Mars and other Black Africanists.

Second, Firmin analyzes what he considers the prompt evolution of the Black in the New World from slavery to independence, privileging the case of Haiti and the example of the intellectuals, military figures, and heroes of its independence movement. Firmin states:

> Nous allons voir ce qu'ont pu faire dans les hautes régions de l'esprit les arrière petits-fils tirés de la Côte-d'Or, du Dahomey, du pays des Aradas, des Mandingues, des Ibos et des Congos, pour être jetés en Haïti couverts de chaînes et maudissant leur destinée! (P. 438)
>
> [We shall see what in the lofty regions of the mind has been accomplished by the great-grandchildren of those dragged from the Gold Coast, from Dahomey, from the land of the Arada, the Mandingo, the Ibo, and the Congo peoples, to be cast down into Haiti covered in chains and cursing their fate.]

Third, Firmin's goal is to denounce the moral, intellectual, and scientific relativism of Europe: first, through a systematic refutation of the false ethnography of slavery and postslavery racism and second, through a grandiose affirmation, with examples, of the humanity of Blacks. According to Firmin in 1885, one must

> détruire les prétentions que la race caucasique affiche au monopole de l'intelligence et de toutes les aptitudes supérieures." (P. 452)
>
> [destroy the claims flaunted by the caucasian race to a monopoly on intelligence and all superior aptitudes.]

In Firmin's phrasing, one discerns the beginning utterances of Aimé Césaire's assertion in *Notebook of a Return to the Native Land:* "Et aucune race ne possède le monopole de la beauté, de l'intelligence, de la force . . . et il est place pour tous au rendez-vous de la conquête" [And no race posesses the monopoly of beauty, intelligence, strength . . . and there is space for everyone at the rendezvous of victory]. In fact, much of Firmin's heroic defense of Black humanity prefigures many of the revolutionary positions later taken by many twentieth-century francophone writers.

Throughout *De l'égalité des races humaines,* Firmin qualifies as "specious," "suspicious," "perverse," "monstrous," "stupid," and "fanciful" the contemporary scientific claims that asserted the differences between Black and White humanity. Before Césaire's *Discourse on*

Colonialism (1950) and his denunciation of "the big lie" of the civilizing mission, of anthropological hypocrisy, and of the dishonest equations that tried to prove that Christianity equals civilization and that Black culture equals savagery and paganism, Firmin had asserted that the work of Gobineau and others was in no way

> une réponse scientifique, c'est un pur jeu de rhétorique à réduire à sa juste valeur. . . . j'aurai droit de lui dire, à cette anthropologie mensongère: Non, tu n'es pas une science! (Pp. 227, 230)
>
> [a scientific response, it is a pure game of rhetoric to be reduced to its just value. . . . I shall reserve the right to say to this lying anthropology: No, you are not a science!]

Before the Martinican ethnopsychiatrist Frantz Fanon wrote his 1961 sociodiagnostic *Black Skin, White Masks,* in which he analyzed much of the behavior of the colonized as a consequence of colonial processes of socialization and brutalization, Firmin had posited a similar analysis:

> Les Européens qui ont le courage de reprocher à l'esclave noir son infériorité intellectuelle ne se rappellent-ils donc pas d'avoir employé tous les artifices pour empêcher que l'intelligence ne se développât jamais en lui. Après avoir brisé tous les ressorts de la volonté, toute énergie morale, toute élasticité de l'esprit, ne laissant que la brute là où l'homme menaçait de s'affirmer, ne savait-on pas, sans l'ombre d'un doute, qu'il ne restait plus rien d'élevé dans cet être méthodiquement dégradé? C'est pourtant en s'adressant à lui, le prenant comme terme de comparaison qu'on a établi les bases du jugement par lequel on déclare que les races ne sont pas égales, que les Nigritiens sont au-dessous de l'échelle et les Caucasiens au dessus! Une science qui s'est édifiée au milieu d'un tel renversement de la nature et qui y a cherché ses règles d'appréciation et de raisonnement ne pouvait offrir rien de sérieux, rien de solide. Dans cette pénible occurrence, la science, par une lâche complaisance ou par insuffisance d'observation, s'est rendu complice du plus sot des préjugés et du plus inique des systèmes. (Pp. 488–89)
>
> [Those Europeans who have the audacity to reproach the black slave for his intellectual inferiority do not therefore recall having employed every ingenious device in order to prevent intelligence from ever developing

in him. After having broken all the resilience of his willpower, every bit of his moral energy, all elasticity of the mind, leaving only a brute there where a human being threatened to affirm itself, did they not know, without a shadow of a doubt, that there remained nothing more of the lofty in this methodically degraded being? It is, however, in addressing that being, taking him as the basis of comparison, that they have established the bases of judgment by which they declare that the races are not equal, that the Negroes are at the bottom of the ladder and the Caucasians are at the top. A science that erects itself in the middle of such a reversal of nature and that searches therein its rules of appraisal and reasoning can offer nothing serious, nothing solid. In this painful instance, science, by a cowardly connivance or a lack of observation, has made itself complicitous with the most stupid of prejudices and the most iniquitous of systems.]

Before the poet Léon Gontran Damas denounced the highly imitative form and unexamined content of early-twentieth-century Caribbean literature, Firmin had already begun a critique of the state of Haitian literature in 1885:

> Malheureusement dans cette première floraison de l'intelligence des Noirs, on ne s'occupa que de la littérature. On aima mieux cultiver la forme dans laquelle les idées doivent se présenter que d'étudier le fond de ces idées. Beaucoup de brillant littéraire et presque pas de science. Louis-Philippe disait de Villemain qu'il faisait ses phrases tout d'abord et cherchait ensuite l'idée qu'on pouvait y mettre. C'est une saillie qui contient plus de finesse que de vérité; mais il n'est pas moins vrai que les hommes de 1830, en France, sacrifiaient souvent trop à la forme. Imitant tant donc l'éloquence fleurie avec laquelle les doctrinaires français parlaient de la liberté et des principes, les Haïtiens se mirent à parler admirablement du droit, sans y croire aucunement, sans même s'occuper de ce qui le constitue, ni dans quelles limites il doit s'exercer, ni à quel point, il est respectable. (P. 584)

> [Unfortunately in this first flowering of the intelligence of Blacks, one was interested only in literature. One preferred to cultivate the form in which ideas must be presented rather than study the substance of these ideas. Lots of literary brilliance but almost no science. Louis-Philippe used to say of Villemain that he fashioned his phrases first then searched

> for the idea that one could put into the phrase. It is a witticism that contains more finesse than truth; but it is no less true that the men of 1830, in France, often sacrificed too much to form. Consequently imitating, to quite an extent, the florid eloquence with which the sententious French doctrinarians spoke of liberty and its principles, Haitians began to speak admirably of law, without believing in it in the least, without even dealing with what actually constituted it, nor in what parameters it should be exercised, nor to what extent it is honorable.]

While pondering the bloody past of the slave trade, the wretched conditions of slave life, and the self-serving claims of nineteenth-century anthropology, Firmin resists melancholy and draws strength, pride even, from the slave past and the survival and progress of New World Blacks, thus anticipating the Negritude movement of the 1930s and 40s.

> Pour moi, j'avoue bien franchement que je ne puis m'empêcher d'être fier de mes pères, quand je me reporte par la pensée à cette époque de misère où, rivés à une existence infernale, ayant le corps brisé par le fouet, la fatigue et les chaînes, ils gémissaient en silence, mais conservaient dans leur poitrine haletante le feu sacré qui devait produire l'explosion superbe de la liberté et de l'indépendance! (P. 533)

> [For me, I must confess quite frankly that I cannot keep myself from being proud of my forefathers, when through thoughts I am transported back to that period of misery during which, tied to a hellish existence, being broken by the lash, by weariness and chains, they moaned in silence but preserved in their panting breast the sacred fire that would produce the splendid explosion of liberty and independence.]

While the word "negritude" is of twentieth-century coinage, Césaire maintains in the *Notebook* that it "stood up for the first time and declared its humanity" during the Haitian Revolution of 1802–1804. With that in mind, it is perhaps later in the same century, in 1885, with the publication in Haiti of *On the Equality of the Human Races* by Anténor Firmin—in direct response to the indictment of Black humanity by European physical and moral anthropology—that one can place the beginnings of a francophone literary consciousness and the countermoves of the denunciatory tradition.

In 1921 Maran's existence dramatized a variation of the double consciousness explicated by W. E. B. DuBois in 1902. In DuBoisian double consciousness one is dealing with the tensions between individual racial or ethnic identity and values and collective national identity and values. Specifically, the conflict in DuBois emerged from the existential twoness of being: "One ever feels his twoness,—an American, a Negro; two souls, two thoughts, two unreconciled strivings; two warring ideals in one dark body, whose dogged strength alone keeps it from being torn asunder." In Maran's case, it is the twoness of being Negro and French. Maran's life in 1921 was one of remarkable mobility. His dilemma, knowing colonial history while not identifying with Africa and Africans, prefigures today's dilemma of Parisian-born Blacks who have no memory or experience of Africa or the West Indies. This predicament crosses linguistic boundaries to include anglophone and other francophone Blacks who have been inculcated with Western values and are living in world capitals. Maran's dilemma is expressed today by writers like Caryl Phillips, who shuttles between St. Kitts and London and captures the sense of the contemporary manifestation of Maran's experience:

> The question leaps out: "When will it end?" The problem occurs when you don't have any memory of the Caribbean, and you have been told that's where you are from. That's why Alvin in *Strange Fruit* goes back to the Caribbean, returns to England and actually discovers that the Caribbean is not for him. It's a real problem to have no memory of the Caribbean, and it's a problem to have a memory of the Caribbean. If you seek to discover the Caribbean in somebody growing up in North America or Britain, then nine times out of ten, you will be disappointed.[6]

In Maran's *Batouala,* the tension between the vision in the preface compared to the contents of the novel is of particular interest, as is the psychocultural location of Maran himself. There is a dissonance or contrapuntal discontinuity between the probing and denunciatory analysis of colonialism in the preface and the content of the novel proper. Maran the novelist is unable or unwilling to write himself out of the traditions, gaze, aesthetics, and position of a Europeanized Black looking upon Africans as an outsider. With a French heart and worldview, Maran sensed that he was in the land of his ancestors, ancestors from whom he distanced himself because he did not share their condition, mentality, or tastes, but whom he recognized, nonetheless, as his ancestors.[7] Today many successful minorities have difficulty recognizing themselves in the socially, educationally, and economically disenfranchised members of their racial or ethnic group, and class asserts itself.

Subtitled in French *Véritable roman nègre* (A True African Tale), in the English edition the novel is subtitled, *An African Love Story*.[8] Essentially, it describes a love triangle between Batouala, the chief, Yassigui'ndja, his ninth wife, who is, however, "first" among equals, and the robust young hunter Bissibi'ngui. Yassi and Bissi are sexually overdetermined as characters, and Batouala is "naturally jealous, vindictive and violent." The African woman is portrayed as being of easy virtue and is condemned to promiscuity and infidelity because she acts only according to instinct. In fact, the text states, "The only law is instinct." Thus, Africans cannot rid themselves of innate savageness, and relationships between the African men and women are one-dimensional—reduced to sexual pursuit and satisfaction. Relationships between men in the novel are competitive and deadly; the same is true of the relationships between women. Perhaps the only moment in which the novel echoes the anticolonialist criticisms and preoccupations of the preface is when Batouala pronounces an extended discourse on the character of the Boundjous, or Whites, during preparations for the celebrations of Ga'nza, the ceremony of circumcision and excision.

Maran's writing is important because, although his depiction of Africa in 1921 reinforces the colonialist textualization of Africa as pagan and savage, the novel and, in particular, the preface constitute the beginning in francophone literature of deterrent dissent against French colonial practices. Maran's honesty is uncompromising, at times disturbing, heroic, and instructive. Maran is caught between two competing sets of impulses that contribute to the slipknot of the assimilation process.[9] The slipknot of the assimilation-alienation process manifests itself in crises of alternating admiration and revulsion, national identification and racial identification, self-identification and social classification, mimetic desire and self-aversion, blindness and insight. The often resultant sense of alienation and shame is contemplated in the image of the complicitously dirty hands of a colonialized cultural elite in the poem "Solde/Sellout" by Léon Damas: "les mains effroyablement rouges du sang de leur ci-vi-li-sa-tion" [my hands horrifically red with the blood of their ci-vi-li-za-tion].

In his burgeoning but unsustained consciousness, Maran's 1921 preface foreshadows aspects of Césaire's *Discourse on Colonialism.* In his person and in his literary dilemma as writer-thinker, Maran presages the crisis of double consciousness in the novel *The Ambiguous Adventure.* Maran and his work are instructive lenses through which to view many of the fundamental preoccupations of francophone literary culture, of this study, and indeed of issues in African, Caribbean, and American societies as they struggle with questions of class, social mobility, assimilation, memory, self-identification, classification, and allegiance to race and nation.

Maran's work is significant because it sketches many of the dilemmas with which future francophone writers would have to contend, as well as the positions they would assume: a condemnation of colonialism; a condemnation of complicitous silence; a double consciousness on the part of the Afro-French person; an awareness of the double standard of libertarian, egalitarian European *domestic* values and the practice of brutality, inequality, repression, and exploitation *abroad;* and, ironically, a recurrent need to believe in the perfectibility of France.

Consciously or unconsciously, many major African novelists concerned with African tradition and the status of African women would rewrite the chapter concerning the circumcision-excision ritual, most often depicting the practice in its extremely dehumanizing and brutalizing dimensions.[10] Yet, certain impulses would set Maran apart from most of his successors, most notably his tendency to what might be called "deracialization," the desire in the words of his novel's title to be *Un Homme pareil aux autres* (A Man Like Any Other Man).[11]

As an act of defiance against the banning of literature, certain African and French West Indian students, such as Joseph Zobel, the future author of *La Rue Cases-Nègres* (*Sugar Cane Alley*),[12] felt duty-bound to read *Batouala.* From among these students a political and literary movement emerged that, on the eve of World War II and the French occupation, would be highlighted by the publication in 1937 of *Pigments* by Léon Gontran Damas and in 1939 of *Cahier d'un retour au pays natal* (Notebook of a Return to the Native Land) by Aimé Césaire.[13]

Beginning with denunciation and defiance, francophone literary culture is inaugurated, also, under the sign of tragic struggle. The Malagasy poet Jean-Joseph Rabéarivélo, for example, was torn between his passionate embrace of French culture and the love that bound him to his colonized Madagascar homeland. Deep in financial debt, rejected for promotion in a French administrative post, and ultimately unable to reconcile his painful conflicts, Rabéarivélo committed suicide on June 22, 1937.

Thus, the years from 1885 to 1921 and from 1937 to 1987 constitute historical frames around my study, with particular focus given to the latter fifty-year period. As I attempt to map some of the issues of this period as exemplified by six writers, my point is not to be encyclopedic but rather synthetic.[14] Cheik Hamidou Kane orients the beginnings of this effort as his protagonist, Samba Diallo, philosophizes on the complex and tragic process of self-discovery and transformation that permeates this literature:

> Il arrive que nous soyons capturés au bout de notre itinéraire, vaincus par notre aventure même. Il nous apparaît soudain que, tout au long de notre cheminement, nous n'avons pas cessé de nous métamorphoser, et que nous voilà devenus autres. Quelquefois, la métamorphose ne s'achève pas, elle nous installe dans l'hybride et nous y laisse. Alors, nous nous cachons, remplis de honte. . . . Quand j'y réfléchis maintenant, je ne puis m'empêcher de penser qu'il y a eu un peu de l'attrait morbide du péril. J'ai choisi l'itinéraire le plus susceptible de me perdre.[15]

> [And so it happens that we arrive at the end of our itinerary, vanquished by the *adventure* itself. And, suddenly, it appears to us that all along as we were making our way, we were in a process of *metamorphosis.* So here we are . . . becom[ing] something other. Sometimes the metamorphosis is not complete and it propels us into a space of *hybridity* and leaves us there. And so we try to hide ourselves, filled as we are with *shame*. . . . When I reflect upon it now, I can't help but think that there was a bit of the morbid appeal of danger. I chose *the itinerary the most likely to confuse me.*] (emphases added)

The metamorphosis, the hybridity, and the shame will be principal preoccupations in the writing of Ken Bugul and Gérard Etienne. The preoccupation with the shame that results from a sense of complicitous participation in the process of one's own alienation is a recurring motif, echoed thirty-four years after *The Ambiguous Adventure* in Tahar ben Jelloun's novel *L'Enfant de sable* (The Sand Child):

> Aux point et lieu où je suis arrivée je m'arrête un moment, je me dépouille de mes oripeaux, j'enlève une à une toutes mes peaux, tel un oignon je m'éplucherai devant vous jusqu'à l'ultime substance pour dire la faute, l'erreur et la honte. (P. 179)

> [At the point and place I've come to, I pause for a moment, take off my finery, remove all my skins one by one; like an onion I'll peel away before you until I come to the ultimate substance—sin, error, and shame.] (P. 140)

The paradoxical reversals of fortune and threats to psychological well-being during the colonial and postindependence moments made authors and their characters aware of having undergone an adventure (Kane), of having followed an itinerary (Jelloun), of errancy (Etienne), and of beings and a world turned upside down (Bugul). These insights in turn lead Césaire, in poetry, and later Bugul, in a novel, to contemplate the baobab tree ("the upside-down tree") as an apt image. As an image of heroic survival against disproportionate odds, the baobab is part of the network of images associated with the slipknot and will be helpful later in forming a theory about the francophone condition.

The adventure of francophone literature is, in many respects, composed of deadly and passionate fascination, suspicion,[16] and struggle with the French language and the system of values it implies. In my view, the discussion must begin with three primary observations:

1. Language is a powerful tool of acculturation, assimilation, and domination for the colonizer in that it is the primary means for the implantation of culture and, perhaps more important, for the implantation of a system of command, persuasion, coercion, and exploitation. Language includes and excludes individuals in ways that have a pervasive set of consequences for individuals "outside the power language."

2. The power of language is like that of a double-edged sword, for it also provides a potent means of empowerment for the oppressed.

3. In a multiethnic shared environment where the subordinate class is excluded from the status and the material benefits conferred by the economy on the superordinate class, the imperative for the oppressed is to *expropriate* the language imposed upon them.

The process and adventure of linguistic expropriation, as well as political and psychological empowerment through language, constitute, in my opinion, the essence of the short history of the emergence of francophone literature since the 1930s. This expropriation is a therapeutic process of disalienation. It implies the modeling, engineering, and dissemination of new concepts of self—both male and female, native and European. In studying francophone literature, one cannot avoid confronting the complexity of transitional social realities. To speak of "francophone" literature or of the "francophone" world is to raise a host of complex and interlocking questions that in their totality capture the idea of a geography, a sociology, and a psychology of the French language *in contact* and *in contestation* with other cultures. An understanding of francophone literature begins with a consideration of the implantation of French administration, culture, and, above all, language outside of metropolitan France. Only then is it possible to study the voluminous body of literature written in French that is extravagant in the way it interfaces with multiple ethnic, geographic, and cultural variants and temporalities. A few examples of such interfaces are French with Polynesian, Asian, North African, West African, Caribbean, and Canadian; Catholicism with Islam, Voodoo, and Protestantism; tradition with modernity, surrealism, and African worldviews—specifically Dogon notions of continuity, transcendence (*muntu*), and language (*nommo*); gender; assimilation; alienation—as well as the interface of native, colonial, postcolonial, and modern temporalities. These interfaces give rise to perplexing spaces of historical, geolinguistic, and cultural instability, hybridity, conceptual fusion, and confusion. People, life, and cultural moorings become "unhinged" and, in turn, give rise to the francophone expression of status inconsistency, role conflict, and divided consciousness.[17]

In *The Wretched of the Earth,* Frantz Fanon writes, "Culture has never the translucidity of custom; it abhors all simplification."[18] Perhaps one could go even further and suggest that culture—especially francophone culture—*defies* simplification. This caveat notwithstanding, Fanon poignantly characterizes culture as "the fluctuating movement that the people are *just* giving shape to." According to Fanon, there exists "this zone of occult instability where the people dwell that we must come to; and it is there that our souls are crystallized and that our perceptions and our lives are transfused with light" (p. 227). He points out that "it has always happened in the struggle for freedom that such a people becomes unhinged, reorganizes itself, and in blood and tears gives birth to very real and immediate action" (56).

Francophone literature, as a body of literary expression, is fundamentally concerned with what Erikson called, in *Everything in Its Path,* "the axis of variation"[19]; that is, the wandering from culture to culture in the wake of regional catastrophe and the "in-betweenness" that results from competing ethnicities, nationalisms, and the expression of cultural differences. It is, therefore, precisely this "axis of variation," "fluctuating movement," and "zone of occult instability" that orient signification and representation in francophone literature.[20]

Eventually a relationship evolved between francophone literary culture and French modernism as a consequence of the juxtaposition of the French poet and theorist of modernism, Charles Baudelaire (1821–67), and the francophone poet and theorist of Negritude, Aimé Césaire (1913–). It is fitting to explore that relationship here.

Cygne/Signes/Singe, or Modernism and Signs of Cultural Difference

Je pense à la négresse, amaigrie et phtisique,
Piétinant dans la boue, et cherchant, l'œil hagard,
Les cocotiers absents de la superbe Afrique
Derrière la muraille immense du brouillard;

A quiconque a perdu ce qui ne se retrouve

. . . .

Aux captifs, aux vaincus! . . . à bien d'autres encor![21]

[I think of the lean consumptive negress trudging through the mud, with her haggard eyes peering in vain through the huge wall of fog for the absent palm-trees of her noble Africa;

I think of all those who have lost what they can never, never hope to find again;

Of those who are captive, those who are defeated—and of many another]

In the poem quoted above, "Le Cygne" (The Swan) by Charles Baudelaire, the reader encounters the poet as decipherer and translator of the universe as text. The focus is particularly on the cityscape of Paris with its crowds of people parading in misery, marginality, and alienation through the urban streets. The title of the poem is suggestive of sound-sense and homonymy. *Cygne/Signes* (Swan/Signs) are represented identically in phonetic transcription, and in fact, contain and predict the drive of the poem's creative impulse: SIGNS of difference and sameness. Of special interest is the double action or simultaneous postulations of the poem. On the one hand, the poem acknowledges the haggard and tubercular Black woman as a sign that is in dramatic counterpoint to the white and wandering swan, both of whom are out of place in the streets of Paris, and signs of death and misery. And yet the poem levels the Black woman's difference as a sign and inserts it into the generalized state of exile, loss, nostalgia, and desire to effect an Edenic return to some original state of bliss as lived and represented by the poet Victor Hugo, to whom the poem is dedicated; by the swan, the ostensible subject; by Andromache, the widow wandering in exile; and all captive and lost souls. In using the Black woman, Baudelaire inserts the colonized subject into the general symbolic social order; difference is represented and promptly subsumed, approached only to be absorbed. The poem can be read as an aestheticization of the colonial politics and sociology of assimilation, a process of dedifferentiating that Francophone literature will resist.

One must, however, recognize what seems to be Baudelaire's ambiguity on the subject of mystical correspondences. In the article entitled "L'Exposition universelle de 1855," Baudelaire is careful to characterize his system as one that "courait sans cesse après le beau multiforme et versicolore qui se meut dans les spirales infinies de la vie" (p. 955) [was chasing ceaselessly after the multiform and variegated beauty that moves about in the infinite spirals of life]. Baudelaire states in this article on Victor Hugo that "tout, forme, mouvement, nombre, couleur, parfum, dans le *spirituel* comme dans le *naturel,* est significatif, réciproque, converse, *correspondant*" (p. 705) [everything, form, movement, number, color, perfume, in the *spiritual* realm as well as in the *natural* realm, is significant, reciprocal, converse, and *analogous*]. Charles Baudelaire, it would appear, was aware of the consequences of his vision of correspondences, equivalences, and analogies and its nullifying double action. For abstract and systematic critics, writes Baudelaire, "tous les types, toutes les idées, toutes les sensations se confondraient dans une vaste unité, monotone et impersonnelle, immense comme l'ennui et le néant" (p. 956) [all character types, all ideas, all sensations would melt into one another in a vast unity, monotonous and impersonal, as all-encompassing as boredom and nothingness].

The Martinican poet Aimé Césaire would agree with Charles Baudelaire that the true poet is a decipherer and translator. However, as a counterpoint to dedifferentiating equations of sameness, analogy, and correspondences into which signs of difference dissolve and lose their specificity, Aimé Césaire wishes to cultivate and invoke and convoke particularity and precision. The modernist Baudelairean or Swedenborgian system of homologies and correspondences is ultimately a system of *containment.* Césaire's goal is to recover that which signifies difference and to tease it out into the highest relief that grasps Black francophone difference in all of its irreplaceable specificity.

> Disons que si je nomme avec précision (ce qui fait parler de mon exotisme), c'est qu'en nommant avec précision, je crois que l'on restitue à l'objet sa valeur personnelle (comme quand on appelle quelqu'un par son nom); on le suscite dans sa valeur unique singulière; on salue sa valeur de force, sa valeur-force. Ici, c'est le vague qui dissout, qui anéantit, c'est la précision qui individualise. En nommant les objets, c'est un monde enchanté, un monde de "monstres" que je fais surgir sur la grisaille mal différenciée du monde; un monde de "puissances" que je somme, que j'invoque et que je convoque.
>
> En les nommant, flore, faune, dans leur étrangeté, je participe à leur force; je participe de leur force.[22]

[Let us say that if I name with precision (which makes for talk about my exoticism), it is that in naming with precision, I believe that one restores to the object its personal value (just as when one calls someone by his name), one calls it forth in its unique value; one hails its quality of strength, its value-strength. Here it is vagueness that dissolves, that destroys—it is precision that individualizes. In naming objects, it is an enchanted world, a world of "monsters" that I cause to surge forth on the poorly differentiated grayness of the world, a world of "powers" that I summon, that I invoke and that I convoke.

By naming them, flora, fauna, in their strangeness, I participate in and of their strength.]

Césaire wishes to underscore the importance of the sign that is lost against the disorienting background of the world. There is resistance on all levels in francophone literature, but here it is specifically the refusal of insertion into the dominant symbolic social order, for there can be no such insertion without the loss of the specificity of experience. The transformation of the specific into the generalized makes for the leveling of difference, a subsuming of the specificity of the colonized experience into the totalizing first-world view. In its countermoves, francophone literature resists the digestive, intestinal, assimilating, political, social, and aesthetic processes of first-world modernism. Césaire would appear to be addressing this point in his letter of resignation from the French Communist Party in 1956. The letter, addressed to Maurice Thorez, protests the slipknot of assimilation that European Communism has put like a noose around the neck of Martinique, Césaire's country:

Singularité de notre "situation dans le monde" qui ne se confond avec nulle autre. Singularité de nos problèmes qui ne se ramènent à nul autre problème. Singularité de notre histoire coupée de terribles avatars qui n'appartiennent qu'à elle. Singularité de notre culture que nous voulons vivre de manière de plus en plus réelle. . . .

C'est assez dire que pour notre part, nous ne voulons plus nous contenter d'assister à la politique des autres. Au piétinement des autres. Aux combinaisons des autres. Aux rafistolages des consciences ou à la casuistique des autres.

L'heure de nous-mêmes a sonné. . . .

Ici que l'on me permette de penser plus particulièrement à mon malheureux pays: la Martinique.

J'y pense pour constater que le communisme a achevé de lui passer autour du cou le nœud coulant de l'assimilation. . . .

Je préviens une objection.

Provincialisme? Non pas. Je ne m'enterre pas dans un particularisme étroit. Mais je ne veux pas non plus me perdre dans un universalisme décharné. Il y a deux manières de se perdre: par ségrégation murée dans le particulier ou par dilution dans l' "universel."

Ma conception de l'universel est celle d'un universel riche de tout le particulier, riche de tous les particuliers, approfondissement et coexistence de tous les particuliers.

Alors? Alors il nous faudra avoir la patience de reprendre l'ouvrage; la force de refaire ce qui a été défait; la force d'inventer au lieu de suivre; la force "d'inventer" notre route et de la débarrasser des formes toutes faites, des formes pétrifiées qui l'obstruent.[23]

[The exceptional nature of our "situation in the world" which is not to be compared to any other. The peculiar nature of our problems which can be likened to no others. The remarkable nature of our history fraught with enormous avatars peculiar only to it. The uniqueness of our culture which we wish to assume in a more and more genuine way . . .

Suffice it to say that for our part we no longer wish to content ourselves with witnessing the politics of others. Witnessing the marking of time of others. The arrangements of others. The adjustments of consciences or the casuistry of others.

Our time has come . . .

Here do allow me to pause to focus more specifically on my unfortunate country: Martinique.

I think about my country in order to point out that communism has succeeded in putting around its neck the slipknot of assimilation. . . .

I can foresee an objection.

Provincialism? Not in the least. I do not intend to bury myself in a narrow particularism. But nor do I wish to lose myself in some bare and fleshless universalism. There are two ways of losing oneself: by a walled-up apartheid sense of identity or through dilution into "universals."

My conception of the universal is that of a universal rich with all particularity, enriched by all the details, a deepening and a coexistence of all individualities.

And so what? And so, we must have the patience to get back to work; the strength to redo what has been undone; the strength to create rather than to follow; the strength to "invent" our way and to rid it of ready-made formulas, those petrified ideas that can obstruct our path.]

The imperative for francophone literature is to reevaluate, to restage, and to redescribe the themes of modernism. This does not represent an outright rejection of modernism, and certainly not of Baudelaire, but rather a desire to recapture Black subjectivity by salvaging, qualifying, and above all, modulating the themes of modernism in harmony with the realities of the colonized subject's experience. Modulation is perhaps the key maneuver, for it suggests the counterpoint of a differing voice, rhetoric, affect, pitch, and melody. This francophone voice is the articulation of difference that refuses the imposition of the dominant imaginary and proposes different signs. Thus the image of the Martinican Narcissus gazing into the mirror framed by the specificity of Antillean culture makes the point.

Nous cherchons notre vrai visage. Nous avons suffisamment condamné la littérature artificielle qui prétend nous en donner l'image: poètes attardés, héros du poncif, superstitieux faiseurs d'alexandrins, très lâches diseurs de rien. Narcisse martiniquais où donc te reconnaîtras-tu? Plonge tes regards dans le miroir du merveilleux: tes contes, tes légendes, tes chants. Tu y verras s'inscrire, lumineuse, l'image sûre de toi-même.[24]

[We are searching for our true visage. We have sufficiently condemned fake literature that claims to give us a reflection of ourselves: behind-the-times poets, heroes of hackneyed convention, overly scrupulous crafters of twelve-syllable verses, quite cowardly sayers of nothing. Martinican Narcissus, where then will you recognize yourself? Plunge your gazes into the mirror of the marvelous: your short stories, your legends, your songs. You will see inscribed therein, luminous, the unfailing image of yourself.]

The specular invitation extended to the Martinican Narcissus is to desire and seek the self, to delve systematically into the amorous captivation of the Black self. I began with the Poet as translator and decipherer of the universe as text. The sphere here is restricted: The

Narcissus is Black and declared decipherable. The mirror suggests the will to isolate a set of signs and significances necessarily perceived in a cultural frame. The frame isolates the gaze and defines the text. The realizations are that the observation of sameness is disabling and that the articulation of difference is enabling.

Exile, Language, and Consciousness

The existential and economic themes of francophone literature elucidate such events and experiences as the deracination and marginalization of populations, migration, the bordering of cultures, the sense of loss, displacement, lost harmonies, lost communities, homelessness, traditions redefined, survival, experimentation, and the attempts to recover a wholeness from cultural fragments. The overwhelming sensation communicated in this literature is that of being neither, of residing between two worlds, of being neither here nor there. The ambiguous experience of life and language is that of the "plate glass window" of syllepsis:[25] reflection, transparency, opaqueness, and, especially, separation at the moment of contact. There is a yearning for reconciliation of the warring strivings and paradoxical impulses as one lives on the hyphen of cultural identity. Ultimately, francophone literature is a representation of a liminal state.

With words, song, desperation, wisdom, and music, Black Americans have expressed in the blues their depression and alienation when the world, life and the self seemed to have come unhinged. Léon Gontran Damas expresses his sense of desperation as he recognizes his geographically, culturally, and psychologically *dislocated* state in a poem entitled "Limbé" (Blues).

Rendez-les-moi mes poupées noires
    qu'elles dissipent l'image des catins blêmes
    marchands d'amour qui s'en vont viennent
    sur le boulevard de mon ennui . . .
    Donnez-moi l'illusion que je n'aurai plus à contenter
    le besoin étale
    de miséricordes ronflant
    sous l'inconscient dédain du monde . . .

Rendez-les-moi mes poupées noires
    que je joue avec elles
    les jeux naïfs de mon instinct
    resté à l'ombre de ses lois
    recouvrés mon courage
    mon audace
    redevenu moi-même
    nouveau moi-même
    de ce que Hier j'étais   hier
        sans complexité
                    hier
    quand est venue l'heure du déracinement[26]

[Give me back my black dolls
    to dissipate the picture
    of pallid wenches
    merchandising love
    who stroll along
    the boulevard of my ennui . . .
Give me the illusion I shall no longer
    have to satisfy
    the sprawling need
    for mercy
    snoring beneath the world's disdainful nose
Give me back my black dolls
    so that I might play with them
    the simple games of my instincts
    instincts that endure
    in the darkness of their laws
    with my courage recovered
    and my audacity
    I have become myself once more
    myself again
    out of what I used to be
    once upon a time
        once
    without complexity
                once upon a time
    when the hour of uprooting came. . . .]

The liminal state emerges as a consequence of the difficult process of assimilation, the failed integration into the European language —meaning culture and the repression of one's original condition— which implies alienation from languages, history, and ethnic culture including attitudes, beliefs, norms, values, aesthetics, lifestyles, accumulated knowledge, actions, and material objects. In "Blues," Damas insists on this consciousness of the loss of culture for the Afro-French assimilado:

Le sauront jamais cette rancune de mon coeur
À l'oeil de ma méfiance ouvert trop tard
ils ont cambriolé l'espace qui était le mien
la coutume
les jours
la vie
la chanson
le rythme
l'effort
le sentier
l'eau
la case
la terre enfumée grise
la sagesse
les mots
les palabres
les vieux
la cadence
les mains
les piétinements
le sol (*Pigments,* p. 44)

[Will they never know the rancor in my heart
opened to the eye of my distrust too late they did away
with what was mine
ways
days
life
song
rhythm

effort
footpath
water
huts
the smoke-gray earth
the wisdom
the words
the palavers
the elders
the cadence
the hands
the feet
marking time
upon the ground][27]

This condition of assimilation, marginality, alienation, and dislocation leads to the predicament of "double consciousness," so deftly defined and eloquently expressed by the twentieth-century Black American intellectual W. E. B. DuBois (1868–1963):

> After the Egyptian and Indian, the Greek and Roman, the Teuton and Mongolian, the Negro is a sort of seventh son, born with a veil, and gifted with second-sight in this American world,—a world which yields him no true self-consciousness, but only lets him see himself through the revelation of the other world. It is a peculiar sensation, this double-consciousness, this sense of always looking at one's self through the eyes of others, of measuring one's soul by the tape of a world that looks on in amused contempt and pity. One ever feels his twoness,—an American, a Negro; two souls, two thoughts, two unreconciled strivings; two warring ideals in one dark body, whose dogged strength alone keeps it from being torn asunder.
>
> The history of the American Negro is the history of this strife,—this longing to attain self-conscious manhood, to merge his double self into a better and truer self. In this merging he wishes neither of the other selves to be lost. He would not Africanize America, for America has too much to teach the world and Africa. He would not bleach his Negro soul in a flood of white Americanism, for he knows that Negro blood has a message for the world. He simply wishes to make it possible for a man to be both a Negro and an American, without being cursed and spit upon by

> his fellows, without having the doors of Opportunity closed roughly in his face.[28]

At the center of the adventure of francophone literary culture is the self-contradictory double consciousness of the formerly colonized writing subject. DuBois articulates the ambiguous identity of the American who is Negro. This DuBoisian state of double consciousness embraces the condition of the Black or colonized being *worldwide in the twentieth century*, for DuBois insists on the antagonism, incoherence, and contradictions at the core of the articulation of *identity* when identity of self with *race* is in some measure *in conflict* and in contestation with identity of self with *nation:* "Herein lie buried many things which, if read with patience, may show the strange meaning of being black here at the dawning of the twentieth century. This meaning is not without interest to you, Gentle Reader, for the problem of the twentieth century is the problem of the color line" (359).

DuBois's binocular analyses insist on the paradoxes of the dynamics of nation, race, and, ultimately, narration. The tensions between nation and race are parallel and separable, yet inextricably bound, oppositional yet permeable, elevating yet humbling, empowering and stifling, enabling and disabling, leaving the subject compartmentalized and, thus, conscious of being simultaneously *inside* and *outside* the nation, a condition that gives rise to a kind of "double vision." To be an American Negro, to be Afro-French, burdened and endowed with a double consciousness and double vision is to be, in a certain sense, "a twisted signifier." DuBois's color *line* analysis is sociological, and yet it is also of linguistic and psychoanalytic consequence, since it anticipates a Lacanian analysis of the division and unity of consciousness and repression, using the Möbius *strip* as illustration.

> Lacan uses "signifier" in a contextual theory of meaning, and would obviously subscribe to Wittgenstein's slogan: "The meaning is the use." Thus he also uses "signifier" to avoid the implication that any given word "contains" or "has" a meaning of its own, outside its diacritic reference to other signifiers. In this sense, even Saussure's distinctions give rise to ambiguities, for if the meaning of a signifier is its differentiation from other signifiers, it can nevertheless be defined by them. Thus the loose use of signified to mean "signification" is just another way of saying the signified is a signifier after all.

> Saussure likens the relationship of signifier (sound) and signified (sense) to the two sides of a single piece of paper. This image brings to mind the analogy of the Moebius strip sometimes employed by Lacan to describe the subject, where the apparent division of conscious and repressed turns out to be the unity of the writing on one continuous side. Analogies are of course the weakest and most dangerous form of argument, however valuable they may be as illustration. It is in this restricted latter sense that one might liken the relationship between signifier (word-concept) and reality, which is the essentially irresolvable problem here, to that between a map and the countryside it represents. One might then recall the assertion of topologists that if a map is crumpled up and thrown down on another identical map, at least one point will be exactly where it would be if the two had been simply superimposed. For Lacan, the symptom is a twisted signifier, but it is still related somehow to the original map, just as the nodal point of the dream in analysis is a transferential point aimed at the "significant other" the analyst represents.[29]

Frantz Fanon (1925–61) specifies the complications of self-awareness that result from the necessity of mastering the French language. For the colonialized subject, to write and to speak in French is to inscribe the self into the worldview of the Other and therefore to exist for and through the Other. The result is the sensation of loss, betrayal, even shame. The challenge to the francophone writer, therefore, is to translate, in the archaic sense of *translatio studii*—that is, to carry over into the French language or the culture of the Other—the particularity of self and culture, as well as the sense of "home."

> In a more limited group, when students from the Antilles meet in Paris, they have the choice of two possibilities:
>
> —either to stand with the white world (that is to say, the real world), and, since they will speak French, to be able to confront certain problems and incline to a certain degree of universality in their conclusions;
>
> —or to reject Europe, "Yo" and cling together in their dialect, making themselves quite comfortable in what we shall call the *umwelt* of Martinique, by this I mean—and this applies particularly to my brothers of the Antilles—that when one of us tries, in Paris or any other university city, to study a problem seriously, he is accused of self-aggrandizement, and the surest way of cutting him down is to remind him of the Antilles by exploding into dialect. This must be recognized as one of the reasons

why so many friendships collapse after a few months of life in Europe . . . A Senegalese learns Creole in order to pass as an Antilles native: I call this alienation.[30]

Language, exile, and consciousness are complementary problematics in the colonized outsider writers' search for precise elaboration of their culture in a European language. This linguistic dilemma often leads to the cognitive, psychological, social, linguistic, symbolic, and political implications of the coercive imposition of another language upon an individual, a culture, and a region. The internalization of that language by the individual, with the language's implicit worldview and core values, can have deleterious consequences for ethnicity, culture, and nationality, because the process involves the interpenetration of cultures and their respective systems of knowledge. The colonialized discourse expresses cultural difference in the attempt to rearticulate the aims of knowledge from the perspective of the resisting Other. Put differently, the goal of the discourse of cultural difference is to disturb the calculation of the colonial power holder and the production of knowledge, thereby producing other spaces of signification.

The first francophone voices of difference sprang from the liminal, minority position, where, as Foucault would say, the relations of discourse are tantamount to warfare. It is a question of *Légitime défense*,[31] for the first generation of Black francophone student poets did not consider themselves poets but rather fighters.[32] The French-language poetry of this generation is sui generis in its political stance. Its aesthetic has to do with aggressivity, opposition, and insurrection, which inform the stylistic choices and constitute a pragmatics of rejection, rebuttal, and repudiation, and which are antiimperial, anticanonical, and anticolonial in register. Consider Léon Damas, writing in the mid-1930s:

C'est qu'aujourd'hui, il ne s'agit plus d'être consciencieux, de s'appliquer à ne pas violer les règles, de jouer au nombre de pieds qui se comptent, de travailler à des sonnets impeccables. Les héritiers de Leconte de Lisle, de François Coppée, de Sully Prudhomme, de Catulle Mendès, de Léon Dierx, ont vécu, bien vécu de leur legs.

Le temps du refoulement et des inhibitions a fait place à un autre âge: celui où l'homme colonisé prend conscience de ses droits et de ses devoirs d'écrivain, de romancier ou de conteur, d'essayiste ou de poète.

La pauvreté, l'analphabétisme, l'exploitation de l'homme par l'homme, le racisme social et politique dont souffre l'homme de couleur noire ou jaune, le travail forcé, les inégalités, les mensonges, la résignation, les escroqueries, les préjugés, les complaisances, les lâchetés. les démissions, les crimes commis au nom de la liberté, de l'égalité, de la fraternité, voilà le thème de cette poésie indigène, d'expression française.

De plus en plus, politique et littérature s'entrepénètrent et leur synchronisme se fait de plus en plus apparent dans les oeuvres des représentants de la nouvelle école.[33]

[Today it is no longer a question of being conscientious, of trying hard not to break the rules, of keeping the meter, and working on impeccable sonnets. The heirs of Leconte de Lisle, François Coppée, Sully Prudhomme, Catulle Mendès, and Léon Dierx have lived, and lived well, on their inheritance.

The time of repression and inhibitions has given way to a different age: one where the colonial subject realizes his rights and duties as an author, novelist, short story writer, essayist or poet. Poverty, illiteracy, the exploitation of man by man, social and political racism weighing on the black and yellow races, forced labor, inequality, lies, resignation, tricks, prejudices, complacency, cowardice, responsibilities shirked, crimes committed in the name of liberty, equality, and fraternity: these are the subjects of this native poetry expressed in French.

More and more, politics and literature are becoming interwoven and their synchronism is becoming more and more obvious in the works of representatives of the new school.][34]

The problem lies in the absorption of the difference, the literal, and the specific into the generalized (metaphoric) malaise resulting from the European modernist exaltation of individuality, marginality, and alienation as the markers of superiority, genius, and election. It is in this direction that Frantz Fanon, the Martinican ethnopsychiatrist, orients his analysis of decolonization and "the colonized intellectual dusted over by colonial culture."

All the Mediterranean values—the triumph of the human individual, of clarity and beauty—become lifeless, colorless knickknacks. All of those speeches seem like collections of dead words; those values that seemed

> to uplift the soul are revealed as worthless, simply because they have nothing to do with the concrete conflict in which the people is engaged. Individualism is the first to disappear. . . . the idea of a society of individuals where each person shuts himself up in his own subjectivity and whose only wealth is individual thought. . . . The native intellectual takes part in a sort of auto-da-fé, in which the destruction of all his idols; egoism, recrimination that springs from pride and the childish stupidity of those who always want to have the last word. . . . The motto "look out for yourself" the atheist's method of salvation is in this context forbidden.[35]

A questioning of European values does not mean a return to a precolonialist society. "Je pense à quiconque a perdu ce qui ne se retrouve" [I think of all those who have lost what they can never, never hope to find again]. This verse places us in the realm of pure nostalgia, for among other things, "la superbe Afrique." And yet, Baudelaire's poem "Le Cygne" ambiguously undercuts the modernist desire for a return to some preindustrial, Edenic home of origins. Francophone literature will emphatically deny the possibility of a return of any kind, especially to an antecolonial state. There can be *no* return to precolonial Africa, as Césaire makes clear.

> This being said, it seems that in certain circles they pretend to have discovered in me an "enemy of Europe" and a prophet of the return to the ante-European past.
>
> For my part, I search in vain for the place where I could have expressed such views; where I ever underestimated the importance of Europe in the history of human thought; where I ever preached a *return* of any kind; where I ever claimed that there could be a *return*.[36]

Francophone artists are not exiles in the aesthetic modernist sense. According to a basic trope in the composite presuppositions of first-world modernist aesthetics, exile predicts or implies a nostalgic longing and return, but this exile-return trope is precisely what is unavailable to the colonized subject. Exile in francophone literary culture is grounded in the inability, even the lack of desire, to return to the native land as it was in its abject colonial or postindependence state. Under the conditions that are the consequences of colonialism, or postindependence kleptocracies, there is no nostalgic reverie of a utopian pastoralism in the native land. Reminiscences abound, as well as fond recollections of family and communal existence, but they do not constitute a longing to return, for the overwhelming resultant recognition is of a past that demands a better future. Home is a wellspring of cultural values and an inspiration to action that will engineer a just future. If the son and daughter return, it is not because of a longing for the way things were, but rather because they wish to change the social, political, and economic realities that are the legacies of the colonial incursion.

Léon Laleau, a Haitian poet of the 1930s, has written very instructively about what goes into the experience of writing in French by the colonized.[37] In the collection *Musique nègre,* Laleau captures, with painful eloquence, the difficulty of inscribing oneself into a nonnative language.[38] One very brief poem in particular, "Trahison," crystallizes the situation of marginality, liminality, and perplexity:

TRAHISON

sentez-vous cette souffrance
et ce désespoir à nul autre égal
d'apprivoiser, avec les mots de France
Ce cœur qui m'est venu du Sénégal?

[BETRAYAL

Do you know this suffering
and this despair comparable to no other
of attempting to calm and to tame with words from
France
this heart of mine from Senegal?]

The Negritude movement and the voices of francophone literature emerging from the period of French political and social assimilation offer a different reading of displacement. In this instance, exile and alienation are not situated within modernism, but rather constitute a category and precondition continuous with and counter to first-world modernism. Language and writing are recognized as a predescription and prescription that are experienced and dealt with as difficulty, effort, struggle, work, resistance, and war. There is a desire to return to the individual the power to live *in* and *through* language and *not* to submit to it. From the Laleau poem we learn that minority discourse sets the act of emergence in the antagonistic *in-between* of image and sign. The act of creation in the francophone world is a contentious performative space. Cultural difference addresses the jarring of meanings and values generated in between the variety and diversity associated with cultural plenitude. Cultural difference is to be found where the "loss" of meaning enters as a cutting edge. In *L'Enfant de sable,* the Moroccan writer Tahar ben Jelloun has one of his characters declare: "One cannot step from one life into another with a simple stride across a footbridge" (p. 130). Cultural difference emerges from the borderline moment of translation, in the foreignness of languages. From consciousness emerges the awareness that the transfer of indigenous meaning can never be total between different systems of knowledge or knowing the world. Consciousness here is tied to a sharpened existential awareness of place—and of displacement—of location and dislocation; of having been forcibly moved out of (*ex salire,* the Latin root of exile) one place and into another, but of not having successfully negotiated the transfer, the crossover, of not having been successfully carried "home" to the new place, as Laleau suggests in the rest of his poem "Trahison":

Ce cœur obsédant, qui ne correspond
Pas à mon langage ou à mes costumes,
Et sur lequel mordent, comme un crampon
Des sentiments d'Emprunt et des coutumes
D'Europe

[This haunted heart that doesn't fit
My language or the clothes I wear
Chafes within the grip
Of borrowed feelings, of European ways]

These verses point to a sensation of cultural *transvestism* in, as Laleau and Walter Benjamin would say, this "ill-fitting robe of language." Transvestism, like assimilation, is often a voluntary act undertaken with exuberance. It is the consciousness of one's eternal lack, of the impossibility of ever becoming what one is imitating, that can lead to the tragic despair of feeling ridiculous. After Laleau, Damas would exploit the *ridiculus sum* vestmental code.

SOLDE/SELLOUT

J'ai l'impression d'être ridicule
dans leur souliers
dans leur smoking
dans leur plastron
dans leur faux-col
dans leur monocle
dans leur melon
. . . . . .

J'ai l'impression d'être ridicule
dans leurs salons
dans leurs manières
dans leurs courbettes
dans leur multiple besoin de singeries

J'ai l'impression d'être ridicule
parmi eux complice
parmi eux souteneur
parmi eux égorgeur
les mains effroyablement rouges
du sang de leur ci-vi-li-sa-tion (*Pigments,* p. 41)

[I feel ridiculous
in their shoes
their dinner jackets
their starched shirts
and detachable collars
their monocles and
their bowler hats
. . . . . .

I feel ridiculous
in their drawing rooms
in their manners

their bowings and scrapings
in their manifold need of monkeyshines

I feel ridiculous
among them
like an accomplice
among them
like a pimp
like a murderer among them
my hands hideously red
with the blood of their
ci-vi-li-za-tion][39]

Transvestism becomes the satiric representation of hyper-assimilation or, stated otherwise, the colonized subject's *divestment* of his original cultural values. The awareness of a certain transvestism in the ill-fitting robe of language leads, however, to a need for a second divestment of language and the culture it signifies—an imperative to strip down to the nakedness that recovers a state of nonknowledge.

The Game of Slipknot

Consciousness occurs in the relay of inscription into one language accompanied simultaneously by an erasure of content or effacement of self from the language of one's origins. There is an awareness of an infidelity that leads some writers to make seemingly innocent and coquettish statements like those of Tahar ben Jelloun that Arabic is his wife and French is his mistress.[40] Consciousness, then, is an awareness that one has shifted levels. This awareness of the secondariness of the expression of the imaginary and the expression of "home" leads to a nexus of concerns where writers can find themselves in a knot of confusion and despair, in a slipknot of assimilation, under the stranglehold of language. My perhaps seemingly excessive pressuring of color *line,* Möbius *strip, twisted* signifier, double consciousness, and double vision, as well as my teasing out of the seme *nexus,* knot, slipknot, and stranglehold of language, is tragically borne out in the now celebrated example of another Haitian poet, Edmond Laforest.

Often it is a single, singular incident that dramatizes the complexities of a dilemma—especially the dilemma presently under discussion. The insurmountable agony of living, the incommensurable experience of struggle and survival in the construction of a national culture, and the failures—psychological, spiritual, existential, metaphysical, aesthetic, literary and stylistic—of the ambiguous adventure and of linguistic marginality in the French language coalesce in the fate of Edmond Laforest (1876–1905), a composer of classical alexandrines and limpid, romantic verse. The students who became the first generation of Negritude poets—Léon Gontran Damas, Léopold Sédar Senghor, Aimé Césaire—were poignantly aware of the extent to which a schooled resemblance underscores how emphatically one is not French.

According to the *Anthologie d'un siècle de poésie haitienne, 1817–1925* (1924) by Louis Morpeau, "the heart of Edmond Laforest bled in crafted verses imbued with a distinguished melancholy and a deep pessimism, and his heart must have bled in real life, if it is true according to accounts that two or three months after the occupation of the Haitian Republic by American marines, Monsieur Laforest, who in verse and in prose had defended his native land, took his own life."[41] A concern for propriety obviously motivated the anthologist to spare the reader an important detail: Edmond Laforest symbolically tied a Larousse French dictionary around his neck and drowned himself in the great Artibonite River.

A response of irrepressible laughter is almost inevitable upon hearing this account. Laughter is often the only defense in the face of the absurd, the paradoxical, and the nonrational. Edmond Laforest's life and suicide concretize the seriousness of the relation of colonized writers to the act of writing in their effort to find a voice in a European language. Laforest calls attention to the suffocation and drowning of many other writers who succumbed under the weight of the language of the European Other.

Similarly caught in the slipknot of his profound appreciation of France and French culture and an abiding love for his colonized homeland, the Malagasy poet Jean-Joseph Rabéarivélo committed suicide in 1937. Frantz Fanon instructs us:

> I ascribe a basic importance to the phenomenon of language. To speak means to be in a position to use a certain syntax, to grasp the morphology

> of this or that language, but it means above all to assume a culture, to support the weight of civilization. The problem we confront is this. . . . The Negro of the Antilles will be proportionately whiter—that is, he will come closer to being a real human being—in direct ratio to his mastery of the French language. A man who has a language consequently possesses the world expressed and implied by that language. What we are getting at becomes plain: Mastery of language affords power. Paul Valéry knew this, for he called language "the god gone astray in the flesh (Charmes)."[42]

Laforest's dramatic suicide warns us that language is a potent force, a force of domination by the conqueror-colonizer—domination of a people, of a mind, psyche, and spirit, of life even. Laforest succumbed to this domination entirely. For the present generation of Black literary critics,[43] his death is emblematic. He died agonistically of irredeemable frustration—of silence, of mutism, of the feeling of having lost his voice, caught in the slipknot that is the division and unity of consciousness and repression.

At the conceptual crossroads, Laforest could not meet the challenge, it would seem, of "incomplete signification," that is, of a turning of boundaries and limits into the in-between spaces through which the meanings of cultural and political authority are negotiated. At the perplexing crossroads of language, history, culture, and consciousness, Laforest perhaps could not negotiate that in-between space "containing" thresholds of meaning that must be crossed, erased, and translated in the processes of cultural production, minority discourse, and cultural differences. Although Aimé Césaire does not succumb, he recognizes the challenges of inscription of self into the French language. Césaire becomes the potently ignorant being again, working his way through the divestment of language, a pawning of language, toward the eventual expropriation of the previously imposed language and a fascination in the face of its power:

> Il y a des tas de choses dont je ne sais pas le nom et que
> je voudrais te dire.[44]
>
> [There are so many things the names of which I do not know and that
> I would like to tell you.]
>
> Pour penser à toi j'ai déposé tous mes mots au mont-de-piété.[45]

[In order to think about you I have turned all of my words in to the pawnshop.]

> Il faut plier le français au génie noir. Ou bien on n'utilise pas le français et on emploie carrément sa langue. C'est une possibilité: J'ai voulu l'employer dans des conditions très particulières. J'ai voulu mettre le sceau imprimé, la marque nègre, la marque antillaise comme vous voulez sur le français. J'ai voulu lui donner la couleur du créole.[46]

[One must make the French language yield to the bent of the Black genius. Or else one does not use French and one's own language straight out. That is a possibility: I wanted to use it in very particular conditions. I wanted to put the Black stamp, the Negro brand, the Antillean mark, as you like it, on the French language. I wanted to give it the color of Creole.]

> Je n'ai jamais cessé d'être fasciné par la magie des mots. Le mot est démiurge, c'est lui qui organise le chaos. C'est avec les mots que nous passons de l'existence toute simple à l'être.[47]

[I have never ceased to be fascinated by the magic power of words. The word is the creator of the world, it is that which organizes chaos. It is with words that we pass from mere existence into being.]

To ponder the dilemma described in the foregoing is to ponder the complexity of the contact between France and its former colonies, a contact that paradoxically has led to an enrichment, a revitalization even, of the French language in the twentieth century. The process of cultural change and psycholinguistic evolution that has led to this felicitous development of a flourishing body of francophone literature has been fraught with difficulties and failures, however.

The fascination with language in the cultural zone of instability, perplexity, and the liminal, "where the people dwell," pervades francophone literature, even, perhaps especially, in the densest sites of cultural complexity, such as in immigrant-cosmopolitan-student neighborhoods, cafés, and universities of sophisticated capitals. Such is the backdrop of the novel *Sans la miséricorde du Christ*. In this 1985 novel by the francophone Argentinian writer Hector Bianciotti, who is of Italian origin and makes his home both in Paris and Buenos Aires, there is a further description of the ambiguous adventure of linguistic exile and consciousness of the ill-fitting robe of language.

> J'ai tout de suite aimé sa façon de parler . . . la géographie n'est que la forme apparente . . . toute de surface . . . de l'exil . . .
>
> Moi, qui n'ai plus de langue mais me tourmentent plusieurs ou qui, parfois bénéficie de plusieurs, j'ai des sentiments qui varient selon les mots que j'emploie. Il m'arrive d'être désespéré dans une langue et à peine triste dans une autre. Chaque langue nous fait mentir, exclut une partie des faits, de nous-mêmes; mais dans le mensonge, il y a une affirmation, et c'est une façon d'être à un moment donné; plusieurs langues à la fois nous désavouent, nous morcellent, nous éparpillent en nous mêmes. . . .
>
> J'embarassai Adélaïde Marèse par quelques questions sur ce sujet—on ne peut pas poser de question plus intime. En fait, ce que je pris sur le moment pour de l'embarras n'était peut-être que le reflet d'un souci d'exactitude, le scrupule du croyant qui s'avance parmi les révérences et cautèles de la théologie. La langue peut être une théologie.[48]
>
> [Instantly, I fell in love with her way of speaking. . . . Geography, having primarily to do with surfaces, is only the most obvious form of exile.
>
> I who no longer have a language, but rather am tormented by several, or who sometimes benefit from several, have feelings that vary according to the words I use. Sometimes it happens that I am utterly devastated by the words in one language and made hardly if at all sad in another. Each language makes us lie, excludes a part of the facts, a part of ourselves. But in the lie there seems to be an affirmation, and the lie is a way of being at a given moment; speaking several languages simultaneously fails to translate us, splits us, scatters and fragments us within ourselves . . .
>
> I embarrassed Adélaïde Marèse by asking some questions on this subject. One cannot, you know, pose more intimate questions. Yet in fact what I had taken at the moment for embarrassment was perhaps only the reflection of a concern for exactness, the scruples of an acolyte who makes her way carefully through the reverences and casuistries of theology. A language can be a theology.]

Under conditions of exile and postcolonialism, conflict between the superordinate and subordinate ethnic groups is inevitable. The inability to give voice to a group's aspirations, to invent new traditions, to give expression to the silent, flowing, secret life of the heart, of the soul, of the unconscious; the feelings of fragmentation and isolation, and the immobility of one's treadmill existence in a society of speed, technology, rapid communication, and unprecedented mobility; the disconnectedness from one's past and traditions, the solitude amid the urban crowd where one sought contact and communion, and the sense of loss and homelessness, wandering and ruin—these are not merely modernist commonplaces but rather constitute the poetry of powerlessness, the poetry of speechlessness.

In a shared environment where between the oppressor and the oppressed there is little sharing of the benefits of the economy, as already stated, expropriation of the language is empowering. Language has the potential of becoming an ideological tool for ethnic autonomy. In the painful assertion of political independence, confronting the psycholinguistics of the experience of the imposed language, language has healing, therapeutic, and redemptive powers not to be underestimated. Poets have always understood the redemptive healing power of the word and have notably declared it in the twentieth century. T. S. Eliot exclaimed:

> For last year's words belong to last year's language
> And next year's words await another voice[49]
>
> You cannot say, or guess, for you know only
> A heap of broken images[50]
>
> These fragments I have shored against my ruin[51]

Aimé Césaire entitled his most experimental volume of poetry *Les Armes miraculeuses* (Miraculous Weapons), which are none other than words. For words have the power to reveal and transform by means of symbols, metaphor, and the forging (in the sense of a blacksmith) of images that invent the future and express the world not as it is but as it should be. Through images there is a power of parthenogenesis, a veritable giving birth—in the case of the poet, rebirth—to one's self. Césaire declares: Images think for me; I think myself into being through images.

> À Paris, en même temps que je découvrais la culture, j'ai mieux compris les raisons de mon insatisfaction; j'ai pris conscience de mon ap-

partenance à la condition originale du Nègre. Ma poésie est née de cette connotation.

Le *Cahier,* c'est le premier texte où j'ai commencé à me reconnaître; je l'ai écrit comme anti-poême. Il s'agissait pour moi d'attaquer au niveau de la forme, la poésie traditionnelle française, d'en bousculer les structures.[52]

[In Paris, at the same time that I was discovering culture, I better understood the reasons for my dissatisfaction. I became aware of my belonging to the original condition of the Negro [Black]. My poetry was born out of this acknowledgment.

The *Cahier [d'un retour au pays natal]* is the first text where I started to recognize myself; I wrote it as an anti-poem. For me it was a question of attacking traditional French poetry on the level of form, of upsetting its structure.]

Je tire un pied, oh je tire l'autre pied, laissez-moi sans m'insulter de promesses me dégluer de la charogne et de la boue.[53]

[I withdraw one foot, oh I withdraw the other, allow me, without insulting me with promises, to unglue myself from the putrid carcass and from the mire.]

Je saute ancestral aux branches de ma végétation, je m'égare aux complications fructueuses.[54]

[I leap ancestral to the branches of my vegetation. I stray through fruitful complications.]

Nous avons bondi nous les esclaves, nous le fumier nous les bêtes au sabot de patience[55]

[We have leaped forward we the slaves, we the dung
We the beasts with the hoof of patience.]

Césaire expresses his frustration with the shopworn valuelessness of words and the impotence of language to capture and contain that which is felt and perceived yet is nonarticulable and untranslatable. After writing *Notebook,* Césaire declared that he had the sensation of having given birth to himself—through language. Naturally one might wonder to what extent this preoccupation with words could lead to an esoteric poetic experience akin to "art for art's sake." However, this is rarely the case with the better, committed minority poets who have a clear sense of their role as theorists of a new aesthetic. In the case of *Notebook,* we see that it is paradoxically through a hatred of traditional poetry and traditional literature as art for art's sake that Césaire became a poet.

> I don't think I had found a form that was my own. I was still under the influence of the French poets. In short, if *Return to My Native Land* took the form of a prose poem, it was truly by chance. Even though I wanted to break with French literary traditions, I did not actually free myself from them until the moment I decided to turn my back on poetry. In fact, you could say that I became a poet by renouncing poetry. Do you see what I mean? Poetry was for me the only way to break the *stranglehold* the accepted French form held on me.
>
> In other words, for me French was a tool that I wanted to use in developing a new means of expression. I wanted to create an Antillean French, a black French that, while still being French had a black character.[56] (Emphasis added.)

Speechlessness as a trope of first-world modernism is inflected by francophone literary culture as one of the untranslatabilities of cultures and, particularly, cultural signs. The sense is that European languages are not propertied in the way that renders them easily habitable, thus leaving the third-world subjectivity nonspeakable and inaudible in these conventional linguistic sites.

The purpose for Césaire's generation of poets was to reinvent language. The French poet Apollinaire shouted the cry of liberation and frustration in his *Calligrammes* when he exclaimed: "Oh mouths man is looking for a new language which grammarians will have no say about." A poem should be a demonstration of protest, according to André Breton and Césaire. The surrealist formula was that "beauty [art] will be convulsive or it will not be," but as she contemplated the miserable state of poetic mimicry on her island, Suzanne Césaire proclaimed, "Martinican poetry will be cannibalistic or it will not be."[57] It was felt that the poet could no longer concentrate on what was said while neglecting how it was said. In addition to the role of theorist of a new aesthetic, the poet was also pilgrim, quaestor, archaeologist, museum, library, visionary, silence broken, penetrating eye, sonorous ever-expanding and contracting sympathetic echo at the center of all experience, sensation, and sensibility. In a 1959 article Aimé Césaire was unequivocal concerning the ideological and utopian intent of his poetry:

> "Notre devoir d'hommes de culture, notre double devoir est là: Il est de hâter la *décolonisation,* et il est, au sein même du présent, de préparer une bonne *décolonisation,* une *décolonisation* sans séquelles.
>
> Il faut hâter la *décolonisation,* qu'est-ce à dire? Cela veut dire qu'il faut, et par tous les moyens, hâter le mûrissement de la prise de conscience populaire, sans quoi il n'y aura jamais de décolonisation. . . .
>
> Certains ont pu dire que l'écrivain est un ingénieur des âmes. Nous, dans la conjoncture où nous sommes, nous sommes des propagateurs d'âmes, des multiplicateurs d'âmes, et à la limite des inventeurs d'âmes.[58]

> [Our responsibility as men of culture, our double responsibility is the following: it is to hasten decolonization and it is at the very present time to prepare a sound decolonization, a process of decolonization that leaves no post-traumatic scars.
>
> That we must hasten decolonization is to do what exactly? It means that we must by every means available to us hasten the raising of consciousness of the masses, without which there will be no decolonization.
>
> . . . Some have said that the writer can be an engineer of souls.
>
> In our present situation we are propagators of souls, multipliers of souls, and to a certain extent almost inventors of souls.]

For Césaire the transformation of language is inextricably linked to social transformation. The ideologizing of language enables an ethnic group to play desired roles in symbolic mobilization and unification; it also leads to the expropriation, transformation, and development of these languages themselves into fitting instruments of high culture. In the psychological and social domain, language, as an ideological weapon, advances the mission of full self-realization, self-hood, self-determination, and political autonomy. Historically, the first step toward self-esteem is evident in *Notebook of a Return to the Native*

Land, when Césaire evokes the geography of suffering, enslavement, and colonialism, ending with an allusion to the first successful slave rebellion in Haiti, and when this classical-studies major coins the word *négritude.*

> What is mine, these few thousand death-bearers who mill in the calabash of an island, and mine, too, the archipelago arched with an anguished desire to negate itself as if from maternal anxiety to protect this most delicate tenuity separating the two Americas; and these loins which secrete for Europe the hearty liquor of a Gulf Stream, and one of the two slopes of incandescence between which the Equator tightropewalks towards Africa. And my nonfence island, its brave audacity standing at the stern of this Polynesia; and before it, Guadeloupe split in two down its dorsal line, and equal in poverty to us, Haiti where Négritude rose for the first time and stated that it believed in its humanity; and the funny little tail of Florida where the strangulation of a nigger is being completed, and Africa gigantically caterpillaring up to the Spanish foot of Europe, its nakedness where Death scythes widely.[59]

It is a step toward the unification of the commonwealth of Black speakers of French when they, by virtue of their linguistic particularity, bear the mark of the colonial experience and must share the experience of the internalization of their language so as to transcend it. Paradoxically, this shared experience and language overarches colonial national boundaries, as well as boundaries of precolonial tribal Africa, so as, in a quite unforeseen fashion, to lend a resonant, unified voice to hundreds, perhaps a thousand, linguistically distinct ethnic groups. In this commonwealth phase, the poets write for survival, catharsis, and expression in French rather than retreating into regional languages or into the humiliated and humiliating languages that bear the scars of the slave experience—languages such as Creole, which can be described as the linguistic crumbs of European languages tossed to the slaves for the most rudimentary, functional communication. There can be *no* return to precolonial Africa.

In every work of Aimé Césaire's the relation of language, words, and ethnicity is explicitly discussed. In *A Tempest,* an adaptation of Shakespeare's *The Tempest* for Black Theatre, Ariel, a mulatto sprite, is a hesitant intellectual and indentured servant to Prospero, the magician colonizer of an island inhabited by Caliban, a black radicalized native who has been taught his master's language. In Ariel and Caliban, the spectator-reader recognizes Martin Luther King and Malcolm X, respectively, and the play addresses the imperial will to power in the Americas. The tone is tragicomic. Caliban (phonetic echo of "cariban" and anagram of cannibal) uses his newly imposed language to curse his master rather than to sing his praises. Césaire saw in Shakespeare, Prospero, and Caliban the paradigm of the relationship between the colonizer and the colonized, the master and the slave. Caliban is also aware of the foreign worldview (weltanschauung) that resonates in every syllable of the language of this newly arrived oppressor:

Une Tempête (*my translation*)

A TEMPEST

Caliban enters

Caliban: Uhuru.

Prospero: What are you saying?

Caliban: I am saying Uhuru.

Prospero: Ah, once again your barbarous language is surfacing. How many times have I told you that I do not approve of it? Besides, you could be courteous, a polite hello would not kill you.

Caliban: Ah! I forgot myself. . . . Hello . . . But a Hello covered as much as possible with wasps, toads, running sores, and shit. Let today hasten by ten years the day when birds of prey from the sky and the wild beasts of the earth satisfy their appetite on your rotting carcass.

Prospero: Ever the gracious spirit, I see, you wretched monkey. How can one be so ugly?

Caliban: So you find me ugly. Well, I don't find you cute at all, with your hook nose you look like an old vulture. Hee Hee! Yes an old vulture with a skinny shaven neck!

Prospero: Since you have mastered the art of curses and insults, perhaps you wish to bless me for having so masterfully taught you the art of speech. A barbarian. A brutish beast that I have trained, educated, that I have lifted up from the base animal instincts that still defile your being through and through.

Caliban: First of all, none of that is true! You have taught me absolutely nothing. Except, of course to jabber a few words in order to obey your orders: cut the wood, wash the dishes, fish, plant the vegetables, because you are too lazy to do it. Now as for your science and technology, have you ever taught me any of that, huh! Ho Ho, you have taken great pain to keep that to yourself. Your science and technology you have quite egotistically kept for you and yourself alone, locked up in those big books over there.

Prospero: Without me, where and what would you be!

Caliban: Without you? Quite simply I would be the King. The King of the island, the king of my island that you took from my mother Sycorax. (Act 1, sc. 2)

Prospero: All this is so amusing! You have tried in vain, in vain, for you will never succeed in convincing me that I am a tyrant.

Caliban:
You must understand a few things, Prospero:
For years I have bowed my head
For years I have accepted my condition
Accepted, accepted it all!
Your insults, your ingratitude
Worse still, more degrading than all the rest
Your condescension
But now, it's all over.
Finished, do you understand?
Your power, I don't give a damn.
The same goes for your bloodhounds,
Your police force, your riot-control intervention
And do you know why I don't give a damn?
Do you want to know why?
It is because one day I know that I am going to have you
Impaled. And on the very stake that you will have
Sharpened for me. Impaled upon yourself
Prospero, you are a magician, a prestidigitator, an illusionist

Deceiving yourself.
Ah lies, you are familiar with lies
And you have lied to me so thoroughly
Lied to me about the world, lied to me about me
So much so that you imposed upon me an image of myself
that I almost was convinced of.
Me—underdeveloped as you say, incapable of mastering basic skills.
That is how you would have me see myself.
And this image you have given me of myself, I loathe it
And it is false
But now, and oh it has taken such a long time, now I know
You, you cancer in my heart and I also know myself
By the way, you do have the opportunity to get out now.
You can break camp, get the hell out
You can return to Europe
Ah you aren't listening to me
I am certain you won't leave
Oh it makes me laugh, your so-called "mission"
Your "vocation"
Your calling is to make my life miserable,
To stay on my ass
To give me shit.
(Act 3, sc. 5)[60]

The foregoing scenes illustrate what Marianne Wichmann Bailey describes in her insightful study of Césaire's theatre as "a process of refusal-devaluation and reversal-revaluation" in which there is a "smelting of new values in the crucible of old injuries."[61] Césaire explains his purpose in refashioning Shakespeare's *Tempest:*

> I was trying to "de-mythify" the tale. To me Prospero is the complete totalitarian. I am always surprised when others consider him the wise man who "forgives." What is most obvious, even in Shakespeare's version, is the man's absolute will to power. Prospero is the man of cold reason, the man of methodical conquest—in other words, a portrait of the "enlightened" European. And I see the whole play in such terms: the "civilized" European world coming face to face for the first time with the world of primitivism and magic. Let's not hide the fact that in Europe the world of reason has inevitably led to various kinds of totalitarian-

> ism. . . . Caliban is the man who is still close to his beginnings, whose link with the natural world has not yet been broken. Caliban can still *participate* in a world of marvels, whereas his master can merely "create" them through his acquired knowledge. At the same time, Caliban is also a rebel—the positive hero, in a Hegelian sense. The slave is always more important than his master—for it is the slave who makes history.[62]

Césairian *négritude* entails the consciousness of being Black, the simple recognition of this fact, which implies acceptance, and the assumption of one's identity, destiny, history, and culture as a Black.[63] For Césaire, *négritude* is a philosophy, a psychological posture, and a stance that is, at one and the same time, political and moral. It involves three affirmations: the affirmation of the Black identity, the affirmation of a solidarity with other Blacks, and the affirmation of faith in and faithfulness to a system of values distinctly Black and historically African in origin. Today, these affirmations might appear to some to be obvious and needless, because we are all in our outlook the intellectual grandchildren of *négritude*. We must caution ourselves against losing a sense of historical relativity, however, and realize that in the political, social, and cultural milieu of the 1930s, these affirmations constituted revolutionary postures. Today we live in a postindependence era, and perhaps we are living in a post-Negritude era as well—perhaps. While asserting that Negritude should be considered as a historical cultural movement that preceded contemporary cultural forces such as Antillanité and Créolité, Maryse Condé recalls, "Césaire said as long as there are Negroes there will be Négritude"[64] (see p. 275).

The first affirmation of identity is particularly important for Césaire as a new-world Black belonging to a country in which the structure of domination led to an aggressive politics of assimilation (and continues to do so). As a consequence of the domination, many Martinicans lost a sense of their identity as Blacks. In 1939, when *The Notebook* was published, such an affirmation of blackness in the Martinican milieu was provocative. The poet Léon Damas published equally scandalous volumes, entitled *Black Label* and *Pigments,* which drew attention to the fact that the melanin content of the skin could not be altered, despite the process of assimilation, that is, whitening, or "lactification," as Frantz Fanon refers to it.

As to the second affirmation, as a Black Césaire feels solidarity with all Blacks and all oppressed peoples. He asserts, "The world does not spare me. There is not one single lynched man in the world, not one tortured man in whom a part of myself is not murdered and humiliated."[65] This expression typifies the sympathetic phenomenon of simultaneity and unanimism that is seen in much of early-twentieth-century literature. It makes for a sense of the oneness of human life containing the multiple, thus encouraging the individual to embrace simultaneous, multiform human experience at different points in space, just as one encompasses all past times through one's ancestry.

Thus, according to Césaire:

> [There is a solidarity] through time and space with our black ancestors and with this African continent of which we are the issue, and there is a horizontal solidarity across geographic boundaries with all blacks who come from the continent for the reasons we know well and who have in common this heritage. This heritage and collective experience weighs still heavily upon us, but we must not deny it, we must transcend the pain and make it blossom and multiply.[66]

Following the example of the Negritude poets, poets could no longer remain aloof wisps of narcissistic, solipsistic meditation. It became necessary to quit the ivory tower and undertake roles of involvement that made them modern alchemists searching in their laboratories for the secret algebra, calculus, formulas, processes, dynamics, and pragmatics of social transformation. And where do words fit into this scheme? Ah, yes, words.

> *I would rediscover the secret of great communications and of great combustions.* I should say storm. I should say river. I would say tornado. I should say leaf. I should say tree. I would be drenched by all rains, moistened by all dews. I would roll like frenzied blood on the slow current of the eye of words turned into mad horses, into fresh children into clots into curfews into vestiges of temples, precious stones remote enough to discourage miners. Whoever would not comprehend me would not understand any better the roaring of the tiger.
>
> Words? while we handle quarters of the earth, while we wed delirious continents, while we force steaming gates, words, ah! words, but words

of fresh blood, words that are tidal waves and erysipelas and malarias and lava and brush fires, blazes of flesh, and blazes of cities.[67]

Finally, Negritude must also be recognized as a psychoanalytic process, the purpose of which is to summon up from the unconscious, untapped forces of the black psyche and genius. Césaire was aware of this necessity of plunging "into the depths":

—I said to myself: it's true that superficially we are French, we bear the marks of French customs; we have been branded by Cartesian philosophy, by French rhetoric; but if we break with all that, if we plumb the depths, then what we will find is fundamentally black.

In other words, it was a process of disalienation. Yes, a process of disalienation, that's how I interpreted surrealism.

—That's how surrealism has manifested itself in your work: as an effort to reclaim your authentic character, and in a way as an effort to reclaim the African heritage.

—Absolutely.

And as a process of detoxification.

A plunge into the depths. It was a plunge into Africa for me.

—It was a way of emancipating your consciousness.

—Yes, I felt that beneath the social being would be found a profound being, over whom all sorts of ancestral layers and alluviums had been deposited.[68]

As a psychoanalytical process of disalienation and detoxification, therefore, Negritude is a means for Black people to come to terms with the double consciousness of their condition. In European terms it is therapy; in ancient African and West Indian ceremonial and ritualistic terms it is a laying on of the hands, healing of the scars, and exorcism of the demons that, through the centuries of colonization and slavery, locked up access to the Black psyche and projected the Black spirit into a space of radical divorce from the self. The embrace, a familiar motif in Césaire's poetry, characterizes Negritude, a cyclical and circular process of ever expanding and contracting embrace of the self, of one's people across national boundaries, of all oppressed peoples, of one's history, and, eventually, of all humankind.

Qu'on le sache: en articulant notre effort de libération des peuples colonisés, en combattant pour la dignité de nos peuples c'est en définitive pour le monde tout entier que nous combattons et pour le libérer de la tyrannie, de la haine et du fanatisme. . . . Alors et alors seulement nous aurons vaincu et notre victoire finale marquera l'avènement d'une ère nouvelle. . . . nous aurons aidé à fonder l'humanisme universel.[69]

[Let it be known: while articulating our effort of liberation of colonized peoples, while fighting for the dignity of our people, it is definitely for the whole world that we are fighting and to liberate it from tyranny, hatred and fanaticism. . . . Then and only then shall we have been victorious, and our final victory will mark the coming of a new era. . . . we shall have assisted in founding universal "humanisme."]

In enumerating the aspects of the poet's role, I specifically did not include that of teacher, because the term is not exact. Césaire would not have the man of culture, the poet, be a pedagogue but rather a "psychogogue," that is, a molder of souls, a healer and mender of psyches. This purpose is manifest in the much anthologized, eroticized rhetoric of the "virile" prayer in *Notebook:*

and here at the end of these wee hours is my virile prayer that
I hear neither the laughter nor the screams, my eyes fixed on
this town which I prophesy, beautiful,

grant me the savage faith of the sorcerer
grant my hands power to mold
grant my soul the sword's temper
I won't flinch. Make my head into a figurehead
and as for me, my heart, do not make me into a father
nor a brother,
nor a son, but into the father, the brother, the son,
nor a husband, but the lover of this unique people.

Make me resist any vanity, but espouse its genius as the
fist the extended arm!

Make me a steward of its blood
make me trustee of its resentment
make me into a man for the ending
make me into a man for the beginning
make me into a man of meditation
but also make me into a man of germination

make me into the executor of these lofty works
the time has come to gird one's loins like a brave man—
But in doing so, my heart, preserve me from all hatred
do not make me into that man of hatred for whom I feel
only hatred
for entrenched as I am in this unique race
you still know my tyrannical love
you know that it is not from hatred of other races
that I demand a digger for this unique race
that what I want
is for universal hunger
for universal thirst[70]

2

Toward a Sociology of Humor

Léon Gontran Damas and Body Talk

There can be no going back in time: the destinies of Europe/America and Africa will never again be separate. Mano a mano, like a couple of wrestlers or lovers, they are inextricably bound to one another geopolitically in the ambiguous adventure of the global economy.

Instead of projects revolving around nostalgic return, francophone literature explores the new cultural ties, bonds, links, knots, nooses, hybrid spaces, and beings that result from the contact between the first world and Africa, the Caribbean, Asia, Polynesia, and the Indian Ocean. The destinies of Europe and the third world are permanently entangled by the experience of colonialism, decolonization, and independence. This tie, which threatens to strangle the alienated couple, is nowhere better illustrated than in the poem "Pour toi et moi" by Léon Gontran Damas:

> Pour toi et moi
> qui ne faisions l'un et l'autre
> qu'un seul pris hier encore
> au jeu du nœud coulant
> à moins que ce ne fût
> au nœud coulant du jeu
> ou encore au jeu coulant du nœud
> voici que chante pour nous deux
> la rengaine de l'un sans l'autre
> tous deux désormais dos à dos

Dos à dos je ne
dos à dos tu ne
dos à dos je ne sais
dos à dos tu ne sais
je ne
tu ne
nous
nous ne savons l'un l'autre
plus rien de l'un
plus rien de l'autre
si ce n'est ce grand besoin que nous avons l'un l'autre

défait
dé-lié
dé-noué
le coulant du nœud
le nœud coulant du jeu
le jeu du nœud coulant (*Pigments,* 146–47)

[For you and me
who just yesterday were only one caught
in the game of slipknot
unless it was
the slipknot of the game
or even the game slipping the knot
Here sings for the two of us
the chorus of one without the other
the two of us henceforth back to back

Back to back I can't quite
Back to back you can't quite
Back to back I don't know quite
Back to back you don't know quite
I don't
You don't
We
We don't know the one the other
nothing more of the one

nothing more of the other
if it isn't this great need that we have the one for the other

undone
un-tied
un-knotted
the slipping of the knot
the slipknot of the game
the game of slipknot] [1]

Damas's poetry illustrates Frantz Fanon's assertion that "the violence with which the supremacy of white values is affirmed and the aggressiveness which has permeated the victory of these values over the ways of life and thought of the native mean that, in revenge, the native laughs in mockery when Western values are mentioned in front of him." [2]

With Damas we move from the homonymity of cygne/signe to the paronomasia of signe/singe (sign/monkey). What is bound in one world is loosed in another. It is the game of slipknot. The poetry of Léon Gontran Damas reveals the sociology of a humor that is a form of radical social critique. A poetics of *indigestion* is articulated in this universe of coughing, hiccuping, bleeding, vomiting, vertigo, and sleeplessness. An important figure in Damas's universe is Singe (Monkey):

> Tu as beau ressembler à l'Homme, dit Perroquet un beau jour à Singe, tu es incapable de parler, comme lui et moi.
>
> Assurément tu parles. Et même tu parles beaucoup, rétorqua Singe. Mais s'il en est ainsi, insupportable bavard, c'est que tu n'as pas de mains, comme moi qui en ai quatre, et que dès lors, on ne peut pas t'obliger à travailler. Si je voulais parler, je m'en tirerais sans nul doute mieux, beaucoup mieux que toi. Mais je serais—comme tes pareils—enfermé dans une cage, et il me faudrait payer l'impôt. Par surcroît . . ."
> "Grand merci" [3]

> [Try as you may to resemble man, said Parrot one fine day to Monkey, you are unable to talk like him and me.
>
> Most assuredly you can talk. And you even talk a lot, responded Monkey. But if such is the case, you insufferable chatterbox, it is that you

have no hands, unlike myself who has four of them, and so you can't be made to work. If I wanted to speak, I daresay, I would do a much better job than you. But then I would be—like you and your kind—locked up in a cage and I would have to pay the price. What's more . . .
"Thanks a lot . . . go screw yourself!"]

There is considerable mischievousness behind Damas's ironies, burlesque, caricatures, pastiches, and virulent satire. Damas seeks to explode the stereotypes and clichés by his example and through his analyses. In the foregoing "Palabre," the monkey must be understood as representing the antithesis of man and also of the parrot, while the parrot represents a hyperassimilated colonized person. Although accused by the parrot of inhabiting the margins of discourse, the monkey asserts himself as a Master of Discourse with enormously generative semiotic powers. The monkey's response to the parrot and his kind constitutes an act of aggressivity against language for being shopworn, obscurantist, a hollow repetition of clichés, and a marker of superiority—and of course against the colonized beings who have become parroting parodies of a French person. Monkey is poignantly aware of the extent to which a schooled resemblance underscores how emphatically one is not French. The monkey is a great linguistic jester who completely disorganizes language and wreaks havoc among signifiers on the level of so-called indissolubility of relationships between the signifier and the signified or the sign. The monkey names, signifies, and criticizes through indirection!

In his poetry, Léon Gontran Damas rejects the forced Frenchification or *francisation*—the French politics of assimilation:

HOQUET

Et j'ai beau avalé sept gorgées d'eau
trois à quatre fois par vingt-quatre heures
me revient mon enfance
dans un hoquet secouant
mon instinct
tel le flic le voyou

. . . .

Cet enfant sera la honte de notre nom
cet enfant sera notre nom de Dieu

Taisez-vous
Vous ai-je ou non dit qu'il vous fallait parler français
le français de France
le français du français
le français français
. . . .
Ma mère voulant d'un fils très do
. . . .
très do
ré-mi-fa
sol-la-si
do
Il m'est revenu que vous n'êtes pas allé
à votre leçon de vi-o-lon
Un banjo
vous dites un banjo
comment dites-vous
un banjo
Non monsieur
vous saurez qu'on ne souffre chez nous
ni ban
ni jo
ni gui
ni tare
les *mulâtres* ne font pas ça
laissez donc ça aux *nègres* (*Pigments,* pp. 35–38)

SOLDE

J'ai l'impression d'être ridicule
dans leur souliers
dans leur smoking
. . . .
Jai l'impression d'être ridicule
parmi eux complice
parmi eux souteneur
parmi eux égorgeur
les mains effroyablement rouges
du sang de leur ci-vi-li-sa-tion (*Pigments,* p. 42)

[HICCUPS

I gulp down seven drinks of water
several times a day
and all in vain
instinctively
like a criminal to the crime
my childhood returns
in a rousing fit of hiccups
. . . .
This child will disgrace our family name
This child will be our in the name of God!
be quiet
have I or have I not
told you to speak French
the French of France
the French that Frenchmen speak
French French
. . . .
My mother wanted her son to be
very do
. . .
very do-re-mi-fa-so-la-ti-do
I see you have not been to your vi-o-lin lesson
a banjo/did you say a banjo
what do you mean a banjo
you really mean a banjo
no indeed young man
You know there will be no ban-
or jo
or
gui
or tar
in our house
they are not for mulatto people
leave them to the niggers!

SELLOUT

I feel ridiculous in their shoes
their dinner jackets
. . . .
I feel ridiculous among them
like an accomplice
like a pimp
like a murderer among them
my hands hideously red with the blood of their
ci-vi-li-za-tion.] (Kennedy, pp. 48–51)

Uncompromisingly, Damas, representative of the first generation of Black francophone poets, analyzes the emasculation, masquerade, and complicity of the colonized Black; he mocks the values of the French colonialist politics of assimilation, which he hiccups, coughs up, vomits, and rejects in his poetry. Images of malnutrition, insomnia, and vertigo further express his malaise.

If Aimé Césaire conjures the Black Narcissus toward cultural "detoxification" of the superficially French self and "disalienation" by framing the self in the particularity of Antillean culture, it is Léon Gontran Damas who will live and die in contemplation of the chiasmatic image of self reflected in the mirror of Afro-French culture. In the person and poetics of Damas, there is something, in the Baudelairean sense, of the Dandy, who is aware of the functioning of the extravagant mask as a weapon of protest and protection against a hostile society. Certain titles of poetry collections reveal Damas's dandyism in another sense: *Pigments* and *Black-Label* were considered by some, at the time of their publication, to be inelegant, indeed, in poor taste, because they brought undue attention to difference, and particularly to the melanin content of the skin. In the assimilationist milieu of the thirties, this was scandalous for Blacks as well as Whites. Damas's intentionally impertinent, provocative subjects suggest the intoxicating, aristocratic pleasure the Dandy derives from choices, extravagances, excesses, and tastes that displease and unsettle bourgeois notions of convention and propriety. It is this pleasure taken in displeasing that in part inspires the aggressive, dark humor of the Dandy. Baudelaire theorizes that the concept of the Dandy implies an extraordinary refinement of character and a highly nuanced understanding of the moral dynamics of the world and the moment in which one lives.[4] These qualities are apparent in the poetry of Léon Damas, professor and representative to the French National Assembly. The Dandy, in the nineteenth-century tradition of Baudelaire and Barbey d'Aurevilly, is torn between narcissistic preoccupation with the rare, superior, and individual quality of his postures and actions and, at the same time, the desire to provoke, to be daring and to shock rather than please a normative public.

The poetic universe of Damas is bitter, tragicomic, noisy, and musical. From his poems (which typographically meander across, up, and down the page, resembling musical scores at times) rise pianistic melodies, the hammering cadences of African and Harlem drums, and the stammerings, stutterings, and moans of a Louis Armstrong muted trumpet. Damas confronts the poetics of the mask in his contemplations. The Negro American poet Paul Laurence Dunbar (1872–1906), who was appreciated for his dialect poetry and not his crafted verses of American poetry, expressed his disappointment in his poem "The Poet":

> He sang of love when earth was young
> And Love itself was in his lays.
> But ah, the world, it turned to praise
> A jingle in a broken tongue.[5]

Personal despair and historical and racial consciousness, as well as moral, philosophical, and religious questioning, lent Dunbar's poetry a deep pessimism and irony, as the following lines show:

> We wear the mask that grins and lies
> It hides our cheeks and shades our eyes
> This debt we pay to human guile
> With torn and bleeding hearts we smile
> And mouth with myriad subtleties. . . .
> But let the world dream otherwise
>   We wear the mask[6]

Damas dedicated a poem to Louis Armstrong, who in many ways was a Dandy, in the sense that he assumed certain stereotypical characteristics of the "Darky," such as the big eyes, the gleaming complexion, the enormous smile, and the "sportin' life wardrobe." These he was able to transmute, because of his jazz trumpet and singing virtuosity, into an inimitable and ironic Negro elegance and eloquence of which many "enlightened" Negroes and whites did not approve. The poem "Shine" reflects Damas's empathetic understanding of Armstrong's mask and of the complex position taken by this musician of the French Quarter in New Orleans.

Avec d'autres
des alentours
avec d'autres
quelques rares
j'ai au toit de ma case
jusqu'ici gardé
l'ancestrale foi conique

Et l'arrogance automatique
des masques
des masques de chaux vive
jamais n'est parvenue à rien enlever jamais
d'un passé plus hideux
debout
aux quatre angles de ma vie

Et mon visage brille aux horreurs du passé
et mon rire effroyable est fait pour repousser
        le spectre des levriers
                traquant le marronnage
et ma voix qui pour eux chante
et douce à ravir
l'âme triste
de leur por-
            no-
                gra-
                    phie (*Pigments,* p. 65)

[With others
from the neighborhood
a few rare friends

till now I have kept
the conical ancestral faith
high among the rafters of my hut

And the automatic arrogance
of masks
masks of living chalk never has been able to remove
anything
ever
of a past
more hideous
here
at the four corners of my life

And my face gleams with the horrors of the past
and my dreadful laughter would repel
    the specter of the hounds
                    pursuing runaways
and my voice which sings for them
is sweet enough to soothe
the soul saddened by their
    por-
        no-
            gra-
                phy] (Kennedy, p. 58)

Stylistically and syntactically, Damas's poems rely on repetitions and reversals, with subtle permutations and modulations of inverted repetitions of phrases or entire verses, thereby producing a poetic vertigo that is uniquely Damasian. It is a discourse that unfolds from a semantic and syntactic nodal point, or kernel, spiraling in linguistic knots, like riffs and musical chiasmus in jazz, toward cohesion and signification. Too often, Damas's poetry is characterized as "simple"; but if the rhetorical figures to which Damas instinctively returns are among the simplest kind, it is in their orchestration that his virtuosity is demonstrated. Antithesis, oxymoron, chiasmus, synonymy, homonymy, paronomasia, and irony progressively overlay each other and, indeed, emerge out of each other as the poem pushes toward signification in a symbolic enactment of the entanglement of cross-cultural, political, racial, and philosophical struggles. From the standpoint of the Freudian analysis of humor, Damas's "playfulness" might be seen as based on "manifold applications" derived from the exploitation of the "plasticity" of language—double-meanings, ambiguities, allusions, "the contrast of ideas," "sense in nonsense," and "confusion and clearness." The result is a productive, insightful, and revelatory ambiguity of states and emotions in which language affirms itself no longer as a simple tool of command and coercion and a perfect univocal means of communication, but as a space of exploration, self-examination, evocation, aggression, punning, intellectual and aesthetic creativity, or, simply put, poetry. And, consequently, one understands with Damas the Wittgensteinian notion that the "limits of my language mean the limits of my world."[7]

Ostensibly a love poem, "Pour toi et moi" ultimately reflects Damas's position vis-à-vis the West. The poem is a politicization of the intimate and the familial, as well as an eroticization of the political. As previously noted, the destinies of Africa and the West are, like those of lovers, inextricably linked, despite their state of divorce. Herein lies the significance of Césaire's ending in his *Tempest*. In contrast to the ending in Shakespeare's *Tempest*, in which Prospero returns to Europe, Césaire's Prospero has remained on the island with Caliban and years later mutters: "Odd how the climate has changed. Cold on this island . . . Have to think about making a fire . . . Well, Caliban, old fellow, it's just us two now, here on the island, only you and me. You and me. You-me . . . me-you!"[8]

Damas's neuralgic, noisy poetry also features the taste of blood that rises in the throat, coughs, nausea, vomiting, dizziness, spasms, insomnia, drunkenness, sobs, stuttering, suffocation, burping, and, of course, hiccups. The poet's entire nervous and digestive being rebels against the French politics of assimilation, as is evident in the poems "Solde" (Sellout), "Nuit Blanche" (Sleepless Night), "Hoquet," "Limbé," "Blanchi" (Whitewashed), "Black-Label," and "Trêve" (Truce).

Trêve de blues
de martèlements de piano

de trompette bouchée
de folie claquant des pieds
à la satisfaction du rythme
. . . .

Trêve de lâchage
de léchage
de lèche
et
d'une attitude
d'hyperassimilés (*Pigments,* 21)

[Enough of blues
piano banging
muted trumpet
mad feet tapping
to satisfy the rhythm
. . . .
Enough letting-go-of
licking-up-to
taking-the-leavings
and
enough
of that attitude
of hyperassimilation]

In the poem "Hiccups" Damas recalls the intensely painful effects he suffered as a child from parental and cultural authority, which, from the vantage point of adulthood, he can treat humorously rather than repress. The poem illustrates a principle in the Freudian psychoanalysis of humor, for, as Freud wrote: "Humor can now be conceived as the loftiest of these defense functions. It disdains to withdraw from conscious attention the ideas which are connected with the painful affect, as repression does, and it, thus, overcomes the defense automatism. It brings this about by finding the means to withdraw the energy from the ready held pain release, and through discharge changes the same into pleasure."[9]

Langston Hughes (1902–67) places a slightly different spin on the psychoanalysis of humor:

> Humor is laughing at what you haven't got when you ought to have it. Of course, you laugh by proxy. You're really laughing at the other guy's lacks, not your own. That's what makes it funny—the fact that you don't know you are laughing at yourself. Humor is when the joke is on you but hits the other fellow first—before it boomerangs. Humor is what you wish in your secret heart were not funny, but it is, and you must laugh. Humor is your own unconscious therapy.[10]

Hughes's analysis explains the functioning of ironic laughter in the following lines by Damas:

> Ils ont si bien su faire
> si bien su faire les choses
> les choses
> qu'un jour nous avons tout
> nous avons tout foutu de nous-mêmes
> tout foutu de nous-mêmes en l'air (*Pigments,* p. 73)

> [They did their thing so well
> did their thing
> that one day we let all
> all that once was ours
> go
> we threw it all away] (Kennedy, p. 59)

Damas does not write from a settled state, and his texts elaborate a poetry of indigestion and indisposition. Yet while there is the irrepressible hiccup, there is also the inextinguishable Damasian laughter.

Laughter raises a plethora of questions concerning its origins and what motivates and drives it. With Damas, it is a question of the laughter that emerges from the spiritual and historical experiences of a people: the uprooting, slavery, colonialism, the abolition of slavery, segregation, miscegenation, exile into another language, assimilation, double consciousness, even triple consciousness—for Léon Damas, who is ever aware of the triangulated history of the Caribbean, and his triracial origins.

> Trois Fleuves
> trois fleuves coulent
> trois fleuves coulent dans mes veines

. . . .
de tous ces riens qui font une âme euphémiquement
créole.[11]

[Three Rivers
three rivers flow
three rivers flow in my veins
. . . .
of all the bits of everything that make a soul
euphemistically Creole]

The triangulated history of the Caribbean involves the slave trade triangles drawn from Europe to Africa and the Caribbean as well as from the Caribbean to the United States and Europe. The triangulation of anglophone, francophone, and hispanophone cultures in intimate contact creates a distinct multicultural Caribbean identity. The specific reference in the poem, however, is to the Amerindian, African, and European ancestry of many Caribbean and American Blacks.

Of the three theorists of Negritude, it is Damas who most compellingly orients one toward a sociology of humor. Wit, laughter, comedy, parody, and humor function as revolutionary gestures, acts of provocation, unconscious therapy, and aesthetic freedom in Damas's poetry. Damas's poetry is one of negation. Damas declares himself to be against the farce of French social and political hypocrisy and the "host"ipophagic (as in anthropophagic) church, "the holy history of which is not very catholic." From Damas's work, with its negativity and tragic dimensions, there erupts the engulfing philosophical laughter of dark humor. The treatment of serious issues seems to give coherence to the comical or satiric, and thus humor takes on a philosophic, political, and ethnic cast. The bitter, black, dark humor is an outcry, which conveys that the business of living is absurd and that there is perhaps no more fitting response to the tragedy of man's fate in the twentieth century than caustic, mocking, derisive, and at times desperate, convulsive laughter. Damas's nervous, self-conscious laugh is both protection and protest, an expression of fury and outrage at the misery, exploitation, and reciprocal dehumanization that characterize colonialism, fascism, and Nazism in their original as well as contemporary forms.

As much as it speaks to readers' emotions and animal instincts, Damas's desperate laughter speaks to their intellect and intelligence, thereby functioning as a strong weapon of persuasion, dissuasion, and conversion, as in the horrific laughter of "S.O.S."

S.O.S.

À ce moment-là seul
comprendrez-vous donc tous
quand leur supériorité
s'étalera
d'un bout à l'autre de leurs boulevards
et qu'alors
vous les verrez
vraiment tout se permettre
ne plus se contenter de rire avec l'index inquiet
de voir passer un nègre
mais
froidement matraquer
mais
froidement descendre
mais
froidement étendre
mais froidement
matraquer
descendre
étendre
et
couper leur sexe aux nègres
pour en faire des bougies pour leurs églises

bientôt cette idée leur viendra
de vouloir vous en bouffer du nègre
à la manière d'Hitler
bouffant du juif
sept jours fascistes
sur
sept (*Pigments*, p. 51)

[s.o.s.

At that moment only
will you all finally understand
when their superiority
spreads itself out
from one end to the other of their boulevards
and then
you will see them
truly allow themselves every excess
no longer contenting themselves to laugh with the finger
pointed disturbed
about seeing a nigger go by
but coldly bludgeoning
but coldly killing
but coldly eliminating
but coldly
bludgeoning
killing
eliminating
cutting off niggers' dicks
in order to make candles in their churches
Soon the idea will come to them
of ridding you of niggers
just as Hitler
does away with Jews
seven fascist days a week]

Humor resides in the slipknots of language and its translation. Humor shatters the enveloping, assimilating, leveling mechanisms of domination. Humor calls attention to that which cannot be translated and is a code that must be learned by outsiders. Humor takes place at the site where the civilizers have been thwarted and outdone by the laughter that is speech. The nontranslatability is the elimination of the power of decoding.

In Damas's humor there is a double consciousness not only of Afro-Frenchness but also of the pain informing the laughter.

OBSESSION

Un goût de sang me vient
un goût de sang me monte
m'irrite le nez
la gorge
les yeux (*Pigments,* p. 19)

Il est des nuits sans nom
Il est des nuits sans lune
où jusqu'à l'asphyxie
moite
me prend
l'âcre odeur de sang
jaillissant
de toute trompette bouchée
. . . .
où le dégoût s'ancre en moi
aussi profondément qu'un beau poignard malais (*Pigments,* p. 25)

[A taste of blood comes
a taste of blood rises
irritates my nose
eyes
throat
There are nights with no name
there are nights with no moon
when a clammy
suffocation
nearly overwhelms me
the acrid smell of blood
spewing
from every muted trumpet
. . . .
When the sickness sticks within me like an oriental dagger.] (Kennedy, p. 46)

In Damasian humor one observes what Sigmund Freud referred to as a "Janus-like double-facedness" of wit,[12] which often is dictated by painful emotional feelings but must simultaneously be released by laughter. In this concatenation of affect and release, laughter is the cavernous howl of despair.

Damas's humor is gripping because it stimulates meditation and self-criticism. The laughter is not always immediate. Rare, in fact, are those poems that make the reader guffaw. Most often the reaction does not manifest itself in raucous or even perceptive laughter; there will be instead an almost imperceptible, all-knowing, smug smile of understanding and complicity, and this after an intellectual exercise of social criticism and self-criticism precipitated by the poet's observations and puns. One understands that the purpose of Damas's humor is not to tickle readers lightly, but rather to affect their intellect and psyches, that is, to radically alter the consciousness of people who are often alienated from the problems presented, as for example in the poem "Whitewashed":

BLANCHI

Se peut-il qu'ils osent
me traiter de blanchi
alors que tout en moi
aspire à n'être que nègre
autant que mon Afrique
qu'ils ont cambriolée

Blanchi
Abominable injure
qu'ils me paieront fort cher
quand mon Afrique
qu'ils ont cambriolée
voudra la paix rien que
la paix

Blanchi
Ma haine grossit en marge
de leur scélératesse

. . . .

Ma haine grossit en marge
de la culture

en marge
des théories
en marge des bavardages
dont on a cru devoir me bourrer au berceau
alors que tout en moi aspire à n'être que nègre
autant que mon Afrique qu'ils ont cambriolée (*Pigments,* p. 59)

[WHITEWASH

It may be
they dare to treat me white
though everything within me
wants only to be black
as Negro as the Africa they ransacked

White
Abominable insult
that they'll pay me dearly for
when my Africa
the Africa they ransacked
is determined to have peace
peace
nothing else but peace

White
My hatred swells
at the scope of their villainy
. . . .
My hatred swells
around the limits of the culture
the limits of the theories
the tales
they thought they sought
to stuff me with
from the cradle onward
while all the while
everything within me
wants only to be black
as Negro as the Africa they robbed me of] (Kennedy, p. 56)

Humor also functions as a weapon and shield for the community, particularly in regard to its sociological functions of laughter as defense, protest, and protection. Humor serves as a social bond, reinforcing a collective consciousness by underscoring the heritage, traditions, experiences, ideas, themes, and values shared by a community —specifically, the Afro-French community. Whether Black or White, readers who do not share the community's values will feel immediately excluded—indeed, targeted—by the humor.

ALORS

je vous mettrai les pieds dans le plat
ou bien tout simplement
la main au collet
de tout ce qui m'emmerde en gros caractères
colonisation
civilisation
assimilation
et la suite (*Pigments,* p. 53)

[Then
I'll put your feet in it
or simply grab you by the throat
with all that capital letter shit
colonization
civilization
assimilation
and the rest]

Damas seems very wary of the power of certain racist stereotypes, as in the poem "Pareille à ma légende."

occidentalement
avance mon ombre
pareille à ma légende
d'homme-singe. (*Pigments,* p. 61)

[occidentally
my shadow moves forward

like the legend
of my ape-man past]

Damas seems to be acutely aware of the fine line between mockery that is resistance, revolt, and protection, and the brand of humor that crosses the line and becomes, inadvertently, complicity and reinforcement of stereotypes. Humor must be redemptive, affirming the humanity and the integrity of the so-called inferior and encouraging self-esteem and belief in personal and collective strength and integrity. The formula is very simple: laugh to keep from crying; laugh in order to survive.

Through our participation in the act of reading, Damas's laughter becomes our laughter, shared in the face of the worries, paradoxes, and repulsive, convulsive grotesqueness of human comportment, which is so shamelessly displayed in the colonial drama. Laughter is life. In a single Damasian verse, tears, alarm, confusion, rebellion, tenderness, revelation, and nervous laughter coalesce. What one feels profoundly in Damas is the great potential of laughter and its effectiveness as a strategy for survival, as a shield against oppression, and ultimately, as a form of radical social critique, invective, and counterdiscourse:

voilà
qu'il recommence
qu'il recommence à dire
Merde
. . .
UN POEME POUR SUR S'EN PASSE VOLONTIERS
. . . .
mais il s'agit moins de recommencer à dire
le gros mot
le mot défendu
que de continuer à être
contre
la conspiration du silence autour de moi-même
à moi-même imposée
par moi-même admise
. . . .
Il s'agit moins de recommencer
que de continuer à être

contre
la morale occidentale
et son cortège de préceptes
de préoccupations
de présomptions
de prénotions
de prétentions
de préjugés
Il s'agit moins de recommencer
que de continuer à vous refiler ma nausée
continuer à vous surveiller
continuer à ruer
. . . . . .
continuer à vous navrer
vous décevoir
vous désarmer. (*Black-Label,* pp. 29, 31)

[there he goes
he's at it again
back to saying
Shit.
. .
A POEM CERTAINLY CAN DO VERY WELL WITHOUT THAT
but it is less about starting to say once again
the dirty word
the forbidden word
than it is of continuing to be
against
the conspiracy of silence all around me
that I have imposed upon myself
by myself admitted
. . . .
It is less a question of starting all over again
than it is about continuing to be
against
western morality
and its procession of precepts
of preoccupations

of presumptions
of preconceived notions
of prejudices
It is less a question of starting all over again
than of continuing to pass on to you my nausea
continuing to keep an eye on you
continuing to kick and scream
. . . .
continuing to annoy you
to trick you
to disarm you]

Humor also functions as a psychological safety valve and a means of emotional decompression. It allows for the venting of frustration and provides an opportunity for salutary aggression against, and escape from, the pressure of authority, institutions, and individuals, as well as philosophical and scientific positions. Laughter, acting as a form of release against a system of coercion, domination, and restriction, rechannels frustrated energies into a "passive," or legal, resistance that can expose the grotesque in human behavior and ideologies. As to social conflict, humor functions as sublimation of physical violence and attack, defusing a potentially explosive situation. In Freudian terms, Damas's humor leads to a discharge of psychic irritation, a consciousness of incongruities, and relief from the restraints inherent in a psychically stopped-up being as expressed in the poem "Si souvent."

Si souvent mon sentiment de race m'effraie
autant qu'un chien aboyant la nuit
une mort prochaine
quelconque
je me sens prêt à écumer toujours de rage
contre ce qui m'entoure
contre ce qui m'empêche
à jamais d'être
un homme

Et rien
rien ne saurait autant calmer ma haine

qu'une belle mare
de sang
faite
de ces coutelas tranchants
qui mettent à nu
les mornes à rhum (*Pigments,* p. 49)

[If often my feeling of race
strikes in me the same fear
as the nighttime howling of a dog
at some approaching death
I always feel
about to foam with rage
against what surrounds me
against what prevents me
ever from being
a man

And nothing
nothing would so calm my hate
as a great
pool
of blood
made
by those long sharp knives
that strip the hills of cane
for rum]

For Aimé Césaire humor is a powerful, emotionally unsettling, politically liberating, and socially destabilizing force (humor, force of liberation . . . negation of the world).[13] From its most ancient origins, humor has overturned hierarchies. It is only when the world is turned upside down that we can see ourselves as "other." A grammar of humor then asserts itself, one in which Damas hoists a great ironic smile toward the "enlightened" totalitarian European, who perceives himself as the subject of all predications in which the colored races, which have been reified so as to better serve the demands and exigencies of the colonial machine, would be direct objects of exploitation, and indirect objects to whom the European brings civilization and for whom bridges, railroads, and ports of exportation and importation have been built. In Damas's textual maneuvers, Damas the "nègre" becomes the subject of the discourse, a first-person active voice. The former accusative accuses the European, who is now the object of his scrutiny, his radical critique, and his humor.

At this juncture the "pleasure principle" comes into play, for, as Freud suggests, "the most conspicuous factor of the jest is the gratification it affords by making possible that which reason forbids. . . . From the beginning [wit's] object is to remove inner inhibitions and thereby, render productive those pleasure sources which have become inaccessible.[14] In this sense, humor levels difference, exposes political travesty, upsets artificial hierarchies, and overturns social orders.

Specular chiasmus may be used to see the self's image repeated but reversed, to see it as other. In the humor glass "Je est un autre" ("I is an other," writes Rimbaud).[15] It is perhaps this specular dimension of Damasian humor that is the most exalting—humor as the demythifying, demystifying, revelatory, and sonorous mirror held up to self and society. As a poet, Damas has the mission of unmasking social inequality and of stating the truths that both Black and White society wishes to cloak.

Finally, Damas's humor is not limited to the cynical, the grating, or the uneasy. The second movement of *Black-Label* ends with a great, smiling celebration of the energy, legitimacy, pleasures, and prides of Black life.

car la beauté est nègre
et nègre la sagesse
car l'endurance est nègre
et nègre le courage
car la patience est nègre
et nègre l'ironie
car le charme est nègre
et nègre la magie
car l'amour est nègre
et nègre le déhanchement
car la danse est nègre
et nègre le rythme
car l'art est nègre

et nègre le mouvement
car le rire est nègre
car la joie est nègre
car la paix est nègre
car la vie est nègre. (*Black-Label,* p. 52)

[for beauty is negro
and negro too is wisdom
for endurance is negro
and negro too is courage
for patience is negro
and negro too is irony
for charm is negro
and negro too is magic
for love is negro
and negro too is the swaying of hips
for dance is negro
and negro too is rhythm
for art is negro
and negro too is movement
for laughter is negro
for joy is negro
for peace is negro
for life is negro.]

3

Counterexertions

Theorizing the Francophone Condition

Neither as terms nor as concepts does symbolist, supernaturalist, aesthetic modernism or, especially, parodic, aleatory, absurdist, gimmicky postmodernism appropriately designate the experience, affect, and rhetoric of francophone literature. None of these adequately suggests the combination of negation, negotiation, and reevaluation or the expropriatory acts and the multiple consciousness of the twisted signifier in francophone artistic expression. Especially during its insurrectionary beginnings in the 1920s and 1930s, African and Caribbean francophone text production posited a consciousness that ironized its position within European civilization, examined the liminal spaces of cultural hybridity occupied by the colonized subject, and systematically expressed its sameness (i.e., humanity), as well as its difference (i.e., culture). The themes of modernism were superficially embraced and constituted swinging-door concepts between first-world modernism and francophone literature. Swinging-door concepts at the borderline of cultural difference allow passage from one world into another. Yet there is a hollowness to the terms expressing these concepts, and as one moves from first-world modernism to the specificity of francophone literature these concepts become unhinged. Simply put, the themes are *the same but different.* Poised at the crossroads of consciousness, the francophone artist, aware of the emptiness of language and suspicious of the strange familiarity and the familiar strangeness of terms, grapples with the incommensurabilities.

Metaphoricity has been voided for the francophone artist. Francophone literary culture voids the modernist engine of translation of its operative mechanism of turning every tenor and vehicle into equivalents, correspondences, and facile interchanges. In linguistic terms francophone literary culture stands before linguistic swinging or revolving doors in which significance is translated into the power to play against any single meaning. This constant unhinging of relationships, voiding of meaning, and rejection of language as adequate—this reassessment of significance and pawning of language—is the linguistic conceptual play that partly constitutes the game of slipknot. Francophone literature does not oppose modernism, but in the slipknots of language, intertextualities, and life there is an erasure of metaphoricity as it is employed in European modernism. Frantz Fanon, apparently wanting to distinguish Negritude poetry from the European lyric, observes:

> For, it must be admitted, Aimé Césaire was generous in his *Cahier d'un retour au pays natal.* This town of Fort-de-France is truly flat, stranded. Lying there naked to the sun, that "flat, sprawling city, stumbling over its own common sense, winded by its load of endlessly repeated crosses, pettish at its destiny, voiceless, thwarted in every direction, incapable of feeding on the juices of its soil, blocked, cut off, confined, divorced from fauna and flora." Césaire's description of it is anything but poetic.[1]

The performance of francophone literature constitutes a *deromanticized modernism* in which metaphor is illustrated as literal and lived experience; in which the melting pot of generalized correspondences is deconstructed into its constituent differences; in which marginality, alienation, and disease are not markers of the artistic temperament and the holy wounds of hypersensitivity and intelligence but rather notations of the quotidian realities of a subordinated social, economic, and ethnic class; in which the slave, the colonized worker, the guest worker, the third-world tortured political prisoner are absolute, not metaphorical, embodiments of pain and the racially mixed woman is an absolute embodiment of difference, marginality, and alienation.[2]

For the colonized, subordinated, uprooted elements of the transformed francophone societies, francophone literature does not represent antimodernism. It is instead continuous with modernism, while being in counterposition to it, cautious, suspicious, qualifying, and resistant to further intellectual colonization by this first-world phenomenon. The poet Arthur Rimbaud facilitates the orientation toward this qualification when he writes, "Il faut être absolument moderne" (One must be absolutely modern). This well-known declaration from Arthur Rimbaud's poem "Adieu."[3] has served, when decontextualized, as the slogan and rallying cry for an ultramodern, chic. Because the statement begins with the ambiguous, impersonal "*il faut*" (it is necessary/one must/you must), one can read it in context either as a lamentation, as in "Alas, today one must be absolutely modern," or as an ironic protest, as in "At all costs you have to be absolutely modern." Rimbaud's protest speaks to the tyranny of modernism and would seem to suggest that to be absolutely modern necessitates a shading, an abandonment, an erasure even, of all that is and all that one is. Rather than reflecting an antimodernist position, Rimbaud's statement seems to be cautionary and suspicious, questioning and contesting, and therefore it foreshadows the position of francophone literary culture vis-à-vis European aesthetic modernism.

The counterexertions of francophone literature form what, in my opinion, could properly be called countermodernism. As mentioned earlier, francophone literary culture is neither modernist nor antimodernist; instead, it refuses both labels and slips the knot of binary oppositions, thereby asserting itself as countermodernist. Francophone literary culture is neither a shortsighted solipsistic identity politics nor a type of lyricism. It is not antiurbanism, anticommodification, or antiprogress in the strict sense. Rather, it seeks to confront, to contest, and to counter the dehumanizing excesses and legacies of colonial domination. As previously suggested, the affix *counter* is crucial in describing francophone literary culture's inflection of modernist aesthetic practices and vision. As a prefix, according to dictionary definitions, *counter* posits a relationship of proximity between one action and another and declares an oppositional stance within that relationship of proximity. *Counter* suggests the substitution of an action *as a reply* to that other action, condition, narrative, or discourse that is already in existence and considered inimical. The reply is a critique whose purpose it is to check or frustrate, correct or redefine, rival or outdo the inimical discourse by working in particular within the realm of the unacknowledged, the unrecognized, and the unrealized.

Counterstorytelling is the next facet of the francophone literary cultural experience that we will explore, focusing particularly on questions evoked earlier of status inconsistency, role conflict, and consciousness. Although theorizing is a way of accounting for a phenomenon, it is not only the slipknot and the idea of countermodernism that assist one in hypothesizing the many dimensions of francophone literary culture; one may also look to myth. Myths are clues to one's experience of life in groups and in one's surroundings. They serve as fields of reference and, as such, as the interface between what is known and that which constitutes the mystery of human experience. Myth forms the interface between hidden meaning and the visible.

For example, in studying the baobab, a tree indigenous to northern and western Africa, we learn why this imposing giant of African flora, with its cathectic dimension as cult object, its subsequent diegetical survival in myth, and the rich hermeneutical potential of the myth, is a model for analyzing the nomadic condition.

Attaining at times a circumference of twenty meters, as old as two thousand years (the age of some civilizations), capable of withstanding brush and bush fires, often a solitary giant in a desolate landscape, scarred, scorched, burned, and dusty, this bombaceous tree is shrouded in mystery and surrounded by myth. It is the "generous" giant of the African plain. With a trunk that is often hollow, the tree is a veritable oasis and sprawling zoological garden. It contains bird nests, insect colonies, animal lairs, and, it is believed, offers asylum to errant souls and wandering spirits. In short, it is a community, a small city, a society teeming with life.

Elephants roaming in search of food and water gouge out enormous chunks of the baobab's bark and wood, gorging themselves on these, as well as on the branches, leaves, and gourdlike fruit. On rare occasions an unusual drama is enacted that symbolizes the intertwined fates of the dominant and the subordinate, demonstrating in the process that society's most dangerous creation is that element stripped of all dignity, the oppressed, which harbors but one dream—to bring down the society that oppresses. Occasionally this gigantic tree, already hollow, burned, and deserted, and having, it would appear, nothing further to lose, collapses under the assault of a hungry elephant, crushing the elephant to death in its fall.

Commonly known as "the upside-down tree," the baobab (*Adansonia digitata*) is associated with a startling mythology. The veneration of this spectacular tree by the native peoples allegedly aroused the jealousy and eventually the wrath of the neglected gods. These gods violently uprooted the baobab and thrust it deep into the earth with its canopy, branches, leaves, and fruit so deeply interred that only a portion of the trunk and the root system were visible. Miraculously, going against every design of the gods, the baobab rerooted upside down. The former branches functioned as roots, while the former roots functioned as branches, thus explaining the distinctively withered and atrophied appearance of the tree.

The spreading of foliage and flowering are difficult for the baobab; its fruit is precious and its growth process slow. A schematization of the elements associated with the destiny of this tree reveals: violent deracination, a fall, the instability of status and the reversals of role, full and harmonious fulfillment denied, desires thwarted, difficult reproduction, a society decimated, its upper portion relegated to the world of shadows, its aspiration toward the spiritual directed downward, reenracination, survival under the most adverse conditions and despite the reigning gods' arsenals of suppression, and, finally, the ensuing atrophy.

It can be seen that this schema coincides with the trajectory and history of the slave trade and the survival of Blacks in the New World. Aimé Césaire says succinctly: "Baobab, c'est notre arbre."

> Naissance
> arbre non arbre
> hier renversé
> les laboureurs célestes sont fiers d'avoir changé
> o laboureurs labourants
> en terre il est replanté
> le ciel pousse
> il contre pousse
> arbre non arbre
> bel arbre immense[4]
> . . . .
> bel arbre nu
> en déjà l'invincible départ vers on imagine un sabbath
> de splendeur
> sur les oriflammes sublimes de ta révolte
> . . . .

innocent qui va là
oublie de te rappeler
que le baobab est notre arbre
qu'il mal agite des bras si nains
qu'on le dirait un géant imbécile[5]

les bras trop courts s'allongèrent de flammes[6]

[tree that is not a tree
yesterday overturned
The celestial workers are proud of having changed it
O laboring laborers
In earth it is replanted
the sky pushes
It counter pushes
tree that is not a tree
Beautiful tree immense
. . . .
beautiful tree naked
already embarked upon the invincible departure toward
one imagines a Sabbath
of splendor
on the sublime golden banners of your revolt
. . . .
innocent one who goes there
forget to remember that
the baobab is our tree
how awkwardly it waves its arms so dwarfed
one would almost say it is an imbecilic giant

the arms too short stretched out into flames]

In an interview with Césaire, when I discussed the extended role of the flora in his poetry, he offered:

> The baobab has always fascinated me because it is a tree that I find pathetic. It is quite pathetic because it is monstrous. It most definitely has extremely short arms. It is not at all a harmonious tree. Indeed, it is what you would call your tortured ontology. In particular, the Baobab has an extremely large trunk; it is almost like a prehistoric animal in shape, with

> very short arms. I find it a very painful tree; it is not fully blossomed, not fully realized. Yes, it is a tree in pain. Whence, consequently, the conclusion that it is our tree. Further, it is the tomb of the African storyteller-poet-chroniclers. Yes, the soul of the griot rests in the Baobab tree.[7]

Archetypes of the collective unconscious, myths are expressions of the human psyche that serve as models in analyzing human comportment. The rich hermeneutical potential of this baobab mythology led me to focus on the consequences of certain social and political actualities of the francophone colonial and postcolonial condition, for the dominated, the subordinated, and for their consciousness. Emblematically a tortured ontology, the upside-down tree vegetalizes the existential preoccupations that I daresay characterize much of francophone literature of the last fifty years: the sense of loss, displacement, lost harmonies, lost communities, homelessness, traditions negated and redefined, survival, experimentation, and the reevaluation of concepts of self and society. (The myth and reality of the baobab tree are richly exploited in *Le Baobab fou* [The Abandoned Baobab], which is the subject of close analysis in chapter 7.)

Implicit among the network of existential concerns and social actualities of francophone literary culture are status, role, and consciousness. Countermodernist francophone literary culture ponders the realities of migration, wandering, the bordering of cultures, population drains, the exodus or the transplantation of segments of a population for economic reasons, and the ecological disasters that are the consequences of colonialism as well as the actualities of the postcolonial condition. One of my principal concerns is the extent to which the necessarily uprooted nomadic condition of certain peoples of West Africa, North Africa, and the French West Indies have exacerbated the problems of *status inconsistency,* which leads to *role conflict,* and in turn to *altered consciousness,* issues that, along with questions of sexuality, I shall be examining in Part II.

II

Counterstorytelling

4

Colonialism, Literary Tradition, and Counterstorytelling

In 1921, as *Batouala* by René Maran was being awarded the Goncourt Literary Prize and its preface was being banned in the French colonies, the first pan-African congresses were demanding self-government for the African colonies and calling upon the Société des Nations to undertake the project of promoting the independence of African colonies. From 1921 onward, the emergence of francophone literary culture coincided with the dying days of French colonialism, the bitter trauma of decolonization, and the cooperative phase of neocapitalist postcolonialism. Frantz Fanon asserts, "Every effort is made to bring the colonized person to admit the inferiority of his culture which has been transformed into instinctive patterns of behavior, to recognize the unreality of his 'nation,' and, in the last extreme, the confused and imperfect character of his own biological structure."[1] Francophone literary culture can be analyzed as counterstorytelling, that is, writing, speaking, and performing against the colonial discourse, from the perspective of the colonized.

French Colonialism, the Rise of Anticolonialist Sentiment, and the Push for Nationhood

The term *colonialism* came into being as a derivation of the Latin verb *colere* (to cultivate), through the masculine noun *colonus* (cultivator, peasant, settler), to the feminine noun *colonia,* designating a detachment of Roman citizens sent to populate a deserted territory or conquered land with inhabitants.[2] Eventually *colonia,* or colony, came to designate a settlement that the Romans "founded" and that was composed of an agricultural sector and an urban center replicating the planning of the Roman city itself. The concept of colony implied a legal status for the settlement that combined local municipal autonomy with political subordination to Rome, the "mother" city. The concept of the extended family was fundamental to Roman principles of organization and protection. Thus the hierarchical family metaphor was already in place, with the settling metropolis as a parent figure —matriarchal or patriarchal, empress or emperor, queen or king— and the colonies as the governed, subordinated, dominated woman-child. The Roman model prefigures the nineteenth-century dualistic, anthropological logic of French colonialism in which, as we shall see, the parent-child metaphor is transformed into a conjugal one.

In the twentieth century, colonialism refers to the annexation and exploitation of one people by another. Looking further back, however, it refers to that crusading, missionary, "civilizing," and, above all, entrepreneurial spirit of exploration and commerce that inspired the expansionist politics of most of the European maritime powers from the time of Columbus and Vasco da Gama through the nineteenth century.

The settling of the colonies was conceived of, first of all, as a commercial or economic enterprise designed to procure for the metropolitan center rare goods, precious metals and ores, raw material, spices, and produce from the tropics, the Orient, Polynesia, and the lands bordering the Indian Ocean. Mercantilism was refined to an art so as to enrich the metropolitan center through trade and the sale of goods at increasingly exorbitant prices to foreigners. In this system, the colonies served, on the one hand, as exclusive suppliers of exotic products (coffee, ivory, tobacco, vegetable and nut oils, spices, sugar, cotton, etc.). On the other hand, they served as controlled markets for the products manufactured on the mainland. This system of *exclusive* exploitation of all of the colonies' natural resources as well as the *exclusive* monopoly of the colonial marketplace not only formally and legally outlawed all direct trade among the colonies or with other foreign powers, but also limited local rates and levels of production. This mercantile regime, which assured the sovereignty and enrichment of the colonial power, was known as the exclusive Colonial Pact.[3] Some would maintain that little has changed and that in the "cooperative" postindependence period, the actors merely wear different costumes. This, at least, is the message of the minidrama in the opening scenes of the film *Xala* by Ousmane Sembene. The railroads and ports that were once used primarily for export of raw materials by colonial powers now serve transnational conglomerates for importing and distributing their Western goods to the countries whose natural economies were destroyed through colonial exploitation.

African nationalism would not be clearly articulated until after World War II, but a certain proto-Black ethnonationalism was evident in Senegal as early as 1919. The slogan "Mettre les blancs à la porte!" (Kick the whites out) appeared in this colony during the years 1919–21, when the Société des Nations was being asked to help deliver it from the shackles of French government and exploitation. In the 1920s African intellectuals were particularly attracted by the ideas of the Jamaican American Marcus Garvey, which foreshadowed pan-Africanism. With such rallying cries as "Africa for Africans" and "Wake up, Ethiopia," he initiated the "back to Africa movement." His National Association for the Advancement of Colored People, calling for the eviction of the White race from the Black continent, claimed to sound the death knell for colonialism in Africa. At the same time an international communist movement was aligning itself with Africans by supporting their growing anti-imperialist sentiments and offering a program that called for the emancipation of Black people, the alliance of Blacks everywhere, and solidarity among all pariahs and proletarian classes of the world. In Paris, the Ligue Anti-impérialiste called for the independence of Senegal and the Sudan in 1932, although the Ligue de Défense de la Race Nègre and the Union des Travailleurs Nègres working out of Paris had no real presence in Africa at the time. *Cri des Nègres,* a manifesto written by French Communists, appeared in 1933–34, demanding independence for Senegal and the Sudan.[4] The French Communist "program" for Blacks would be questioned in 1956 by Aimé Césaire, who resigned from the Communist Party in the now famous "Letter to Maurice Thorez":

> Je crois en avoir assez dit pour faire comprendre que ce n'est ni le marxisme, ni le communisme que je renie, que c'est l'usage que certains

ont fait du marxisme et du communisme que je réprouve. Que ce que je veux, c'est que marxisme et communisme soient mis au service des peuples noirs, et non les peuples noirs au service du marxisme.

[I think I have said enough to make it clearly understood that it is neither Marxism nor Communism that I am rejecting, but rather it is the use to which certain people have put Marxism and Communism that I reject. What I want is that Marxism and Communism be placed in the service of the Black peoples of the world, and not the Black people of the world in the service of Marxism and Communism.]

An extraordinary statistic reveals that just prior to the period of decolonization, the French colonial machine in Africa was made up of a surprisingly small core/corps of French administrators. These functionaries governed and controlled more by virtue of their prestige than by force and incorporated traditional African chiefdoms into their system of command. Thus, 593 French colonial administrators controlled 2,200 African canton chiefs, who in turn presided over 48,000 village chiefs.[5]

Between 1939 and 1945 Black Africans were deeply involved in World War II: an estimated 175,000 Africans were mobilized for the armed effort. In 1939, at the outset of the Allied campaign, 17,000 French troops were joined by 80,000 African troops, who, it is said, often served on the front lines as *la chair à canon* (canon fodder). In addition to the troop support, the colonies were called upon to increase production of goods for export to raise revenues for France; in particular, the tonnage of cotton, peanuts, and rubber was increased.[6]

Following World War II the political activity inspired by African nationalism accelerated and violence began to erupt. Black Africans felt that the human and material sacrifices of French-speaking Africa during the war required at least gratitude and recognition from France; instead, in 1944 the return of demobilized Senegalese sharpshooters was marked by a grave incident of mutiny at Tiaroye in which thirty-five rebellious sharpshooters were killed. The Senegalese press reflected the country's growing impatience and militancy. *L'Afrique libre* and *Jeunesse et démocratie* both asserted: "Le colonialisme est terminé" (Colonialism is over) and "Le Toubab a peur" (Whitey is afraid). Another Senegalese newspaper, *La Communauté,* announced: "We will not accept European domination much longer.

It is our hope that Europe will be reduced to dust before a resurrected Africa."[7] The emancipation of Black Africa took place between 1946 and 1960. Compared to Algeria, decolonization in Black Africa was *relatively* peaceful.[8]

A refusal to hate and a willingness to forgive can be found in some francophone poetry in the years before decolonization. For the most part, however, the bitterness runs deep, and hatred is kept in check through prayer and, failing that, through the mordant ironies of the native perspective. For example, Léopold Sédar Senghor evokes the memory of the disregarded Sengalese soldiers who fought so valiantly for France during World War II but who were offered up as so many "Black Hosts," or sacrifices, by the Republic. His poem, "Prière de Paix," is remarkable for its contained bitterness and expression of Catholic pardon. While asking forgiveness for France, it nonetheless records all of the abuses of the colonizer and the ironies issuing from France's double standards, and it reveals the often ambivalent feelings of the colonized subject who loves French culture and hates what France has done to the homeland and the people.

> Seigneur la glace de mes yeux s'embue
>
> Et voilà que le serpent de la haine lève la tête dans mon cœur, ce serpent que j'avais cru mort. . . .
>
> Tue-le, Seigneur, car il me faut pour suivre mon chemin, et je veux prier singulièrement pour la France.
>
> Seigneur, parmi les nations blanches, place la France à la droite du Père.
>
> Oh! je sais bien qu'elle aussi est l'Europe, qu'elle m'a ravi mes enfants comme un brigand du Nord des boeufs, pour engraisser ses terres à cannes et coton car la sueur nègre est fumier.
>
> Qu'elle aussi a porté la mort et le canon dans mes villages bleus, qu'elle a dressé les miens les uns contre les autres comme des chiens se disputant un os.
>
> Qu'elle a traité les résistants de bandits, et craché sur les têtes-aux-vastes-desseins.
>
> Oui Seigneur, pardonne à la France qui dit bien la voie droite et chemine par les sentiers obliques.
>
> Qui m'invite à sa table et me dit d'apporter mon pain, qui me donne de la main droite et de la main gauche enlève la moitié.

Oui Seigneur, pardonne à la France qui hait les occupants et m'impose l'occupation si gravement.

Qui ouvre des voies triomphales aux héros et traite ses Sénégalais en mercenaires, faisant d'eux les dogues noirs de l'Empire.

Qui est la République et livre le pays aux Grands-Concessionnaires.

Et de ma Mésopotamie, de mon Congo, ils ont fait un grand cimetière sous le soleil blanc.[9]

[Lord the mirror of my eye clouds over and there is the serpent of hate raising his head in my heart, the serpent whom I had believed dead. . . . Kill it, O Lord, for I must continue on my way and I want to pray particularly for France. O Lord, among all the white nations, place France on the right hand of the Father. Oh! I know she is also part of Europe, that she has stolen my children as a robber from the north takes cattle, to enrich her lands with sugar cane and cotton, for the Negro's sweat is manure; that she also brought death and the cannon into my blue villages; that she set my people one against the other like dogs fighting over a bone; that she treated resistance as banditry, and spat on the heads that dreamt of greatness. Yes, Lord, forgive France who preaches the straight path but takes the crooked one herself; who invites me to her table yet tells me to bring my own bread, who gives to me with the right hand but takes half away again with the left. Yes, Lord, forgive France who hates occupiers yet imposes occupation so heavily upon me; who opens the triumphal gates to heroes and treats her Senegalese as mercenaries, making them the black watchdogs of the Empire; who is the Republic yet places the country in the hands of big companies. And of my Mesopotamia, of my Congo, they have made a great cemetery beneath the white sun.][10]

Colonialism and the Francophone Literary Imagination

The study of francophone literary culture involves the examination of the sociopolitical and psychosexual challenges imposed by the experiences of colonialism, decolonization, and postindependence. My task is to investigate the consequences of the colonial enterprise for the literary culture or imagination.[11] With texts from French and francophone literary culture, I shall illustrate the set of relationships that form a sequential, transformative, and political *grammar* of metaphors and obsessions orienting the francophone imagination. This task requires citing some lengthy passages from compelling, shocking, even distasteful documents that have exerted a profound influence on the francophone imagination and, particularly, on the dynamics of counterstorytelling. "These facts require to be recalled. . . . these resentments remain with us extremely vivid," asserts Abiola Irele, the Nigerian comparatist of African and Caribbean literature.[12] I have sought to order these texts so that they lead to a reading of a little-discussed musical interlude (act 2, scene 2) in *The Tragedy of King Christophe,* the masterpiece of Césaire's "theater of decolonization."

French colonialism was integral to Europe's ideological will to dominate. Beginning in 1790, France sought to augment its power by land and sea and, through its expansionist, mercantilist policies, to become the focal point of the world. It established its first colony, Algeria, in 1830. By 1878, land under French colonial rule was expanding, according to some figures, at the rate of 240,000 square miles per year. Concerning the speed of this colonialist expansion in Oubangui-Chari, which later became the Central African Republic and Chad, René Maran writes:

> The region was very rich in rubber and very populous. Plantations of all sorts covered its expanses. It abounded in chickens and goats. Seven years were enough to ruin it completely. . . .
>
> Civilization went through there. And Dacpas, M'bis, Maroukas, La'mbassis, Sabangas and N'gapous—all the Bamba tribes—were scattered.[13]

The first point in this political grammar of metaphors and relationships to consider are the clichés that made up the colonial rhetoric. The domination of the African, Asian, American, and Amazonian "hearts of darkness" by the West, coupled with the ability to codify and to disseminate knowledge, led to a perception by the colonizers of a duty to the natives: to establish colonies for their benefit and for the prestige of France. This sense of "duty" gave rise to the rhetoric of the *mission civilisatrice,* the civilizing mission of the French. In a section entitled "The French" in her biography of Léopold Sédar Senghor, Jean Vaillant illustrates these very points when citing Jules Michelet and Senghor:

> The Frenchman wants above all to imprint his personality on the vanquished, not because it is his, but because it is the quintessence of the good and the beautiful—this is his native belief. He believes that he can do nothing that would benefit the world more than to give it his ideas, customs, and ways of doing things. He will convert other people to these ways, sword in hand, and after the battle, in part smugly and in part sympathetically, he will reveal to them all that they gain by becoming French.[14]

Léopold Sédar Senghor seems to agree grudgingly with Jules Michelet, for he states: "The Frenchman wants bread for all, liberty for all; but this liberty, this culture, and this bread will be French. The universalism of this people is French."[15]

Along with the impulse to global dominance, colonialism entailed the will to define, depict, portray, represent, characterize, and textualize the colonized people through the capitalist, Judeo-Christian, and male normative gaze. In his exhaustive study *Le Nègre romantique,* Léon-François Hoffmann reveals the extent to which the French collective consciousness was preoccupied with classifying, organizing, and establishing social and racial hierarchies.[16] His study is essential for understanding many of the literary traditions that francophone artists struggle to counter in their own creative works.

An analysis of the texts and their considerations of alterity discloses a generative, transformational, and political grammar of preoccupations, stereotypes, and metaphors that, to some extent, continue to burden us today. Comte Joseph-Arthur de Gobineau, who served as an inspiration to Adolph Hitler, is perhaps the most well-known author of pseudoscientific texts that sought to justify the exploitation of colored races by the colonial machine. This brings us to the second point in this grammar: the hierarchical codification of colonialist visions of alterity. The scientific literature of the times reinforced the anthropological "logic" of colonialism and, with its binary oppositions between the prelogical and the logical, placed on the one side the yellow, brown, red, and black savage, the child, the woman, and the poet, and, on the other side, the European male.

> La variété mélanienne [i.e., *le Noir*] est la plus humble et gît au bas de l'échelle. Le caractère d'animalité empreint dans la forme de son bas-

sin lui impose sa destinée, dès l'instant de la conception. Elle ne sortira jamais du cercle intellectuel le plus restreint. Ce n'est cependant pas une brute pure et simple, que ce nègre à front étroit et fuyant, qui porte, dans la partie moyenne de son crâne, les indices de certaines énergies grossièrement puissantes. Si ces facultés pensantes sont médiocres ou même nulles, il possède dans le désir, et par suite dans la volonté, une intensité souvent terrible. Plusieurs de ses sens sont développés avec une vigueur inconnue aux deux autres races: le goût et l'odorat principalement. . . .

Mais là, précisement, dans l'avidité même de ses sensations, se trouve le cachet frappant de son infériorité. Tous les aliments lui sont bons, aucun ne le dégoûte, aucun ne le repousse. Ce qu'il souhaite, c'est manger, manger avec excès, avec fureur; il n'y a pas de répugnante charogne indigne de s'engloutir dans son estomac. Il en est de même pour les odeurs, et sa sensualité s'accommode non seulement des plus grossières, mais des plus odieuses. A ces principaux traits de caractère il joint une instabilité d'humeur, une variabilité des sentiments que rien ne peut fixer, et qui annule, pour lui, la vertu comme le vice. On dirait que l'emportement même avec lequel il poursuit l'objec qui a mis sa sensitivité en vibration et enflamme sa convoitise est un gage du prompt apaisement de l'une et du rapide oubli de l'autre. Enfin il tient également peu à sa vie et à celle d'un autre; il tue volontiers pour tuer, et cette machine humaine, si facile à émouvoir, est, devant la souffrance, ou d'une lâcheté qui se réfugie volontiers dans la mort ou d'une impassibilité monstrueuse.[17]

[The negroid variety is the lowest and stands at the foot of the ladder. The animal-like characteristic that appears in the shape of the pelvis is stamped on the negro from birth and foreshadows his destiny. His intellect will always move within a very narrow circle. He is not however a mere brute, for behind his low receding brow, in the middle of his skull, we can see signs of a powerful energy, however crude its objects. If his mental faculties are dull or even nonexistent, he often has an intensity of desire, and so of will, that may be called terrible. Many of his senses, especially taste and smell, are developed to an extent unknown to the other two races.

The very strength of his sensations is the most striking proof of his inferiority. All food is good in his eyes; nothing disgusts or repels him. What he desires is to eat, to eat furiously and to excess; no carrion is too revolting to be swallowed by him. It is the same with odors; his inordinate desires are satisfied with all, however coarse or even horrible. To these qualities may be added an instability and capriciousness of feeling that cannot be tied down to any single object, and which, so far as he is concerned, do away with all distinctions of good and evil. We might even say that the violence with which he pursues the object that has aroused his senses and inflamed his desires is a guarantee of the desires being soon satisfied on the one hand and the object quickly forgotten on the other. Finally, he is equally careless of his own life and that of someone else's: he kills willingly, for the sake of killing; and this human machine, in whom it is so easy to arouse emotion, shows, in the face of suffering, either a monstrous indifference or a cowardice that seeks voluntary refuge in death.]

The third point in a francophone political grammar of the colonial experience would be what the Afro-Americanist Hortense Spillers might designate the legacy of the slave trade:

> The massive demographic shifts, the violent formation of a modern African consciousness, that take place on the subsaharan Continent during the initiative strikes which open the Atlantic Slave Trade in the fifteenth century of our Christ, interrupted hundreds of years of black African culture. . . . the familiarity of this narrative does nothing to appease the hunger of recorded memory, nor does the persistence of the repeated rob these well-known, off-told events of their power, even now to startle. In a very real sense every writing as revision makes the discovery all over again.[18]

Although slavery in its archaic forms is past, it remains a nightmare that haunts the consciousness of all Blacks, however divided they may be by different languages, policies, and histories of colonial experience. Slavery is the collective experience binding Blacks through time and space, and some writers are unable and unwilling to escape the memory and rememory of that experience. The following description of conditions under the French slave trade support Spillers's characterization of the colonial commerce of human flesh as "a 'fall,' a veritable descent into the loss of the communicative force."[19]

PRÉCIS SUR LA TRAITE DES NOIRS

> Un espace ménagé sur l'arrière, entre le logement des noirs et la chambre des officiers, contient les armes du bord, que l'on expose avec inten-

tion aux regards des esclaves. C'est dans cet arsenal, séparé des parcs par une grille, que se promène la sentinelle qui surveille les noirs. Le parc des négresses doit ètre caché à la vue des hommes. L'aspect de ces infortunées suffirait pour porter les africains à des révoltes qu'il est toujours plus facile de prévenir que de réprimer.

Une inspiration, qui pourrait paraître bizarre si elle n'était pas féroce, a fait employer depuis peu un moyen de contenir les esclaves sans le secours des sentinelles. De forts chiens de Terre-Neuve, exercés à la garde des troupeaux d'hommes, sont maintenant chargés de la police intérieure des négriers. Deux de ces animaux suffisent pour garder deux à trois cents africains. . . . Ces parcs, où l'on entasse un si grand nombre d'hommes, sans songer qu'ils ont besoin de respirer, deviennent quelquefois des cloaques d'ou s'exhalent la contagion et la mort. Il n'est pas rare de voir un négrier perdre le tiers ou le quart de sa cargaison dans le cours d'une traversée même rapide. Mais quelques [*sic*] ravages qu'exercent les épidémies sur les africains, le désespoir ou la mélancolie qui les atteint leur devient encore plus funeste: aussi les capitaines ont-ils le soin de faire prendre des distractions aux plus moroses, en les faisant danser sur le pont au bruit d'un tambour et d'un fifre. Pendant cet exercice, qui leur est offert comme un spécifique contre la douleur, des espingoles, braquées sur les danseurs, sont disposées à les foudroyer au moindre signe de rebellion; et cette *triste joie* qu'on leur impose, en leur offrant le plaisir à còté de la mort, est encore plus féroce peut-être que les mauvais traitements dont on les accable.[20]

[PRECIS ON THE SLAVE TRADE

A space arranged at the aft of the ship, between the lodging for the Black males and the officers' quarters, contains the ship's weapons, which are exposed intentionally in the sight of the slaves. It is in this arsenal, separated from the slave quarters by a grid, that the sentinel who keeps watch over the Blacks makes his rounds. The female slave quarters must be hidden from the view of the male slaves. The sight of these unfortunates was enough to incite the African males to revolts that are always easier to avoid than they are to repress.

An inspiration that could appear bizarre, were it not so vicious, led to a recently employed means of controlling the slaves without the need for a watchman. Enormous Newfoundland dogs trained to guard human

> herds are now charged with policing the interior of the slave ships. Two of these animals suffice to guard two or three hundred Africans. . . . These quarters, where such great numbers of men are stacked, without considering that they need space in which to breathe, become at times cesspools from which contagion and death exude. It is not rare to see a slave ship lose one-third or a quarter of its cargo in the course of a crossing, even a rapid one. Yet, however great the ravages inflicted by the epidemics upon the Africans, the despair and melancholy that afflict them is even more devastating. The captains take great care to force the more morose ones to participate in distractions by making them dance on the bridge to the sound of a fife and drum. During this exercise, which is offered them as a tonic to counter their pain, muskets aimed at the dancers are ready to blow them to bits at the slightest sign of rebellion; and this sad joy imposed upon them, by offering them pleasure under the threat of death, is perhaps even more vicious than the other bad treatment that is heaped upon them.]

A francophone grammar of the colonial experience would place at its center the Haitian slave insurrection of 1802, which eventually led to a declaration of independence in 1804. These events mark the first successful slave rebellion, decolonization, and independence of a Black nation:

> Art. 3. Nous concédons . . . par la présente ordonnance, aux habitants actuels de la partie française de l'île de Saint-Domingue, l'indépendance pleine et entière de leur gouvernement, et sera la présente ordonnance scéllée de notre grand sceau.[21]

> Art. 3. We hereby concede . . . with the present order, to the current inhabitants of the French side of the Island of Santo Domingo, the full and total independence of their government, and the present order will be sealed with our imperial stamp.

Aimé Césaire makes the point in *Notebook of a Return to My Native Land* that the Haitian revolution and independence were essential to the formation of a redemptive, revolutionary concept of the Black self and that they exemplify the concept of *négritude*. "Haiti," he writes, "[is] where *négritude* stood up and declared its humanity."[22]

In colonial depictions, the superlative values of those "within God's grace" were opposed to those heathen societies, which were described as "lazy," "degenerate," "primitive," and "unnatural" and should be ruled. As we have seen, Antenor Firmin replied systematically to this discourse. The hierarchies led to the codification of difference among people of color. According to the tortured logic of this rhetoric, New World Blacks were progressively approaching the European model of the human.

> Les nègres Créols [*sic*] naissent avec des qualités physiques et morales, qui leur donnent un droit réel à la supériorité sur ceux qu'on a transportés d'Afrique. . . .
>
> A l'intelligence, le nègre Créol réunit la grâce dans les formes, la souplesse dans les mouvemens, l'agrément dans la figure, et un langage plus doux et privé de tous les accens que les nègres Africains y mèlent. Accoutumés, dès leur naissance, aux choses qui annoncent le génie de l'homme, leur esprit est moins obtus que celui de l'Africain qui, quelquefois par exemple, ne sait pas discerner les subdivisions de la monnoie. . . . Il n'est aucun objet pour lequel on ne préfère les nègres Créols, et leur valeur est toujours, toutes choses égales d'ailleurs, d'un quart, au moins, au-dessus de celle des Africains. Une prédilection assez générale, fait préférer les nègres Créols pour les details domestiques, et pour les différens métiers.[23]

> [Creole Blacks are born with physical and moral qualities that confer upon them a true right to superiority over those who were subsequently transported from Africa. . . .
>
> To natural intelligence, the Creole Black adds grace in form, suppleness in movement, beauty of visage, and a more mellifluous language rid of all those accents that African Blacks mix in. Accustomed, from the moment of their birth, to those phenomena that hail the genius of man, their mind is less obtuse than that of the African, who sometimes does not know, for example, how to discern the subdivisions of currency. . . . There is no area in which one would not prefer a Creole Black, and their value is always, all things considered besides, one-quarter at least above that of Africans. A rather widespread predilection makes Creole Blacks preferable for domestic duties and for different trades.]

The family model implicit in early Roman colonization discussed earlier was perpetuated by the European maritime powers of modern times. The connections between servitude and domesticity, colored races and women, fetishism and emotion, and the manifest domination of the passive colored races and women by the rational white virile race were elaborated in the pseudoscientific literature of the eighteenth and nineteenth centuries that sought to explain the organization of the human family. The observation of the double jeopardy of race and gender for the black woman in the following nineteenth-century text seems prophetic:

> Le noir me parait être la *race femme* dans la famille humaine, comme le blanc est la *race mâle*. De même que la femme, le noir est privé des facultés politiques et scientifiques: il n'a jamais créé un grand état. il n'est point astronome, mathématicien, naturaliste: il n'a rien fait en mécanique industrielle. Mais, par contre, il possède au plus haut degré les qualités du cœur, les affections et les sentiments domestiques; il est homme d'*intérieur*. Comme la femme, il aime aussi avec passion la parure, la danse, le chant. . . . Tandis que le blanc est *panthéiste* et s'absorbe dans la contemplation de l'infiniment grand, le noir est *fétichiste* et adore la puissance infinie dans ses manifestations infiniment petites. . . .
>
> Jusqu'ici *domesticité* et *servitude* ont été des choses à peu près identiques. Aussi le noir, être essentiellement *domestique,* comme la femme, a été jusqu'ici condamné comme elle à un esclavage plus ou moins rude. L'émancipation de la femme devra donc être accompagnée de celle du noir, ou pour parier plus nettement, c'est dans la *femme noire* que l'émancipation de la femme doit complètement se réaliser. On peut dire, encore sous une autre forme, que le couple typique se compose d'un *homme blanc* et d'une *femme noire*.[24]

> [The Black appears to me to be the female race in the human family, just as the White is the male race. Just like women, the black is deprived of political and scientific faculties: he has never founded a great state. He is not an astronomer, mathematician, or naturalist; he has done nothing in industrial mechanics. However, in contrast, he possesses to the highest degree qualities of the heart, affection and domestic feelings; he is a man of interiors. Like the woman, he likes trinkets for self-adornment, dance, song. . . . Whereas the White man is pantheistic and absorbs himself in the contemplation of the infinitely great, the Black is fetishistic and adores the infinite power in its tiniest manifestations. . . .
>
> Up to this point domesticity and servitude have been more or less identical concepts. Also, the Black, an essentially domestic being, like the woman, has been condemned heretofore to a slavery that is more or

less rude. The emancipation of the woman will consequently be accompanied by that of the Black, or perhaps to state it more pointedly, it will be in the emancipation of the Black woman that the liberation of woman will be fully realized. One can also say, in another way, that the typical couple is composed of *a White man* and *a Black woman*.]

When the emphasis is pointedly racial, colonialist writers have transformed the original Roman parent-child metaphor into a spousal metaphor. In so many ways, this text by d'Eichtal and Urbain states the unsayable, indeed the unspeakable, as it addresses the political and ideological assignment of gender to Europe and to the rest of the globe. In wielding power, the European culture, the European man *or* European woman, will function as male. In power relations, the Black, Brown, Red, and Yellow cultures, the women *or* the men will always already be female.[25] It is clear also that the d'Eichtal and Urbain text is not a ringing endorsement of *racial* miscegenation; rather, it presents an economic and a hegemonic model of *marriage* between European civilization and the natural resources, ports, commercial routes, and labor potential of non-European cultures that are there to be unveiled, opened up, and raped. The marriage model between the metropolitan center and the colonies is that of polygamy.

While distancing themselves from the native assimilationist poetics that slavishly imitated French literary traditions, the Negritude poets began to challenge and "signify" upon certain pseudoscientific literature and the romantic and modernist stereotypes that literature engendered: the faithful, contented, and dependent domestic servant; the demonic, rebellious, savage slave; the sexually overdetermined Black male and female; the beautiful, tragic, and demonic mulatto.

Of all the female figures and presences—feminine essences and forces—in the work of Aimé Césaire, perhaps the most haunting is the one whose intertextual destiny migrates between French romantic literature, francophone literature, feminist theory, and film. She is Ourika, the Black nun of despair, from the 1824 French novella *Ourika*, by Claire Durfort, duchesse de Duras, noble friend and spiritual companion of Châteaubriand. Ourika, saved from drowning by the French governor of Senegal after being dropped into the sea by her mother, is pressed into slavery. The anonymous two-year-old Black girl is reared in Paris by the governor's sister, Madame de B., a noblewoman who loves the Black child as if she were her own daughter. Ashamed of her Black skin, embarrassed by the bloody, successful revolt of her Haitian revolutionary brothers, Ourika becomes suicidal because her blackness, she is convinced, prevents her adopted French brother from loving her passionately.

Ourika the text as well as Ourika the female figure inspired the depiction of the solitary cloaked female figure in the opening frames of John Fowles's film *The French Lieutenant's Woman.* Fowles also translated *Ourika* into English in a limited deluxe edition. The embedding of the novella *Ourika* in Césaire's *The Tragedy of King Christopher* (1963) directs us to read this nineteenth-century text. Césaire's incorporation of this figure into his play anticipates the discovery of this text by the French feminists who republished it in 1972 with a lengthy preface. In his play, Césaire uses the tragic self-discovery of a character fatefully named Ourika (Eureka, or "I discover") to study slavery, the Haitian revolution, racial shame, the tension of the white male and the Black female "couple," and the figuration of the Black woman as a split subject. Ourika illustrates the mobility of existence and experience across boundaries of geography, culture, and genre, and the resultant network of significance woven into francophone literary culture. *Ourika*'s fate is an exciting example of the deterritorialization and expropriation of a text and literary figure.

In *The Tragedy of King Christophe,* during an Elizabethan musical interlude (act 2, scene 2), Césaire recalls the name and the tragedy of Ourika in order to explain the significance of King Christophe's tyrannical love and exceptional demands on his recently decolonized Haitian people. After the successful slave rebellion against the French, King Christophe has challenged his people to build an impregnable citadel atop an almost unscalable peak on a cape in northern Haiti.

> *Première Dame:* . . . assez de politique! Isabelle, mettez-vous au clavecin. Elle a une voix ravissante, cette enfant. Isabelle, chantez-nous donc cette jolie romance, la romance d'Ourika.
>
> *Vastey:* Et qui est cette charmante enfant, Ourika?
>
> *Première Dame:* L'héroine d'un roman qui fait pleurer tout Paris . . . C'est l'histoire d'une petite noire élevée dans une grande famille blanche, et qui souffre de sa couleur et en meurt.

Vastey: Ah! Intéressant! Très intéressant!

Isabelle, chantant:
Enfant de la noire Guinée
D'un ciel brûlant lointaine fleur,
Ourika, fille infortunée,
Déplorait ainsi son malheur
France, toi qui m'avais charmée
Toi que saluaient mes transports
Tu me cachais que sur tes bords
Je ne serais jamais aimée.
Blanche couleur, couleur des anges,
Mon âme était digne de toi,
O Dieu puissant, que de louanges
Si tu l'avais faite pour moi!
Mais pour l'oubli tu m'as formée!
D'Ourika termine le sort:
C'est un si grand bien que la mort
Pour qui ne peut pas être aimée.

Première Dame: Bravo! Bravo! C'est à mourir. Qu'en pensez-vous, Monsieur Vastey?

Vastey: Je pense à Christophe, Madame. Savez-vous pourquoi il travaille jour et nuit? Savez-vous, ces lubies féroces, comme vous dites, ce travail de forcené . . . C'est pour que désormais il n'y ait plus de par le monde une jeune fille noire qui ait honte de sa peau et trouve dans sa couleur un obstacle à la réalisation des vœux de son cœur.[26]

[*Première Dame:* Enough of politics! Isabelle, do play the harpsichord. She has a ravishing voice, this child. Isabelle, sing for us that beautiful romance, the story of Ourika.

Vastey: And who is this charming child, Ourika?

Première Dame: The heroine of a novel that has all of Paris crying. It is the story of a little black girl reared in an important white family, who suffers because of her color and dies consequently.

Vastey: Ah! Interesting! Very interesting!

Isabelle, singing: Child of Black Guinea / Distant flower of a scorching sky / Ourika, unfortunate girl / thus deplored her misfortune. / France, you who had charmed me / You who greeted my transport / You hid me on your shores / Where I would never be loved. / White color, color of angels / My soul is worthy of you / O powerful God, what praises to you / If you had granted me that. / But for oblivion you made me / The fate of Ourika is ending / Death is such a great deliverance / For one who cannot be loved.

Première Dame: Bravo! Bravo! It is to die for! What do you think of it, Monsieur Vastey?

Vastey: It makes me think of Christophe, Madame. Do you know why he works day and night? Do you know why he undertakes these wild whims, as you call them, this work of a madman. It is so that henceforth, there will no longer be anywhere in the world any little black girl who is ashamed of the color of her skin and who finds in her color the obstacle to the realization of the wishes of her heart.]

The extravagant dream of the Black King of Haiti has not yet been realized, for the problems treated in the dilemma of Ourika persist today:

Journalist: Who is better? White people or Black?

Black South African schoolgirl: White people.

Journalist: Why?

Schoolgirl: Because they can do whatever they want.

Journalist: What would you prefer to be: White or Black?

Schoolgirl: I would prefer to be White, but there is nothing I can do about it because I am Black.

Journalist: How do you feel about that?

Schoolgirl: Sad.[27]

It is not only the self-hatred revealed by this child's dilemma that should be noted, but also the sense of powerlessness that pervades and burdens the entire being of a little girl because of the consequences of the color of her skin. This profound alienation is repeatedly meditated upon in francophone literature, be it through Mayotte Capécia in *Négresse blanche* (White Negress) or *Je suis Martiniquaise* (I am Martinican); Ken, the confused Senegalese girl in *Le Baobab fou* (The Abandoned Baobab); Kim, the rejected French Vietnamese girl in *Métisse blanche* (The White Mestizo); or the Haitian author Gérard Etienne in *La pacotille* (The Wretched One) and *Le Nègre crucifié* (The Crucified Black).

Aimé Césaire, Frantz Fanon, and Edward Said have demonstrated in their analyses that colonialism entails control of territory, populations, material goods, labor forces, commercial routes, markets, attitudes, minds, and desires. As a concept, francophone culture implies the primacy of language and geography. It is a geolinguistic concept. The geographic underpinnings imply social and political space. From this primacy of geography emerges a structure of attitudes in which valid places are affirmed with such prestige as to hold within their power—the peripheral spaces, that is, the territories, protectorates, colonies.[28] The local bourgeoisie, the collaborating elites, and the class of *évolués* in the colonies made possible the continuing domination and interdependence between the metropolis, Paris, and the peripheries. Militarily, commercially, imaginatively, fashionably, aesthetically, socially, morally even, absolute ideological, cultural, and geographic boundaries of distinction between the Western and the Native would be maintained. It was the creation of a violent Manichaean universe that, according to Frantz Fanon, only the counterviolence of emancipatory decolonization could shatter.

> The colonial world is a world cut in two. The dividing line, the frontiers are shown by barracks and police stations. In the colonies it is the policeman and the soldier who are the official, instituted go-between, the spokesman of the settler and his rule of oppression. In capitalist societies the educational system, whether lay or clerical, the structure of moral reflexes handed down from father to son, the exemplary honesty of workers who are given a medal after fifty years of good and loyal service, and the affection which springs from harmonious relations and good behavior—all these aesthetic expressions of respect for the established order serve to create around the exploited person an atmosphere of submission and of inhibition which lightens the task of policing considerably. In the capitalist countries a multitude of moral teachers, counselors and "bewilderers" separate the exploited from those in power. . . . the agents of government speak the language of pure force.
>
> The zone where the natives live is not complementary to the zone inhabited by the settler. The two zones are opposed, but not in the service

> of a higher unity. Obedient to the rules of pure Aristotelian logic, they both follow the principle of reciprocal exclusivity. . . . The colonial world is a Manichean world. It is not enough for the settler to delimit physically, that is to say with the help of the army and the police force, the place of the native. As if to show the totalitarian character of colonial exploitation the settler paints the native as a sort of quintessence of evil.[29]

The violence of the colonial enterprise inherent in the complexity of its double standards was clearly analyzed in 1921 by René Maran. What perplexed and anguished this West Indian colonial administrator were what Césaire, Fanon, and Said analyzed subsequently—the double standards of metropolitan Western liberty and egalitarian values and standards produced domestically, versus authoritarian imperial control, repression, terror, massacre, and brutality practiced abroad.

> After all if they break down from hunger by the thousands like flies, it is because their country is being developed.
>
> Civilization, civilization, pride of the Europeans, and their burying ground for innocents. . . .
>
> You build your kingdom on corpses. Whatever you may want, whatever you may do, you act with deceit. At your sight, gushing tears and screaming pain. You are the might which exceeds the right. You aren't a torch, but an inferno: everything you touch, you consume. . . .
>
> . . . The negro question is relevant . . . in the course of a challenge in the Chamber of Deputies. The Minister of War, Mr. André Lefèvre, was not afraid to declare that certain French civil servants had thought that they could conduct themselves in reconquered Alsace-Lorraine as if they were in the French Congo.
>
> Such words pronounced, in such a place, are significant. They prove two things—that it is known what is going on in foreign lands and that until now, no one has tried to remedy the abuses, the corruptions and the atrocities which abound there. . . .
>
> . . . Let your voice be raised! You must help those who tell things as they are and not as one would want them to be. . . .
>
> How right was Montesquieu, who wrote in a passage whose contained indignation vibrates under the golden irony; "They are black from head to toe and they have such flattened noses that it is almost impossible to pity them."

> . . . Rare, even among the civil servants, are the colonialists who cultivate their minds. They don't have the strength to resist the atmosphere. They take up alcohol. . . . These and other excesses lead those who indulge in them to the most despicable slackness. That baseness can only cause worry to those who are charged with representing France. . . . They assume the responsibility for the evils which certain parts of the country of the Blacks suffer, right now.
>
> That is because, to advance in rank, it was necessary that they make no waves. Haunted with that idea they gave up all pride, they hesitated, they procrastinated, lied and embellished their lies. They did not want to see. They wanted to hear nothing. They did not have the courage to speak. And moral debility adding itself to their intellectual anemia, with no remorse they wronged their country.
>
> I am appealing to you in order to set to rights everything the administration designates under the euphemism "follies." The fight will be close. You are going to confront slave dealers. It will be harder to fight them than to fight windmills.[30]

René Maran's preface to *Batouala* foreshadows by some thirty years Césaire's *Discourse on Colonialism* (1950). The primary difference between the documents is one of identification. Césaire, unlike Maran, does not align himself with his misguided colonial "brothers of France." Maran's document is an appeal to the moral and social conscience of France, whereas Césaire's discourse is an unambiguous indictment in which the native places the settler on trial. More explicitly than Maran, Césaire underscores the "boomerang effect" of *mutual* dehumanization that is the inevitable consequence of colonial violence:

> For my part, if I have recalled a few details of these hideous butcheries, it is by no means because I take a morbid delight in them, but because I think that these heads of men, these collections of ears, these burned houses, these Gothic invasions, this steaming blood, these cities that evaporate at the edge of the sword, are not to be easily disposed of. They prove that colonization, I repeat, dehumanizes even the most civilized man; that colonial activity, colonial enterprise, colonial conquest which is based on contempt for the native and justified by that contempt, inevitably tends to change him who undertakes it: that the colonizer, who in order to ease his conscience gets into the habit of seeing the other man

> as an animal; accustoms himself to treating him like an animal and tends objectively to transform himself into an animal. It is this result, this boomerang effect of colonization, that I wanted to point out.[31]

Counterstorytelling

> Ce peuple doit se procurer, vouloir,
> réussir quelque chose d'impossible.
> Contre le Sort, contre l'Histoire,
> contre la Nature[32]
>
> [This people must come into its own, must desire,
> must achieve something impossible.
> Against fate, against History,
> against Nature]

In general, francophone literary culture is counterstorytelling. As implied by many of the texts on colonialism and racial inequality just examined, most exploitative domination does not *seem* to be oppression to those perpetrating it. Colonialism, economic exploitation, oppression, and patriarchies are rationalized into systems that cause few considerations of conscience. Counterstories attack smugness, self-serving rationalizations, complacency, blindness, and cultural amnesia. Stories, both oral and written, are the oldest, most primordial meeting ground of human experience. Their effectiveness often provides the means for forming a new collectivity based on the shared story. Thus, in *So long a letter* Mariama Bâ has the character Ramatoulaye declare, in effect, the dynamics of counterstorytelling:

> Books knit generations together in the same continuing effort that leads to progress.
>
> They enabled you to better yourself. . . . *What society refused you they granted.*[33] (emphasis added)

I began this section by stating that francophone literary culture can be analyzed as counterstorytelling, that is, writing, speaking, and performing from the perspective of the colonized against the colonial discourse. Counterstories dream, imagine, and construct new realities, new communities, and new traditions against history, against fate, and against nature as it has been defined. Counterstories reveal that what is inevitable, natural, just, and best for some, in fact can be full of pain, exclusion, and both petty and major tyranny for others.[34] It is through this process that societies can overcome the unthinking conviction that their worldview is the only one and should be the universal.

From this discussion of French colonialism and francophone literary culture, I now turn to discussions of decolonization, independence, and postcolonialism as treated in three representative francophone counterstories.

5

Postscripts

Mariama Bâ, Menopause, Epistolarity, and Postcolonialism

> L'Histoire marchait, inexorable. Le débat à la recherche de la voie juste secouait l'Afrique occidentale. Des hommes courageux connurent la prison; sur leurs traces d'autres poursuivirent l'œuvre ébauchée. Privilège de notre génération, charnière entre deux périodes historiques, l'une de domination, l'autre d'indépendance. Nous étions restés jeunes et efficaces car nous étions porteurs de projets. L'Indépendance acquise, nous assistions à l'éclosion d'une République, à la naissance d'un hymne et à l'implantation d'un drapeau.[1]
>
> [History marched on, inexorably. The debate over the right path to take shook West Africa. Brave men went to prison: others following in their footsteps, continued the work begun. It was the privilege of our generation to be the link between two periods in our history, one of domination, the other of independence. We remained young and efficient, for we were the messengers of a new design. With independence achieved, we witnessed the birth of a republic, the birth of an anthem and the implantation of a flag.][2]

The early phases of francophone literary culture are characterized by assertion of identity, the reinvention of language, the quest for self-hood, the unification of Blacks in the commonwealth of the French colonial experience, and the struggle for decolonization and nationhood. The emphasis on language is crucial, for the expropriation of the French language by the early francophone writers was a first step in the decolonization of the mind. The transformation of language is inseparable from social transformation and the reinvention of concepts of the European and the emancipated self. Decolonization, independence, and postcolonialism are redefinitions of nation, self, and what it means to be a man or a woman in the formerly colonized spaces of the globe.

During the French colonial phase, African and Antillean men and women demonstrated a fierce solidarity, and their combined voices formed a univocal expression of the aspirations of a people to end colonial domination. As Frantz Fanon points out, "Decolonization unifies the people by the radical decision to remove from it its heterogeneity, and by unifying it on a national, sometimes a racial, basis."[3] A consequence of decolonization and nationhood has been that African women have become accustomed to speaking out, alongside their men, have come in revelatory contact with the world, notably with other women on a worldwide scale, and have become aware of the improved status of women in other societies. African women now have the perspective, privilege, political space, and right to attend to their own agenda, apart from that of the African male. The social transformation in Africa involves not only the couple Europe and Africa, but the African man and the African woman vis-à-vis traditional African society and mores. The agenda has shifted from the raising of the consciousness of the masses to the expression of intracultural difference and consciousness, or perhaps, as Julia Kristeva would say, to "the demassification of cultural difference."[4] The perplexing new space is that of the African woman in postindependence society.

In broad terms, francophone literary culture is concerned with transitional social realities and the ever-shifting construction of the francophone identity as it responds to the pressures of the political, the economic, the social, and the legal. In this sense the letter should not be a surprising form of literary expression for a francophone woman writer. As an artifact the letter is *in transit,* crisscrossing borders and barriers, negotiating the national and international *in-between* places where, in francophone literature, difference, displacement differ*ance,* change, and conflict are signified.

As in the plot of the film *Xala* (1975) by the Senegalese writer and film director Ousmane Sembène, at the center of *Une si longue lettre* is the problem of multiple marriages, failed marriages, divorce, decolonization, and independence. The confessional epistle of the Senegalese woman writer, Mariama Bâ, becomes not only a recovery of the letter as an art form, but also an intense psychodynamic exploration and exploitation of the letter as the locus of self-discovery and healing. Beyond this, what is unique in Bâ is her peculiar yoking of the experience of the middle years of a Black woman's life to the traumas of decolonization, independence, and the transition to the state of postcolonialism. The result is that *Une si longue lettre* constitutes a prolegomenon to a distinctly African poetics of gender, menopause, and the postcolonial condition. In the deeply personal missive of her revelations, Ramatoulaye's mentations bridge the gap between the personal and the social symbolic. Ramatoulaye's menopausal transition is experienced as the female embodiment of the African national experience of independence.

I shall discuss *Une si longue lettre* in ways that might seem unorthodox to some. My aim is to attempt to catch some of the complexity that lies beneath the surface sentimentality of the text.

Menopause and Decolonization

Menopause and decolonization have a shared rhetoric. Old medical descriptions of menopause bear a striking similarity to the rhetoric of the colonizer warning the colonized of the fate of regression that would befall those seeking independence. Certain traditions have also treated both menopause and decolonization as disabilities. Medicine and the colonial powers opposed to decolonization have a shared vocabulary of doom and curse that is potentially disabling to those who internalize it. A cultural analysis of reproduction and an ethnopyschoanalytic analysis of colonialism make the point. First, speaking of menopause, Emily Martin notes the following in *The Woman in the Body:*

> This period during which the cycles cease and the female sex hormones diminish rapidly to almost none at all is called the *menopause*. The

cause of the menopause is the "burning out" of the ovaries. . . . Estrogens are produced in subcritical quantities for a short time after the menopause, but over a few years, as the final remaining primordial follicles become atretic, the production of estrogens by the ovaries falls almost to zero. Loss of ability to produce estrogen is seen [as] central to a woman's life: "At the time of the menopause a woman must readjust her life from one that has been physiologically stimulated by estrogen and progesterone production to one devoid of those hormones."[5]

Moving beyond the physiological bases of menopause, Martin is very direct concerning the descriptive language of menopause.

> What is the language in which menopause is described? In menopause, according to a college text, the ovaries become "unresponsive" to stimulation from the gonadotropins, to which they used to respond. As a result the ovaries "regress." . . . Diminished, atrophied relics of their former vigorous, functioning selves, the "senile ovaries" are an example of the vivid imagery brought to this process.[6]
>
> . . . After the MENOPAUSE a woman is usually unable to bear children. . . . Everywhere else there is regression, decline, atrophy, shrinkage, and disturbance.[7]
>
> Eliminating the hierarchical organization and the idea of a single purpose to the menstrual cycle also greatly enlarges the ways we could think of menopause.[8]

At this point, it is important to consider Frantz Fanon's discussion of the politics of the descriptive language of decolonization:

> During the period of decolonization, the native's reason is appealed to. He is offered definite values, he is told frequently that *decolonization need not mean regression* [emphasis added], and that he must put his trust in the qualities that are well tried, solid and highly esteemed.[9]
>
> The well being and the progress of Europe have been built up with the sweat and the blood of Negroes, Arabs, Indians, and the yellow races. We have decided not to overlook this any longer. When a colonialist country, embarrassed by the claims for independence made by a colony, proclaims to the nationalist leaders: "*If you wish for independence, take it, and go back to the Middle Ages,*" the newly independent people tend to

> acquiesce and to accept the challenge; in fact you may see colonialism withdrawing its capital and its technicians and setting up all around the young State the apparatus of economic pressure. The apotheosis of independence is transformed into *the curse* of independence, and the colonial power through its immense resources of coercion condemns the young nation to *regression.* In plain words, the colonial power says, "*Since you want Independence, take it and starve.*"[10]

Both menopause and colonial independence are transitional watershed experiences. Menopause, as a state, is viewed as regression, decline, atrophy, shrinkage, disturbance, and the negation of reproduction; and, viewed as such, it entails a dramatic change in the identity of the female subject. The move to colonial independence also involves a shift in the identity of the colonized subject in which the social, political, and economic transitions are viewed by segments of the society as "regression, decline, atrophy, shrinkage, disturbance (folly, madness), and the negation of reproduction."[11] The tension is between the loss of the capacity to bear and the birth of the nation. Ramatoulaye, the fifty-year-old letter writer at the end of her childbearing years, dispatches a hymn to the new nation after independence, a hymn to marriage, to the couple and the family, drawing our attention to the tie between personal narrative and the narrative of nation. Mariama Bâ reveals what Edward Saïd would call the "sensuous particularity as well as historical contingency" of a woman living on the borderline of historical transition.[12] Bâ's statement cited at the beginning of this chapter insists upon this point: "It was the privilege of our generation to be the link between two periods in our history, one of domination, the other of independence. We . . . were the messengers of a new design."

Here Bâ's text presents the correspondences and ironies of the coincidence between a woman's change of life and national emancipation. To describe the postcolonial condition as menopausal is to admit a consciousness of the ambiguities in the experiences of struggle for decolonization and independence: it is to view emergent nationhood as a prolongation of trauma and pain, as temporary loss and disablement and deferral of full blossoming. This is the sense of the words of Ben M'Hidi, leader of the National Liberation Front (FLN), speaking to the young revolutionary Ali Lapointe in *The Battle of Algiers:* "It is difficult to start a revolution. . . . More difficult to sustain it . . . and still more difficult to win it. But it's later when we've won that the real difficulties begin. There is still a great deal to do. I hope you are not tired."

The association of the change of life with birth leads to Bâ's refusal of the menopausal state as a psychically, socially, and physically disabling state. The identity and the discourse of the menopausal woman and the postcolonial subject are experienced as altered and enabled: both are ultimately experienced here as emancipation from subjugation. Despite the surface simplicity of expression, *Une si longue lettre* is dense with emotional, political, and ironic complexity springing from defining experiences and from the aftermaths of national trauma, the birth of a nation, abandonment, death of a loved one, and the loss of youth and illusions. Bâ experiences the limits of race and gender and translates the differences, along with her woman's pain, into a kind of solidarity with women of her class and condition as well as with African men.

Bâ's Epistolarity

Mariama Bâ's novel, as its title *Une si longue lettre* suggests, is in fact one long letter with embedded shorter letters, examples of which we shall see within its texture. The letter as a form is silence broken, solitude broken. The epistolary form allows for the dictation of the discourse of the Other; it is a privileged format for inscribing silent awareness and speechlessness into reality, into being, like the experimental poetry of the surrealists and the Negritude poets and *The Color Purple* by the African American novelist Alice Walker.[13]

The epistle is potentially a particularly feminist form. It permits the notation of the social history of a people, that is, the details of domestic life, the female perspective on politics, the inclusion of trivia (by male standards), tangential realities, digressions, and, psychoanalytically, the transcription of stream of consciousness and, ultimately, the liberation of the subconscious and the unconscious self—the Other. In particularly feminist terms, it promotes bonding between the correspondents who share their secrets, intimate fears, aspirations, and political agenda. The letter allows Ramatoulaye a space in which to articulate a wife's feminist pride that includes a song of praise to domesticity and cleanliness:

> Nous sommes vendredi. . . . L'odeur du savon m'enveloppe. Cette netteté de ma personne m'enchante. Les femmes qu'on appelle "femmes au foyer" ont du mérite. Le travail domestique qu'elles assument, et qui n'est pas rétribué en monnaies sonnantes, est essentiel dans le foyer. Leur récompense reste la pile de linge odorant et bien repassé, le carrelage luisant où le pied glisse, la cuisine gaie où la sauce embaume. Leur action muette est ressentie dans les moindres détails qui ont leur utilité: là, c'est une fleur épanouie dans un vase, ailleurs un tableau aux coloris appropriés, accroché au bon endroit. . . . L'ordonnancement du foyer requiert de l'art. (P. 93)

> [Today is Friday. . . . The smell of soap surrounds me. The cleanliness of my body pleases me. Those women we call housewives deserve praise. The domestic work they carry out, and which is not paid in hard cash, is essential to the home. Their compensation remains the pile of well-ironed, sweet-smelling washing, the shining tiled floor on which the foot glides, the gay kitchen filled with the smell of stews. Their silent action is felt in the least useful detail: over there, a flower in bloom placed in a vase, elsewhere a painting with appropriate colours, hung up in the right place. The management of the home is an art.] (P. 63)

Francophone literature is replete with insurrection, anger, suffering, and frustration, but it is also sensuous, sexual, about love, loving, embrace, and, in particular, it contains prayer for deliverance from hatred. Mariama Bâ ends her letter with a litany of one-line observations, versets, in which she expresses the desire to transcend her pain, to articulate courageously the love she cannot suppress or transform into hatred, and finally to underscore the importance of the couple and the family. The tone is not strident. It is the considered reflection of a middle-aged widow too old for first love, wise enough to face the future, and strong enough to keep her eyes and heart open to happiness.

> Les irréversibles courants de libération de la femme qui fouettent le monde, ne me laissent pas indifférente. . . . Mon coeur est en fête chaque fois qu'une femme émerge de l'ombre. Je sais mouvant le terrain des acquis, difficile la survie des conquêtes: les contraintes sociales bousculent toujours et l'égoisme mâle résiste. . . . Instruments des uns, appâts pour d'autres, respectées ou méprisées, souvent muselées, toutes les femmes ont presque le même destin que des religions ou des législatures abusives

> ont cimenté. . . . Je suis persuadée de l'inévitable et nécessaire complémentarité de l'homme et de la femme. . . . L'amour si imparfait soit-il dans son contenu et son expression, demeure le joint naturel entre ces deux êtres. . . . C'est de l'harmonie du couple que naît la réussite familiale. . . . Ce sont toutes les familles, riches ou pauvres, unies ou déchirées, conscientes ou irréfléchies qui constituent la Nation. La réussite d'une nation passe donc irrémédiablement par la famille. . . . (P. 129)
>
> [I am not indifferent to the irreversible currents of women's liberation that are lashing the world. . . . My heart rejoices each time a woman emerges from the shadows. I know that the field of our gains is unstable, the retention of conquests difficult: social constraints are ever present, and male egoism resists. . . . Instruments for some, baits for others, respected or despised, often muzzled, all women have almost the same fate, which religions or unjust legislation have sealed. . . . I remain persuaded of the inevitable and necessary complementarity of man and woman. . . . Love, imperfect as it may be in its content and expression, remains the natural link between these two beings. . . . The success of the family is born of a couple's harmony. . . . The nation is made up of all the families, rich or poor, united or separated, aware or unaware. The success of a nation therefore depends inevitably on the family. . . .] (P. 89)

Une si longue lettre is addressed from Ramatoulaye to her girlhood friend, Aissatou, across the ocean. Also a letter in a bottle tossed into the sea of humanity, *Une si longue lettre* is dedicated "To all women, *and to men of good will*" [p. 1; emphasis added]. It is addressed to all who would see the condition of women improved.

As in most letters, *Une si longue lettre* is punctuated within and especially at the end by incomplete significance: "Tant pis pour moi si j'ai encore à t'écrire une si longue lettre" (p. 131; "Too bad for me if once again I have to write you so long a letter," p. 89). It does not end, but rather stops, in a suspended and elliptical space, perhaps at a threshold of understanding and self-affirmation. The gallant and amorous Dr. Daouda Deng functions to underscore the fact that in African societies, divorce, widowhood, middle age, and menopause are not synonymous with death for a woman and need not foreclose the possibilities of sexuality or marriage. Ramatoulaye has gotten "man off her eyeball" as Sug would say in *The Color Purple,* at least for now, and consequently there is no resolution of the economic, social, and affective dimensions of the marital mourning or menopausal conflicts through a happy remarriage ending. *Une si longue lettre* resists closure by simply stopping inconclusively, because of a sense of exhaustion, because it is the end of the day, or because Ramatoulaye is running out of words. The addressee-reader is offered a brief valedictory tinged with a note of delay, deferment, and disarticulation. While remarriage is forestalled, the letter ends at a point in the process of personal exploration and experimentation heretofore denied Ramatoulaye.

In transitional social realities, the need to write often leads to the search for new forms of expression. Most often, existing art forms are recovered, reformulated, and revalued. The "threshold," "aftermath," or "watershed" literatures of francophone production express their blurred realities and borderline living in mixed genres or hybrid forms. Mariama Bâ recovers and exploits the letter maximally. *Une si longue lettre* is a chronicle of Ramatoulaye's mind, her body, her age, her time, and her nation as a woman thinks them. As judge and defendant, with herself and her society on trial, Ramatoulaye's epistolary apostrophe is, in the jurisprudential sense, a letter missive, a letter dismissory, or a letter of appeal. As a transmission of pain and knowledge to her African woman friend in America, the letter is an S.O.S. both to African women of her class and polygamous condition around the world and to future generations of readers.[14] When addressing the nation, the letter assumes the cadences of Koranic discourse and the biblical form of versets (as in the apostolic Epistles). As Ramatoulaye works her way through the "various sounds and juxtapositions of words," her letter becomes a "mystic writing pad" where she lives in the full sensuous mystery of language, characters, script, and calligraphy, finding refuge and revelation in their interstices and a phonics of difference and affirmation.

Absence, silence, abandonment, solitude, and, one might hazard, a measure of preciousness and sentimentality are the nodal points of European female epistolary expression, as typified in French by *Les Lettres portugaises* (perhaps written by a man) and, to some extent, in the writings of Isabelle de Charrière. *Une si longue lettre* seems to pressure these points differently and thereby wrench women's epistolarity from many of its commonplaces and traditions, moving it from the intimate to the community and from the community to the nation and beyond. Ramatoulaye, the correspondent, is not a passionate woman in love, alone and tormented, who through the *projective* epistolary gesture seeks to turn her lover's absence into an imagined presence and her soliloquy into an imagined, fulfilling dialogue.[15] Ramatoulaye's letter is a *retrospective,* written, indeed, under the traditional epistolary sign of absence, but with the distinction that she has been abandoned *utterly*—through infidelity, remarriage, and her lover-husband's death. There is no hope or possibility ever again of dialogue and presence. Ramatoulaye's letter writing as therapy and retrospective seeks "to penetrate the deepest abysses of being."[16]

Polygamy

The film *Xala* begins with a rapid-fire mini-morality play depicting the stages of African nationalist assertion, decolonization, independence, and neocapitalist cooperation in which, significantly, the same actors very obviously simply change costumes. The bright tomorrow of independence strikingly resembles yesterday's colonialism. The mini-drama is followed by the announcement of the third marriage of El-hadji, a businessman and member of the president's inner circle. On this occasion a brief but important declaration is made concerning the importance of polygamy from the male point of view. The hyperassimilated president, who is dressed in a tuxedo, asserts, "La modernité ne doit pas nous faire perdre notre africanité" [Modernity must not cause us to lose our Africanness]. Later, Rama, the daughter of El-hadji's first wife, not only vigorously protests the suffering that the third marriage is causing her mother, but also denounces as liars all men who practice polygamy. El-hadji slaps his daughter and declares, "La polygamie fait partie de notre patrimoine" [Polygamy is an integral part of our national cultural heritage]. The male position seems to be reinforced by the behavior of certain women in the film who perpetuate the system for an array of personal reasons. On the wedding night, only minutes prior to one of many attempted consummations of the marriage by an impotent El-hadji, the mother of the bride-to-be methodically and explicitly instructs her daughter that "woman is not equal to man" and that as a wife it is her duty to be "quiet, submissive, and available." Mariama Bâ addresses the issue of polygamy, clearly stating her awareness of the complexity of the social fabric that fetters the sustained independence of women in her society.

African Muslim polygamous societies are, by definition, relationships of permanent Koran-sanctioned social inequality in which the power of the husband reinforces the domination, subordination, and submission of women. This power is rationalized by the elders and their Koranic explications of what "ought, should, better" be and of what is "right, good, and bad."[17] As indicated before, Bâ's text is a *letter of appeal,* in the legal sense, to traditional patriarchal societies to rethink the economic, legal, and affective consequences of polygamy and culturally sanctioned gender inequality. Mariama Bâ manages with passion, compassion, and discernment to crystallize the sense of the situation of an educated, professional, intellectual Black mother-wife called to an uncommon destiny by a white woman, her high school teacher, in a polygamous Muslim West African urban center. In *Une si longue lettre,* Ramatoulaye, a fifty-year-old teacher and mother of twelve, is abandoned, after twenty-five years of marriage, by her first and only love, her husband, Modou Fall, who marries Binetou, the best friend of their oldest daughter, Daba. The letter begins with the correspondent in a state of total divorce and wordlessness. Ramatoulaye spins in madness, inertia, and devastation, accepting with difficulty what is not there: no husband and no words that can express her spiritual disarray after having been abandoned. The family, especially Ramatoulaye and their daughter, Daba, reel in pain and disbelief. Ramatoulaye laments:

> Et dire que j'ai aimé passionnément cet homme, dire que je lui ai consacré trente ans de ma vie, dire que j'ai porté douze fois son enfant. L'adjonction d'une rivale à ma vie ne lui a pas suffi. En aimant une autre, il a brulé son passé moralement et matériellement. Il a osé pareil reniement . . . et pourtant. Et pourtant, que n'a-t-il fait pour que je devienne sa femme! (P. 23)

> [And to think that I loved this man passionately, to think that I gave him thirty years of my life, to think twelve times over I carried his child. The addition of a rival to my life was not enough for him. In loving someone else, he burned his past, both morally and materially. He dared to com-

mit such an act of disavowal. And yet, what didn't he do to make me his wife!] (P. 12)

Une si longue lettre systematically analyzes a middle-aged mother-wife's perspective and mode of thinking *in contrast* to those of a man. Ramatoulaye presents the woman's body as a text upon which the abjectness of her social condition is writ large. In contemplating her mirror image, Ramatoulaye regards herself as an abject object:

> L'éloquence du miroir s'adressait à mes yeux. Ma minceur avait disparu ainsi que l'aisance et la rapidité de mes mouvements. Mon ventre saillait sous le pagne qui dissimulait des mollets développés par l'impressionnant kilométrage des marches qu'ils avaient effectuées, depuis le temps que j'existe. L'allaitement avait ôté à mes seins leur rondeur et leur fermeté. La jeunesse désertait mon corps, aucune illusion possible. . . . Alors que la femme puise, dans le cours des ans, la force de s'attacher, malgré le vieillissement de son compagnon, l'homme, lui, rétrécit de plus en plus son champ de tendresse. Son oeil égoïste regarde par-dessus l'épaule de sa conjointe. Il compare ce qu'il eut à ce qu'il n'a plus, ce qu'il a à ce qu'il pourrait avoir. (P. 62)

> [I looked at myself in the mirror. My eyes took in the mirror's eloquence. I had lost my slim figure, as well as my quickness of movement. My stomach protruded from beneath the wrapper that hid the calves developed by the impressive number of kilometers walked since the beginning of my existence. Suckling had robbed my breasts of their round firmness. I could not delude myself: youth was deserting my body. Whereas a woman draws from the passing years the force of her devotion, despite the aging of her companion, a man, on the other hand, restricts the field of tenderness. His egoistic eye looks over his partner's shoulder. He compares what he had with what he no longer has, what he has with what he could have.] (P. 41)

The social context of this fiction is not contrived and as a construct is instructive about the universal condition of women, whether Black, white, yellow, red, brown, European, American, or third world. Traditional twentieth-century Muslim and Black communal societies are hierarchical visions of human connection and, as such, dramatize in the boldest terms the issues, frustrations, concerns, and visions of feminism today.[18] Structured on gender inequality, these groups reveal that, between men and women there are different ideologies (myths, images, concepts, and ideas) of justice, care, sexuality, and economics. These societies allow little recognition of the dual perspectives in these areas. The woman, especially, has little exercise of choice. On the one hand, the "network" or "web" of interconnectedness in these religious, polygamous traditional contexts seems to protect the man from entrapment, betrayal, humiliation, rejection, and deceit by the woman.[19] On the other hand, in exchange for protection from isolation, the society offers women roles of dependence, nurturance, self-sacrifice, submission, and susceptibility to abandonment at the very stage of her development when she is most vulnerable: middle age. The voice in *Une si longue lettre* is that of a middle-aged woman in mourning, struggling to overcome rejection and the image of herself as an "abject object."[20]

The Body Pre-text

The epistolary confession we have been discussing presents the psychopathology of a middle-aged woman who, as an adolescent, had imagined a life of intimacy and activities through which family relationships would be woven and connections sustained in an interdependence of love and care rendered increasingly coherent and safe with the passage of time. Instead, after twenty-five years of marriage, she finds herself in a state of moral nihilism because the loss of affiliation with her husband and the disruption of her family cohesion are perceived and experienced as a veritable loss of self. Before its transcendent closing, *Une si longue lettre* is a statement of mourning in triplicate. The novel begins with the death of Ramatoulaye's husband. This ostensible mourning of her husband's death allows her to mourn the greatest transition of her life that had preceded his death by several years: his abandonment of her for an adolescent girl. Occasioned by the same man, this double mourning gives rise to melancholia, self-deprecation, and despair, which exacerbate the third normal transition of midlife with its attendant crises of menopause. Ramatoulaye struggles to see herself as worthwhile. The contemplation of the mirror image of her body reveals to Ramatoulaye, and perhaps to women universally, the integration of the social being and the personal being. In this case, with its "inscriptions" that record the travail of twelve childbirths and years of walking, aging, and internalized pain, the body itself is the *first text,* the *pre-text* to the actual letter. Indeed, the body is the original secret text in which are encrypted the revelations of the subsequent letter. The letter must be read, then, as a secondary trace, as a *postscript* to the original body text. Here one intuits the potential of a woman's body to become a cult to which she alone is the initiate; it is a secret, a chamber, to which she alone holds the key and through which she thinks.

> *Toutes les femmes ont presque le même destin que des religions ou des législations abusives ont cimenté.* (P. 129; emphasis added)

> [All women have almost the same fate, which religions or unjust legislation have sealed.] (P. 88)

Polygamy and abandonment can entail emotional as well as economic humiliation. The consequences of Modou's newfound passions are economically devastating for the family. Ramatoulaye and the twelve children are left almost destitute except for her teacher's salary. They no longer have the car that Modou drives, while the new mother-in-law drives a new car. Binetou, the new wife, has two new Alfa-Romeos, which she drives according to fancy. And then there is the affective humiliation of the statutory conjugal visits from Modou on a tidy, routine rotational basis. Despite her abiding love, Ramatoulaye can no longer suffer his deceitful embrace. She confides:

> Je n'étais donc pas trompée. Je n'intéressais plus Modou et le savais. J'étais abandonnée: une feuille qui voltige mais qu'aucune main n'ose ramasser, aurait dit ma grand'mère. (P. 77)

> [I was not deceived, therefore. I no longer interested Modou, and I knew it. I was abandoned: a fluttering leaf that no hand dares to pick up, as my grandmother would have said.] (P. 57)

Ramatoulaye describes herself as a fluttering leaf that no one dared pick up. And yet Ramatoulaye picks herself up and reaches out across the distance, across the sea, to her best girlhood friend, Aissatou, who presently lives and works in Washington, D.C. One of the felicitous consequences of Ramatoulaye's abandonment is the bonding that occurs between the two modern women of the same ethnic, national class who share a mutually inclusive reality that neither had theretofore discussed. Aissatou's husband, Mowdo, had inflicted upon her what, despite tradition, was for her an irreparable, unpardonable hurt. Before Modou, Mowdo had also taken a younger wife at the insistence of his mother, who had always despised Aissatou. On the day of his marriage, Aissatou gathered her four children and disappeared without a trace, leaving only a letter:

> Mawdo, Les Princes dominent leurs sentiments, pour honorer leurs devoirs. Les "autres" courbent leur nuque et acceptent en silence un sort qui les brime. Voilà, schématiquement, le règlement intérieur de notre société avec ses clivages insensés. Je ne m'y soumettrai point. Au bonheur qui fut nôtre, je ne peux lui substituer celui que tu proposes aujourd'hui. Tu veux dissocier l'Amour tout court et l'amour physique. Je ne rétorque que la communion charnelle ne peut être sans l'acceptation du coeur, si minime soit-elle. . . . Sí tu peux procréer sans aimer . . . je te trouve vil. . . . d'un côté, moi, "ta vie, ton amour, ton choix," de l'autre, "la petite Nabou à supporter par devoir." . . . Je me dépouille de ton amour, de ton nom. Vétue du seul habit valable de la dignité, je poursuis ma route. Adieu. (P. 50)

> [Mawdo, Princes master their feelings to fulfill their duties. "Others" bend their heads and, in silence, accept a destiny that oppresses them. That, briefly put, is the internal ordering of our society, with its absurd divisions. I will not yield to it. I cannot accept what you are offering me today in place of the happiness we once had. You want me to draw a line between heartfelt love and physical love. I say that there can be no union of bodies without the heart's acceptance, however little that may be. . . . If you can procreate without loving . . . I find you despicable. . . . on one side, me, "your life, your love, your choice," on the other, "young Nabou, to be tolerated for reasons of duty." . . . Clothed in my dignity, the only worthy garment, I go my way. Good-bye.] (Pp. 31–32)

Aissatou's departure is an act of refusal in which she transcends victimization, asserts her dignity, withdraws from participation in a system that humiliates her, and makes the move to self-reliance. Aissatou's example sustains Ramatoulaye.

There is a man willing to pick up Ramatoulaye "fluttering like a leaf"—the handsome, wealthy, intellectual assemblyman, the medical doctor Daouda Deng, who had asked her to marry him when they were teenagers. His love for her has never wavered. He declares that still at age fifty, perhaps at the height of her menopausal transition, her grace has kindled his passion. Ramatoulaye is warmed by his expression of love, but she sends him a letter of regret, explaining that while she holds him in high esteem, esteem is not enough for marriage, whose snares she knows from experience. Perhaps more important, Ramatoulaye's solidarity with other married women and her refusal to be complicit in the perpetuation of the abuses of polygamy lead her to point out that, recently abandoned herself because of a woman, she could not lightly impose herself between Dr. Deng and his family.

> Tu crois simple le problème polygamique. Ceux qui s'y meuvent connaissent des contraintes, des mensonges, des injustices qui alourdissent leur conscience pour la joie éphémère d'un changement. Je suis sûr que l'amour est ton mobile, un amour qui exista bien avant ton mariage et que le destin n'a pas comblé. . . . C'est avec une tristesse infinie et des larmes aux yeux que je t'offre mon amitié. (P. 100)

> [You think the problem of polygamy is a simple one. Those who are involved in it know the constraints, the lies, the injustices that weigh down their consciences in return for the ephemeral joys of change. I am sure you are motivated by love, a love that existed well before your marriage and that fate has not been able to satisfy. . . . It is with infinite sadness and tear-filled eyes that I offer you my friendship.] (P. 68)

Farmata, the messenger, returns to act out the pain apparently displayed by Daouda upon reading the letter. Farmata severely criticizes Ramatoulaye for rejecting Daouda. She does not understand Ramatoulaye's empathy and solidarity with Daouda's wife, or that women who question the justice of polygamy must not perpetuate its injustices, even for, or perhaps especially for, personal comfort. Further, Farmata fails to comprehend Ramatoulaye's deferral, which does not foreclose any relationship with Dr. Deng. Ramatoulaye wishes to assert that sometimes a woman might, as she says, "want to be *something else* besides a mother" or a wife: "Je souhaitais 'autre chose' à vivre.

Et cette 'autre chose' ne pouvait être sans l'accord de mon coeur" (p. 102); "I wanted 'something else.' And this 'something else' was impossible without the full agreement of my heart" (p. 70).

Anance's Web: Weaving the Connections

Through the bonding between two women, both traumatized by abandonment and by the "rights" of men in a polygamous society, the reader observes the variable definition of family. It is the support of her friend in moral, spiritual, and financial terms that sustains Ramatoulaye and her family during their time of stress. Family, including the friend Aissatou, is the "smallest organized, durable network of Kin and non-Kin who interact daily, providing the domestic needs of children and assuring their survival."[21] Often, as in *Une si longue lettre* and in *The Color Purple,* family culminates in a network of women abandoned by men.

Mariama Bâ writes with deft simplicity. In a passage where Ramatoulaye is ostensibly talking about books, one discovers a Riffaterrian "paradoxical depth of the surface":[22]

> Les livres te sauvèrent. Devenus ton refuge, ils te soutinrent. . . . Puissance des livres, invention merveilleuse de l'astucieuse intelligence humaine. Signes divers, associés en sons; sons différents qui moulent le mot, agencement de mots d'où jaillit l'idée, la Pensée, l'Histoire, la Science, la Vie . . . Les livres soudent des générations au même labeur commun qui fait progresser. Ils te permirent de te hisser. Ce que la société te refusait, ils te l'accordèrent. (P. 51)

> [Books saved you. Having become your refuge, they sustained you. . . . The power of books, this marvelous invention of astute human intelligence. Various signs associated with sound: different sounds that form the word. Juxtaposition of words from which spring the idea, Thought, History, Science, Life . . . Books knit generations together in the same continuing effort that leads to progress. . . . They enabled you to better yourself. . . . What society refused you they granted.] (P. 32)

The passage stands out because it seems to be a graft,[23] an intervention, that describes the text's own procedures. It repeats the structures it is analyzing, and it seems an act of deconstruction in that it consists of moving from one concept to another by reversing and displacing a conceptual order. Bâ's meta-writing reveals the dynamics of Ramatoulaye's, as well as her own, writing processes, and it suggests what Bâ hopes will be the reception and interpretation of Ramatoulaye's letter, Bâ's book, by Aissatou, the first of generations of readers. While the passage is very much about the power of reading for all Africans, in context it also suggests metonymically or through displacement the power of writing and the dire need of African women, as represented by Aissatou, to read books written by African women, as represented by Ramatoulaye. Further, the passage pressures differ*ance* in that it underscores and bridges the gap of significance between the letter as correspondence—postal missive—and the letter as correspondence between sound and sense, as printed character, representation of sound. There is a desire to return to the African woman the power to live in language and not submit to it, to find herself in the letters, sounds, and juxtapositions. Writing is difficulty, effort, struggle, work, and resistance to predescription and prescription; but, above all, it is refuge, freedom, and power "granted" when a woman writes the letters that correspond to the sounds emanating from within. *Une si longue lettre* must also be read as the transcription of a phonics of difference.

Ramatoulaye's letter is an epistolary cogito, a groping toward significance, self-determination, self-definition, and subjectivity in which she thinks in order to write—in order to be. This groping for significance is evident in the passage of unusual density cited previously wherein Ramatoulaye searches for a phonics that is distinctly her own. The missive is transmission of knowledge, a sharing of pain, a tracing of feminine affect and a search for a language of her own. It is a letter of grief, transfiguration, and conversion in which Ramatoulaye wishes to shed her capacity for self-sacrifice. Like the journal, the dream, and the daydream, the letter allows intimacy with self and emergence of the unconscious self—the Other that has almost lost its voice under the weight of inequality, subordination, submission, and self-abnegation. As a process of self-examination, the epistolary form allows Ramatoulaye to place herself on trial—dialoguing with herself, quarreling with herself as judge and defendant. As writer, Ramatoulaye is author of self and Other. Ramatoulaye's letter represents the unconscious or the discourse of the Other. The Other is therefore the place, the letter itself, in which is constituted the "I" who speaks with her/herself, and who hears her true voice for the first time. There is, of course, a change in register: epistolarity normally associated with the privacy of the "I" is here socialized, politicized, nationalized, and even internationalized by Aissatou's location. The link between writing, textuality, and difference is enacted. Writing in Bâ's text is performing the construction of an alternative personal consciousness within the nation—the demassification of difference. The postcolonial and the poststructural are conjoined in the correspondents, Ramatoulaye and Aissatou, who are mutually constructed disseminations of pain.

Ramatoulaye finds salvation and refuge through writing: she does not speak out; rather she writes herself out of her passivity of dependence, self-abnegation, and paralysis of initiative, action, choice, and thought. Finally, the mother of twelve gives birth to herself through the process of parthenogenesis that is in fact her act of letter writing for survival. Her life had been oriented toward others: virtue resided in self-sacrifice and a reluctance to judge or hurt others.[24]

Ramatoulaye's letter continues with some reflections on the nature of the mother-daughter relationship and particularly with observations on the distinction between love and friendship.

> L'Amitié a des grandeurs inconnues de l'amour. Elle se fortifie dans les difficultés, alors que les contraintes massacrent l'amour. Elle résiste au temps qui lasse et désunit les couples. Elle a des élévations inconnues de l'amour. (P. 79)

> [Friendship has splendours that love knows not. It grows stronger when crossed, whereas obstacles kill love. Friendship resists time, which wearies and severs couples. It has heights unknown to love.] (P. 54)

One particular friendship, brief but of profound importance, was with her high school teacher—another woman, a white woman. The middle years of a woman's life readily appear to be a time to return to the unfinished business of adolescence. For Ramatoulaye, it is the remembrance of the utopian experience of the girls' school, with its white headmistress who called her girls to an uncommon destiny, the recollection of which helps Ramatoulaye orient her desperate condition toward the future and visions of transformation, self-enhancement, self-development, and a new morality of love that includes obligations to self.

> Aissatou, je n'oublierai jamais la femme blanche qui, la première, a voulu pour nous un destin "hors du commun." . . . Des amitiés s'y nouaient, qui ont résisté au temps et à l'éloignement. Nous étions de véritables sœurs destinées à la même mission émancipatrice. . . . Nous sortir de l'enlisement des traditions, superstitions et mœurs; nous faire apprécier de multiples civilisations sans reniement de la nôtre; élever notre vision du monde, cultiver notre personnalité, renforcer nos qualités, mater nos défauts; faire fructifier en nous les valeurs de la morale universelle; voilà la tâche que s'était assignée l'admirable directrice. . . . Elle sut découvrir et apprécier nos qualités. . . . Comme je pense à elle! . . . c'est que la voie choisie par notre formation et notre épanouisssement ne fut point hasard. Elle concorde avec les options profondes de l'Afrique nouvelle, pour promouvoir la femme noire. (Pp. 27–28)

> [Aissatou, I will never forget the white woman who was the first to desire for us an "uncommon" destiny. Friendships were made that have endured the test of time and distance. We were true sisters, destined for the same mission of emancipation. . . . To lift us out of the bog of tradition, superstition and custom, to make us appreciate a multitude of civilizations without renouncing our own, to raise our vision of the world, cultivate our personalities, strengthen our qualities, to make up for our inadequacies, to develop universal moral values in us: these were the aims of our admirable headmistress. She knew how to discover and appreciate our qualities. . . . How I think of her! . . . it is because the path chosen for our training and our blossoming has not been fortuitous. . . . It has accorded with the profound choices made by New Africa for the promotion of the black woman.] (Pp. 15–16)

Returning to the meta-writing passage cited earlier allows for closure as well as overture: Books / knit / generations / together. . . . The syntagmatic development of this sentence progressively signifies and complicates the idea of text. The field of signification expands from the personal textual (books) to the social, economic, and aesthetic textile (knit), to the corporal and biopsychological network of human connection (generations), and finally to the spirituality of cultural identity, solidarity, and community (together). Perhaps the operative word is *knit,* which invites the contemplation of African literary, genealogical, intellectual, social, political, and textual arachnologies or Anance's web, which finds its correspondence in the telegraph and telephone wires that establish the networks of communication in Simone Schwarz-Bart's novels, especially *Pluie et vent sur Telumee Miracle*. In Dogon mythology, the relationship between text and knitting, or speech and weaving, is made explicit:

> SPEECH WHICH IS INSIDE CLOTH
>
> By now, we expect that the origin of the relationship made in Dogon mythology between speech and weaving has been made sufficiently clear, a relationship of both a physiological order, since the mouth organs are parts of a loom that "weaves" the sound material emitted by the larynx and gives it color and form, and of a social order because all the individual "words" intertwine like threads weaving human relationships together and making, as it were, a wide band of cloth that continues uninterrupted from generation to generation.
>
> If speech is weaving, weaving inversely is "speech" in the broad sense because it is created by human activity. It is also "speech" in the restricted sense because the threads intertwine like elements of language, animated by the regular creaking of the pulley and the sound of the tensors and shuttle. This combination of sounds is "the voice of Nommo who speaks softly." The mysterious message registered in the cloth designs is enigmatic, and in the system of correspondence, this speech type is associated with the "speech of weaving." The thread receives this message and becomes a band of cloth. Before it can be altered, its substance requires speech.[25]

As secondary trace or as postscript to the original menopausal *body* text, *Une si longue lettre* weaves the connections between the middle-aged woman's body and the postcolonial condition, between the personal and the social symbolic. The significances respectively of menopause and of the nation's coming into being are altered by their juxtaposition and friction in the text. Just as independence from colonial rule is experienced as birth as well as the prolongation of trauma and pain, menopause is presented as loss as well as redefinition and rebirth. Writing as a connotative system is progress as well as loss and incomplete significance. Writing is contribution to the progress of society, which is itself "in transit," in transition, moving from state to state as in the situations of the menopausal woman, the birth of the nation, and the trajectory of the letter crisscrossing political, intellectual, psychological, and social boundaries. The letter-book knits a network of understanding between Ramatoulaye and Aissatou, and it dreams that there are possibilities for life other than those of the life lived. The letter is so effective because, in its effect, it is insinuative and noncoercive while seeking to subvert the dominant ideology and mind-set that have been lived and experienced as oppression. The closing of the letter points to the healing dimension of Bâ's epistolarity as therapeutic storytelling, as "a writing cure," and an act of psychic self-preservation and a *counter* to subordination.

"Decolonized" and "postcolonial," not unlike "menopausal," are imperfect markers of change. Neither decolonization nor postcolonialism is a completed act or state. Both decolonization and postcolonialism or postindependence are ongoing temporalities and processes of political, social, and psychological revaluation of nation, race, couple, family, and gender. Letter writing is an act of incomplete significance or severed communication, and, as such, it is appropriate to the transcription of the disjointed temporality and ongoing cultural questioning, revaluation, and healing that is the postindependence condition: Bâ's valedictory suggests that the African woman will take up the pen again if she does not find silence without oppression.

Ramatoulaye lives in a culture with inherited laws that no longer work for her. Her story is a statement of refusal in which she transcends victimization, asserts her dignity, and withdraws from participation in a system that humiliates her. Her love for Africa, her hopes for the nation, and her belief in the importance of the couple and the family are unshakable. The tension is between *changing* and *evolving*. Fundamentally, what Ramatoulaye seems to long for is to see the laws that govern polygamy evolve so as not to be out of sync with, or even in opposition to, gender equality by taking into account the changing economic, political, and cultural forces of postindependence Africa and their impact on the reconstruction of the identity of the African woman.

6

Moroccan Independence

Status Inconsistency, Role Conflict, and Consciousness in Tahar ben Jelloun's *The Sand Child*

Morocco, the Last and the First

> Dieu est clément . . .
> Cette naissance annonce fertilité pour la terre, paix et prospérité
> pour le pays. Vive Ahmed! Vive le Maroc! . . .
> La dernière phrase fit aussi du bruit.
> La police française n'aimait pas
> "Vive le Maroc!"
> Les militants nationalistes ne savaient pas que cet
> artisan riche était aussi un bon patriote.[1]

> [God is merciful . . .
> This birth will bring fertility to the land,
> peace and prosperity to the country. Long Live
> Ahmed! Long live Morocco! . . .
> The last sentence caused a stir.
> The French police did not at all care for the "Long live Morocco!"
> The nationalist militants did not know that
> this rich potter was also a good patriot.] [2]

In *The Sand Child* the peculiar evolution of circumstances surrounding the birth of a child coincides with the final days of Morocco's transition from colony to independent state. Morocco's unique destiny in the history of French colonial domination has a symmetry that verges on the poetic. According to accounts,[3] on November 17, 1955, amid great jubilation, Muhammed V returned to his homeland from imposed exile. His first words called upon God to bless Morocco and its people. Immediately, legal preparations for severance from France began. On March 2, 1956, Morocco became the first Maghrebi country to win formal independence from France, and Muhammad V, the Prince of the Faithful, stepped back onto the Moroccan throne.[4] In 1415, Morocco had been the first country to be attacked when Europe came into its age of colonial domination. In 1912, Morocco was the last Maghrebi country to be colonized. When the slide to colonial domination began, Morocco's culture remained secure and, in time, became the means through which Moroccans ousted the colonialists from the land. The French took Algiers in 1830 and, from their Algerian base, launched attacks against Morocco. The French remained in Algeria until 1962. In 1844, the French troops defeated Moroccan troops at the battle of Isly, the first major defeat for Morocco in almost three hundred years. Yet Moroccans maintained their cultural independence. The strength of Morocco's political identity, as well as the sharifian monarchy's ability to actively set the French, Spanish, German, and American powerholders against each other, were contributing factors in Morocco's continued cultural independence, and in its ability to remain outside the French camp for eighty-one years after Algeria became a colony and thirty-one years after Tunisia fell.[5]

The Moroccan novel *L'Enfant de sable* (The Sand Child), by Tahar ben Jelloun, is a richly puzzling text. What can be said about this novel, which is not one text but many because of a semiotic process of suspension and circularity of meaning, or *mise en abyme* of conflicting narrative subversions by a succession of unreliable trickster storytellers? After the disappearance of the original storyteller, Amar, Salem, Fatouma, and the blind troubadour—each in his own way—offer versions, falsifications, and alterations of the follow-up to the story of the life of Ahmed/Zahra. The competing discourses of the storytellers underscore the nomadic nature of truth.

The conjugal relations, the family drama, and the backdrop of post-independence economic and ecological ruin make *The Sand Child* a culturally complex tale. In the broadest terms, it is concerned with dispossession and thwarted desire. Sociologically, *The Sand Child* is a tale of intragroup and intergroup conflict. Gender, class, language, religion, and nationality interact, collide even, with almost equal force in this Arabic, Muslim, feudal, traditional context. In psychoanalytic terms, *The Sand Child* is a tale of phallic aggression and impotence, male and female role conflict, and gender undecidability. Throughout the text these issues are demonstrated imagistically, thematically, and structurally as two sides of the same ideological and sexual coin. The rare coin is a motif in the text: *le bâttène,* with its image of fraternal twins who are indistinguishable except for a beard on the young man, signifies the inner life, that which is buried in the belly, whereas the *zahir* coin signifies the visible, the apparent. Culturally, *The Sand Child* struggles with issues fundamental to Moroccan society: patrilineality, patriarchy, and the blood-centered rituals of sacrifice, marriage, birth, and circumcision.

The issues that underlie the blood-centered Moroccan rituals are essential to the structure of Jelloun's *The Sand Child* and are of abiding and universal concern. The Prophet's birthday concerns the truth of the universe. Where does truth reside? How can humans connect with truth, the eternal, and the transcendent? First, marriage addresses the lives of individuals on earth. What are human beings? What does it mean to be a man, to be a woman? Is the universe's truth mindful of them? What is the male-female connection to be? How should it be organized so that humans beneficently reproduce themselves on earth?[6] The Great Mountaintop Sacrifice is a richly overdetermined male ritual. In this observance, the ram is used as a substitute for the son Ibrahim, whom the father was willing to sacrifice to God. With his weighty phallus and testicles and his remarkable reproductive capacities, the ram is the epitome of natural maleness. The ram's blood verifies the male's dominance of transcendent birth. The ram represents hope beyond the limits of this world and the infant represents hope within it. The sacrifice myth and practice build a reality in which males give birth to that which is eternal and enduring, in contrast to females who give birth to that which is temporal and limiting.[7] All male heads of traditional households perform the sacrifice.

Blood-centered rituals represent humanity itself, the red lifeblood and the red in which all humans are born. The Great Sacrifice explores the connections between the earthly dilemmas. With knife and slit flesh, the sacrifice metaphorically and metaphysically enacts sexual intercourse and uses its connective power to fuse man to God, to gain immortality, and to achieve birth into transcendence, thereby forever breaking death's bonds and connecting with everlasting truth. Moroccan rituals not only play upon the most basic experiences of life—birth, intercourse, and death—but systematically combine them with the physical attributes of the male form (a single erect figure in white like the father in Jelloun's tale) to create a powerful basic-level experience that physically confirms the male's dominance over these processes.[8] With these observations in mind, we must approach Jelloun's postindependence Morocco with its evolving identities and the power of the blood-centered traditions.

A Tale of Contrasexuality

> On a découvert la véritable identité de mon oncle le jour de sa mort. Depuis nous vivons un cauchemar. J'ai pensé qu'en rendant publique cette histoire on en ferait une légende, et, comme chacun sait, les mythes et les légendes sont plus supportables que la stricte réalité. (Pp. 207–8)
>
> [My uncle's true identity was discovered on the day of his death. Ever since, we have lived through a nightmare; I thought that making this story public might turn it into a legend; as everybody knows, myths and legends are more bearable than harsh reality.] (P. 163)[9]

A Moroccan father and mother have seven daughters. The mother feels inadequate and unfulfilled as a woman, wife, and mother, while the father feels that he is less than a man because they have not produced a son. The mother is pregnant an eighth time. Having consulted the stars as well as a sage, an old midwife, the father announces that the eighth child *will* be a male. In league with the father and having been handsomely paid, the midwife corroborates the father's predictions and at the birth declares the eighth daughter to be a blessed male. The child is named Ahmed. According to Koranic tradition, the rite of circumcision must follow. The father thrusts his index finger where there is not a penis and sacrifices the tip of his finger. Blood spatters on the face of the barber and on the thighs of the heavily swaddled infant, who cries as on cue. The witnesses and onlookers are satisfied.

The circumcision scene is rich and fascinating in its tentacular range of signification for the development of the text as well as for Ahmed, who will later assume the female name Zahra. The excision of the finger as a mock circumcision evokes clitoridectomy as practiced in other patriarchal African societies. Textually, it foreshadows, among other events, the sacrifice of an ox that runs about headless until it drops, Ahmed's obsessive fear of her head being separated from the body, and Ahmed/Zahra's castration of the circus bully who repeatedly had sodomized her. Like the ox, he is frantic until he finally bleeds to death. Ahmed will contemplate his/her first menstruation as "the splash from a belated circumcision" (p. 30). Psychologically and affectively, the scene pre-scribes into her destiny denial of the pleasure principle, thwarted desire, and the extent to which Ahmed will live cut off from Zahra, that is, radically divorced from herself. Thus begins the remarkable de-gendered, ungendered, and cross-gendered existence of Ahmed/Zahra. *The Sand Child* can be read as a tale of "passing," of postmodern transvestism in which masculinity is a performance. It is not a tale of fashionable androgyny, but rather an analysis of the coerced and survivalist *contrasexuality* of the dominated subject in a patriarchal society.

Ahmed/Zahra's life begins as a reversal of roles that turns her status upside-down. She is reared and socialized as a male and the exclusive patrilineal heir to her father's fortune, with all the power and authority over the sisters that is the birthright of Arabic males. Zahra enjoys her station, status, and prestige as male and does not at all wish to trade places or status with the sisters or mother. As time passes, Ahmed becomes more and more determined to give her status an unchallenged legitimacy. To guard the secrecy of Ahmed's gender, fate and/or the father seem to silence the women who are privy to the masquerade. The sage old midwife, Lalla Rhadia, dies suddenly. For the mother, the stress of the life-lie is too burdensome, and as a consequence she retreats into a gentle madness and silence, losing her hearing and sight. The mother's muted madness, with the self walled up in silent submission, stands in counterpoint to the convulsive figure of the female condition, Fatima.

Ahmed/Zahra decides to take a wife and chooses the last among women: an unattractive cousin no other man would choose as a wife, the wretched Fatima with her limp and epileptic fits. Ahmed's gesture raises Fatima to the rank of first among women; as the first of four daughters to marry and to marry well, she is singularly honored. Ahmed, a religious man, assumes that their marriage will be "white," that is, chaste. Being grateful for her elevation and deliverance from the excessively cloistered existence imposed by her family, for whom she was an embarrassment, the epileptic Fatima expected no sexual involvement. "Merci de m'avoir sorti de l'autre maison. Nous serons frère et soeur! Tu as mon âme et mon coeur, mais mon corps appartient à la terre et au diable qui l'a dévasté!" (p. 76) [Thank you for getting me out of the other house. We will be brother and sister. You have my soul and my heart, but my body belongs to the earth and the devil that laid it waste] (p. 53). Fatima's presence eventually enrages Ahmed and occasions the first formulations of protest against the religiously and culturally prescribed and sanctioned submission of women to the will of men. Limping, built into life at an odd angle, Fatima is, moreover, a distorted mirror image of Ahmed/Zahra, and one that Ahmed grows to despise:

> La présence de Fatima me troublait beaucoup. Au départ j'aimais la difficulté et la complexité de la situation. Ensuite je me mis à perdre patience. Je n'étais plus maître de mon univers et de ma solitude. Cet être blessé à mes côtés, . . . cette femme courageuse et désespérée, qui n'était plus une femme, . . . cette femme qui n'aspirait même pas à être un homme, . . . cette femme qui ne parlait presque jamais, murmurait de temps en temps une phrase ou deux, s'enfermait dans un long silence, lisait des livres de mystiques et dormait sans faire le moindre bruit, cette femme m'empêchait de dormir. (P. 77)

> [Fatima's presence disturbed me. At first I liked the complexity and difficulty of the situation. Then I began to lose patience with that wounded creature at my side. . . . that grave, desperate woman who was no longer a woman, who didn't even aspire to be a man, but to be nothing at all, that woman who almost never spoke, murmuring a sentence or two from

time to time, but enclosing herself in a long silence, reading books of mysticism and sleeping.] (P. 54)

There is hardly a character in *The Sand Child* who experiences a fulfilling sexual life, and the details of Fatima's situation dramatize thwarted sexuality in the concretest of terms: "Pudeur et chasteté régnaient dans notre grande pièce. J'essayais un jour de voir pendant qu'elle dormait si elle ne s'était pas excisée ou cousu les lèvres du vagin. Je soulevai les draps et découvris qu'elle portait une espèce de gaine forte autour du bassin, comme une culotte de chasteté, blindée, décourageant le désir ou alors le provoquant pour mieux le casser" (p. 77) [Modesty and chastity reigned in our large room. One day as she lay asleep, I tried to see if she had been circumcised or if the lips of her vagina had been sewed up. I gently lifted the sheet and found that she was wearing a strong girdle around her pelvis, like a steel chastity belt, to discourage desire—or to provoke, and destroy it, all the more] (p. 54). In Fatima the pain of the psyche and the body, unsatisfied desires, and woman's inferior status converge, fuse, and convulse in epilepsy. A twisted reflection of Ahmed's condition with "the inverted emotions that come from a betrayed body," Fatima surrenders to her death wish in an epileptic fit.

As time passes, Ahmed's capacity to mute or silence his woman's will becomes increasingly difficult. Ahmed's bound breasts and late-adolescent physiology place her at odds for the first time with her prior socialization as a male. Ahmed/Zahra experiences, as she states it, "la résistance du corps au nom" (p. 46) [the resistance of the body to the name] (p. 30). The question for Ahmed/Zahra becomes "Who am I and who is the other?" She declares, "Je sentais le besoin de me guérir de moi-mème, de me décharger de cette solitude lourde" (p. 46) [I felt the need to cure myself of myself, to unburden myself of the heavy solitude] (p. 31). Particularly in the chapters "The Houseless Woman" and "The Man with a Woman's Breasts," there are mirrors, mirror stage enactments, private exhibitionism, self-examination, masturbation, orgasm in a steamy bath. The autoerotic acts put *him* literally *in touch* with *her,* the absent *Other.* There are anonymous letters from a secret, trustworthy male admirer. In a secret journal, Ahmed records fears, curiosities, and, above all, desires. The letters and the journal constitute a rich psychoanalytic space of release. They are "the writing cure" that allows the initial surfacing of the unconscious, the release of subjectivity, the expression of the repressed, oppressed, and denied self, the emergence of the Other, as in Julia Kristeva's distinction between Other/other, or the stranger within. The autoeroticism and this writing exercise are in time apparently insufficient release and exteriorization, for Ahmed runs away to life.

Mise en abyme

The narrative strategies of this text are as interesting as the life or fictions of Ahmed/Zahra. In its counterdiscourse on the identity, status, and consciousness of the North African man and woman, *The Sand Child* is not antimodernist in its novelistic techniques, for it builds on many of the characteristics of high modernist prose as exemplified by, for example, James Joyce and William Faulkner: the rejection of narrative objectivity, variations of time sequence, stream of consciousness or interior monologue, experimentation and breaks with traditional storytelling techniques, alternative endings and beginnings. The saga is being recounted in installments on consecutive days of the week beginning with Thursday, the day of male births, and by a troubadour who disappears at this point in the story. However, among those assembled to hear the tale are alleged witnesses to Ahmed/Zahra's fate. Each storyteller discredits his predecessor and claims to have irrefutable evidence. The subsequent installments chronicle Ahmed/Zahra's adventures and protean incarnations, past and present, as, among others, circus performer Zahra Amirat Lhob, that is, Princess of Love and female impersonator and male impersonator, who as leader of a band of thieves, occasionally fancies a male rival of rough beauty whom she has beaten into submission and to whom she bares her splendid, irresistible nakedness.

All the storytellers are devoured or discredited by their own fictions. The narrative strategies almost overdetermine the undecidability of meaning. A hermeneutical impasse seems to result from the multiple, competing interpretative possibilities that are not resolved or do not seem to converge. The text invites certain readings that it subsequently resists, if not jettisons. In *The Sand Child,* like grains of sand too tightly grasped in the palm of the hand, meaning slips away. One might be tempted to suggest that *The Sand Child* is simply an example of the Oriental or Arabian art of storytelling. And yet Tahar ben Jelloun, Moroccan, poet, essayist, and novelist, is also, unknown to many, an ethnopsychiatrist like the Martinican Frantz Fanon, author of *Black Skin, White Masks* and *The Wretched of the Earth.* Fanon, who practiced in Algeria, concentrated in his writing on the study of the alienation, self-aversion, neuroses, and psychoses that can accompany the arbitrary, coercive imposition of a foreign language and the resultant consequences of assimilation and the internalization of the values of the dominating or superordinate Other upon an individual, indeed, upon an entire culture. It is difficult for me to accept that the discourse of *The Sand Child* is innocent, unworldly, or socially, politically, and existentially uncharged. In other words, it is not simply a question of telling an oriental tale. The choice of form implies an ideological stance. Modern thought and experience have taught us to be sensitive to what is involved in representation, in studying the O/other, in racial thinking, in unthinking and uncritical acceptance of authority and authoritative ideas, in the sociopolitical role of intellectuals, and in the great value set on skeptical critical consciousness. The questions, then, for me, are what precisely does Ahmed/Zahra represent as transvestite? More precisely, what does the vestmental code represent? What is portrayed in the suffering for want of love, the sexual inversion, the masturbation, the authoritarian father, the mad mother, the epileptic cousin, and, finally, the absurd wandering from culture to culture? As Ahmed/Zahra stands "une passerelle reliant deux rêves" (p. 173) [on a bridge linking two dreams] (p. 135), the overwhelming sensation for the reader is that of being neither/nor, of residing neither here nor there, of absence that is presence, of being and nonbeing, of yearning to become. Ultimately *The Sand Child* is a tale of liminality.

Tahar ben Jelloun identifies intimately with the human condition of his country in particular, and of the Maghreb in general. I believe that he wishes his work to be a demythification and a demystification of Orientalism. It can be read as a study of competing nationalisms: it is an unveiling of the complexities of existence that result from the cultural overlay of French colonial and postcolonial economic domination upon an Islamic patriarchate. Edward Saïd has noted Orientalism's failure as a human inquiry, compared to its intellectual inquiry, for, according to Saïd, in having to take up a position of irreducible opposition to a region of the world it considered alien to its own, Orientalism failed to identify with the human experience. In his counterdiscourse, Ben Jelloun writes to achieve what traditional Euro-American Orientalism failed to do: to perceive the humanity of the Maghrebi world. He does so by studying ideology and sexuality in *The Sand Child*, illustrating the pervasive impact of intragroup and intergroup conflict that, as political and economic struggle, can dehumanize the subordinate class to the extent of controlling and destabilizing even sexuality. Combining the novelistic techniques of high modernist prose and the traditions of the Oriental tale, Tahar ben Jelloun's countermodernist project is a sociodiagnostic that exposes and denounces the layerings and tyrannies of French, Islamic, royal, and clan patriarchy in Moroccan society and the attendant condition of Moroccan women in postindependence Morocco, as well as the psycho-socio-economic condition of the Moroccan male as guest worker in France.

Latent Textuality

> Je viens de loin, d'un autre siècle, versé dans un conte par un autre conte, et votre histoire, parce qu'elle n'est pas une traduction de la réalité, m'intéresse. Je la prends telle qu'elle est, artificielle et douloureuse. (P. 172)
>
> [I come from afar, from another country, thrown into one tale by another tale. Your story, because it is not a translation of reality, interests me. I take it as it is, artificial and painful.] (P. 134)

Texts challenge assumptions and thereby alter consciousness in ways that are not always obvious. The "latency" of signification can lead to the discovery of a text's "worldliness" or aptness to the political, social, and existential actualities of the contexts in which the text was produced.[10] I subscribe to the surrealist André Breton's perception of the literary experience as an essentially wrenching, disorienting, disruptive, and alienating one, "a demonstration of protest": "Le poème doit être une débâcle de l'intellect. Il ne peut en être autrement"[11] (The poem must be a collapse of the intellect. It cannot be otherwise). Surrealism was not simply a poetic revolution, but also a movement aimed at the total transformation of society. Art openly proclaimed its political and social engagement. These positions orient my reading of Tahar ben Jelloun. Not art for art's sake, the textual experience of *The Sand Child,* which at first glance seems to be such a distortion of reality, is characterized by an uncanny mimesis. And it is semiosis that leads the reader to its discovery. The characteristics of everyday existence (actuality) that assist the reader in making sense of a textual experience such as *The Sand Child,* lead the reader through a process of recognition of forms, equivalents, and correspondences (isomorphism) that take on a strange a posteriori worldliness. A paradoxical fictional truth emerges that, in its hyperreferentiality, is more real than the slavishly mimetic. In texts that are not a direct *translation of reality,* textuality need not be, it would seem, the antithesis and displacement of the historical, social, political, and existential. Rather, texts such as *The Sand Child* are often a distortion, a decentering, and a revalorization of the interpretations and meanings of constructs normally defined for society's consumption by the controlling discourse. Indeed, texts are about other texts. The most obvious intertextual connection that the text invites explicitly is with the writing of Borges. The "wordliness" of the text, however, seems just as profoundly related to "textual latency." Textual latency can be defined as that paradoxical depth of the surface of the text that reveals that it is hiding something and indicates how that something can be found.

The Riffaterrian paradoxical depth of the text's surface and Saïd's affiliative or tentacular network of the text encourage the reader-critic to contemplate and to tease out those suspected gaps, needs, incompletenesses, ungrammaticalities, unintelligibilities, and ambiguities of the text. The combined linguistic, literary, and sociological competence, if not consciousness, of the reader leads to a progressive resolution of these riddles of the text, as well as to (and this must be underscored) *an incremental fascination with and pleasure in the text.* Riffaterre's intertext as well as Said's social text are both texts that exist outside of and prior to the text—focusing and informing the structures, pragmatics, and systems of signification and bafflement in the text. From my first reading of *The Sand Child,* I experienced the sensation of "a strange familiarity" or "a familiar strangeness." The chapter that is most difficult to discuss and that most completely defies summarizing or paraphrasing is chapter 18, "The Andalusian

Night." Yet it is precisely this chapter that orients the reader in the most explicit terms toward a Spanish language intertext. The chapter ends with a *cuarteta* (quatrain) in Spanish; it begins with a sleepwalking promenade through the streets of Buenos Aires, and the subject of dreams and phantoms, or "La vida es sueño," is the organizing principle of the chapter. For this reader the intertexts for *The Sand Child* are two texts by Jorge Luis Borges entitled "Borges y yo" and "Las ruinas circulares." My point is that the short story "Las ruinas circulares"—with its plot structure involving a wizard who dreams a son into existence with the help of Fire, its extended network of images involving Fire, consumption, and consummation, religiosity, appearances, and dreams, its themes of patriarchy, filial rebellion, and independence—seems to serve as one of the kernel inspirations that Ben Jelloun has teased out into the narrative elaboration that is *The Sand Child.*

Three troubling questions orient my discussion of *The Sand Child.* Does not this novel, which was a commercial success, perpetuate the clichés and commonplaces of dated eighteenth- and nineteenth-century Orientalism?[12] One of the tasks of contemporary literary discourse is to penetrate the mythical hegemonic discourse concerning the Maghrebi presence. Yet in *The Sand Child* the reader rediscovers the Orient that is associated with vagabondage, undifferentiated sexual drive, and sexual fantasy and license expressed in stock Oriental clichés: harems, all-powerful males, baths, steam, slaves, veils, rapes, dancers, acrobats, circuses, caravans, exotic spices and perfumes, illusion, and chameleonlike change. Sensuality, promises of vague fulfillment, terror, sublimeness, despotism, and idyllic pleasure all intermingle and dissolve into one another. Behind this traditional Orientalism of the fantastic and playful Oriental tale there is an implicit, or "veiled" analysis of a particular aspect of the postcolonial Maghrebi experience—an appeal to reconsider the economic and social relations within the traditional patriarchal family structure:

> La grande, l'immense épreuve que je vis n'a de sens qu'en dehors de ces petits schémas psychologiques qui prétendent savoir et expliquer pourquoi une femme est une femme et un homme est un homme. Sachez, ami, que la famille, telle qu'elle existe dans nos pays, avec le père tout-puissant et les femmes reléguées à la domesticité avec une parcelle d'au-

torité que leur laisse le mâle, la famille, je la répudie, je l'enveloppe de brume et ne la reconnais plus. (P. 89)

[The great, the huge ordeal through which I am passing has meaning only outside those petty, psychological schemata that claim to know and explain why a woman is a woman and a man is a man. No, my friend, the family, as it exists in our countries, with the all-powerful father and the women relegated to domesticity, with a portion of authority left to them by the male, that family I reject, wrap up in mist and no longer recognize.] (P. 64)

After the death of the father, Hajji Ahmed Suleyman, the potter, Ahmed/Zahra levels one the most ironic and pointed criticisms of gender-ascribed superiority and inferiority in Moroccan society. He summons her seven sisters to establish his/her authority:

"À partir de ce jour, je ne suis plus votre frère; je ne suis pas votre père non plus, mais votre tuteur. J'ai le devoir et le droit de veiller sur vous. Vous me devez obéissance et respect. Enfin, inutile de vous rappeler que je suis un homme d'ordre et que, si la femme chez nous est inférieure à l'homme, ce n'est pas parce que Dieu l'a voulu ou que le Prophète l'a décidé, mais parce qu'elle accepte ce sort. Alors subissez et vivez dans le silence!" (P. 66)

["From this day on, I am no longer your brother; I am not your father either, but your guardian. I have the duty and the right to watch over you. You owe me obedience and respect. Anyway, I do not have to remind you that I am a man of order and that if in this house women are inferior to men it is not because God wishes it or because the prophet decided it thus, but because the women accept this fate. So submit, and live in silence!" (P. 46)

Ahmed then says,

"J'ai un comportement d'homme, ou plus exactement on m'a appris à agir et à penser comme un être naturellement supérieur à la femme. Tout me le permettait: la religion, le texte coranique, la société, la tradition, la famille, le pays . . . et moi-même." (P. 152)

["I behave like a man—or, to be more precise, I have been taught to act and to think as one who is naturally superior to women. Everything allows me to do this: religion, the Coran, society, tradition, the family, the country . . . and myself."] (P. 117)

Dispossession

The Sand Child begins with a crisis under the triple burden of a Koranic patriarchy, the sanctity of the male line, and impotence. We have established that a deeply religious Muslim father after the birth of seven daughters has the mad idea of disguising and rearing the eighth daughter as a son. A cornerstone of the Muslim patriarchy is the belief in the existence of a mystical and procreative bond that is preserved and continued solely through the father. The identity of one's father, the fact of being the "ibn" or "ben," that is, the son of so-and-so, is the single biggest determining factor of status in patriarchal Maghrebi society and in some way explains almost every social aspect of the society.[13] The agnatic lineage, or male hereditary line, constitutes a nation. The family is first in all considerations. Everything is subordinated to the family. The father is the absolute source of all power. He distributes all revenues and assigns all duties, work, or routine responsibilities. It is the patriarch's law that stands; it is the father's will that is law. Many aspects of Moroccan and other traditional patriarchies can be explained in terms of, for example, forms of inheritance, the tendency to disinherit daughters, the taboo of virginity, the veneration of the dead, the association of age with authority and wisdom, the prestige of ancestors, and a host of linguistic facts. If a man does not produce a son, the agnatic line is broken, lost, and a nation disappears. Impotence can be seen as a loss of identity and, indeed, of life. The impotent male finds himself not only separated from but also threatened with losing his identity, not only symbolically but in real and actual terms. Linguistically, therefore, it is quite interesting to note that the male sex organs—the penis and the testicles—are referred to as *nafss* (breath [of life]) and *rouh* (soul, life). Thus, without a son, in spite of his seven daughters, the father feels impotent, that is, diminished, devalorized, devirilized, dispossessed, and dying, with only ashes between his legs or, more aptly, with sand and the desert where there should be life, breath, and the soul. Hence, in part, the title *The Sand Child*. In this sense, then, we see that impotence is associated with sterility and, in terms of legacy, with economic dispossession and racial annihilation.

In the broadest terms, this novel is a long meditation on dispossession, particularly in the form of impotence—economic, affective, and sexual impotence that leads ultimately to a feeling of devirilization and devalorization on the part of the Maghrebi male and female, especially in the postcolonial context of guest workers residing in France. It is clear, then, that I read the protean form of Ahmed/Zahra as the representation of a group, of a class, of a nation.

Migrancy: The Guest Worker in France

The seasonal exodus of migrant guest workers from North Africa to France is a culturally destabilizing movement of dispossession. This relocation of a large, highly gendered segment of the Maghrebi population, this human transplantation and deforestation, this strip-manning, as it were, creates a country of women abandoned by their traditional family leaders. Husbands, fiancés, brothers, uncles, and fathers are forced to seek their economic means of survival far from the native land at the expense of their traditional and harmonious family social order. We know that the desert is expanding its domain on the African continent and that many are fleeing the ecological disasters. With the seasonal departures of the men, the economic stresses of radically transformed postindependence economies have created a human desertification or population drain in the Maghreb. One consequence is that traditional (Koranic) gender-ascribed roles are beginning to be overturned as men and women are *forced* by economic hardship to assume new roles and new lives that at times become a travesty of nature and a grand deceit. In the *Prison Notebooks* Antonio Gramsci points out: "The starting point of critical elaboration is the consciousness of what one really is, and is 'knowing thyself' as a product of the historical process to date, which has deposited in you an infinity of traces, without leaving an inventory. . . . therefore it is imperative at the outset to compile such an inventory."[14] On status inconsistency, role conflict, and consciousness, Fatouma is quite categorical in *The Sand Child:*

J'ai appris ainsi à être dans le rêve et à faire de ma vie une histoire entièrement inventée, un conte qui se souvient de ce qui s'est réellement passé. Est-ce par ennui, est-ce par lassitude qu'on se donne une autre vie mise sur le corps comme une djellaba merveilleuse, un habit magique, un manteau, étoffe du ciel, paré d'étoiles, de couleurs et de lumière?

Depuis ma réclusion, j'assiste, muette et immobile, au déménagement de mon pays: les hommes et l'Histoire, les plaines et les montagnes, les prairies et même le ciel. Restent les femmes et les gosses. On dirait qu'ils restent pour garder le pays, mais ils ne gardent rien. Ils vont et viennent, s'agitent, se débrouillent. Ceux qui ont été chassés des campagnes par la sécheresse et les détournements d'eau rôdent dans les villes. Ils mendient. On les rejette, on les humilie et ils continuent de mendier. Ils arrachent ce qu'ils peuvent. Des enfants. . . , il en meurt beaucoup, beaucoup trop. Alors on en fait, encore et encore. . . . Naître garçon est un moindre mal. . . . Naître fille est une calamité, un malheur qu'on dépose négligemment sur le chemin par lequel la mort passe en fin de journée . . . . Oh! je ne vous apprends rien. Mon histoire est ancienne. . . , elle date d'avant l'Islam . . . . Ma parole n'a pas beaucoup de poids . . . . Je ne suis qu'une femme, je n'ai plus de larmes. On m'a tôt appris qu'une femme qui pleure est une femme perdue. . . . J'ai acquis la volonté de n'être jamais cette femme qui pleure. J'ai vécu dans l'illusion d'un autre corps, avec les habits et les émotions de quelqu'un d'autre. J'ai trompé tout le monde jusqu'au jour où je me suis aperçue que je me trompais moi-même. Alors je me suis mise à regarder autour de moi et ce que j'ai vu m'a profondément choquée, bouleversée. Comment ai-je pu vivre ainsi, dans une cage de verre, dans le mensonge, dans le mépris des autres? On ne peut passer d'une vie à une autre juste en enjambant une passerelle. Il fallait quant à moi me débarrasser de ce que je fus, entrer dans l'oubli et liquider toutes les traces. (Pp. 168–69)

[Thus I have learned to live in dreams, to make of my life a totally invented story, a tale that remembers what really happened. Is it out of boredom that one gives oneself a different life, draped on the body like a marvelous djellaba, a magical garment, a wrap, a heavenly cloth studded with stars, colors, and light?

In my reclusion, I have witnessed, mute and motionless, the razing and removal of my country: men and History, the plains and the mountains, the prairies and even the sky are just about all gone. The women and the

> babies remain. It seems that they stay as shepherd guardians of the country, only they have nothing to watch over. They go and come, stir about and survive. Those who have been driven from the countryside because of drought and the changing course of rivers and streams loiter in the cities. They beg. They are rejected, humiliated and they continue to beg. They eke out the existence they can. And the children . . . , too many, far too many, are dying. And so, we make more, again and again. To be born a boy is a lesser evil . . . to be born a girl is a calamity, a misfortune that we sometime abandon negligently on the wayside where death passes at the end of the day. . . . Ah but I am telling nothing that you do not already know. My tale is ancient. . . , it dates from before Islam. . . . My word has little weight. . . . I am only a woman, I have no more tears. I was taught from the very beginning that a woman who cries is a lost woman. . . . I have developed the willpower never to be that woman who cries. I have lived in the illusion of another body with the habits and the emotions of someone else. I fooled everyone up until the day I realized I was deceiving myself. So I began to look around me and what I saw profoundly shocked and upset me. How had I managed to live such a life? In a glass cage, in a lie, in the scorn of others. One cannot step from one life into another with a simple stride across a footbridge. In my case, I had to rid myself of what had been, enter it into oblivion, erase every trace.] (P. 130)

The conflictual interactions of religion, class, gender, language, and nationality give rise to status inconsistency, which leads to role conflict, which in turn leads to consciousness. Consciousness is defined here specifically as a sharpened existential awareness of levels—that in the experience of being one has shifted platforms, statuses, roles. The experience can be positive or negative in that it can lead to plenitude or fragmentation.

Texts are an affiliative structure of eccentric elements: they are texts not as symbols of something else but as displacements of other things: texts are deviations from, exaggerations, and negations of human presence. What concerns the critic is how language signifies, what it signifies, in what form. The sexual and existential loneliness of Zahra, this female reared as a male and endowed with all of the power and authority of an eldest son, can be read as the schema of the virilization of the woman. The woman becomes the omnipotent family or clan leader in the absence of men, and she explores and comes to appreciate her new role. This status inconsistency, that is, this social performance or behavior contrary to prior socialization, is not, however, looked upon as progress and gender liberation, but as a violation of the traditional social contract and as role conflict. Here the identity of the father begins to take on added meaning as the Muslim patriarch, and also as the Mandarin postindependence multinational corporate State as Patriarch in the global economy.

It is Salem, the Black storyteller who sees Ahmed/Zahra as a victim of social abuse, who orients me eventually toward the social text that informs this tale. Salem's veiled, subversive criticism of Moroccan society orients me toward my eventual decoding of the male/female character of Ahmed/Zahra:

> Ce personnage est une violence en soi; son destin, sa vie sont de l'ordre de l'inconcevable. D'ailleurs on ne peut même pas s'en tirer par une pirouette psychologique. Pour parler brutalement, vous en conviendrez, Ahmed n'est pas une erreur de la nature, mais un détournement social. Enfin, je veux dire, ce n'est surtout pas un être attiré par le même sexe. Annulé dans ses désirs, je pense que seule une grande violence—un suicide avec plein de sang—peut apporter un terme à cette histoire. (Pp. 159–60)

> [This character is in himself an act of violence; his destiny, his life are really inconceivable. You can't get out of it by making some psychological pirouette. To put it crudely, you must admit that Ahmed is not one of nature's mistakes, but a social deviation. Anyway, what I mean is, he isn't someone attracted by his own sex. With his desires totally crushed, I think only a great act of violence—a suicide with lots of blood—can bring this story to an appropriate end.] (P. 123)

Malika, the circus female impersonator whom Ahmed/Zahra replaces, declares: "Nous sommes des nomades, notre vie a quelque chose d'exaltant mais elle est pleine d'impasses" (p. 120) [We are nomads: there is something exciting about our life, but it is not an easy one] (p. 90). In the power relations of colonial patriarchy, the colonized male is always already emasculated, if not feminized (see chapter 1 of part 2, "Eichtal and Urbain"). This state of contrasexuality is often intensified when the male is uprooted from the native land and forced for reasons of economic survival to seek employment in the land of the colonizer.

The nomadic Ahmed/Zahra has an equivalent in the Maghrebi guest worker in France who knows the same displacement, wandering, vagrancy, status inconsistency, role conflict, identity crisis, and the same annulment of marriage, desire, and intimacy. Contrary to conventional assumptions, Jelloun's ethnopsychiatric data reveal that these men neither rape white women, employ whores and prostitutes, nor engage in acts of retributive violence with the frequency alleged, again by conventional wisdom. However, their condition in France can only be described in terms of the most excruciating loneliness—separated from their families, humiliated by their lowered status in metropolitan France, victimized by the long-standing racial prejudice against Arabs in France, despised because of their role as imported labor, stripped of all political power, administrative and systemic nonentities, deprived of affection, sexuality, and their role as procreative beings. In France these men whose gender-specific authority and power in their native land are culturally sanctioned have no one over whom to exert authority. The guest workers experience not only culture shock, but also the absence of cultural reference points. They feel culturally orphaned. Status reversed, lives turned upside down, emotions inverted, these men as Ahmed live as social eunuchs.

France, the new country, is lived and experienced as the absence itself of the mother. It is lived and experienced, La Belle France, as a castrating stepmother. This host society presents itself to the guest worker also as an incessant phallic aggression: it is the repressive, foreign patriarch who haunts the guest worker's reality and psyche. The workers live as the objects of domination in a system that historically valorizes male command. From passport control officer, to police headquarters, to employer and foreman, through the intricacies and frustrations of contentious French bureaucracy, the guest worker is commanded and controlled by men. When the authority figure is a woman, the impact is all the more devastating. This social rapport is mirrored in the text in the aberrant sadomasochistic relationship between Abbas, the circus bully, and his cruel old mother, the circus owner and boss. Many of these North African workers collapse emotionally and psychosomatically in the face of their devalorization, devirilization, and the recognition of their social and economic impotence, their absolute inconsequentiality. Coming from a patrilineal, patriarchal nation that as colony was already feminized in its power relations with the colonizer, North African male guest workers in France undergo a second degendering process. This is their particular form of cultural schizophrenia. In his doctoral thesis, ethnopsychiatrist Tahar ben Jelloun describes succinctly the condition of these transplanted workers:

> Ceux qui ont connu le viol colonial sur leur propre terre et se trouvent aujourd'hui expatriés, subissent, avec quelques variantes, la même domination, la même aliénation. L'ancienne puissance coloniale poursuit sa logique en se modernisant. L'esclavage, la négation de l'être, l'exploitation capitaliste se perpétuent avec subtilité et démagogie. Hier on pratiquait le pillage des terres, aujourd'hui on exploite à domicile les hommes expulsés de leur pays par le besoin et le sous-développement, séquelles de la colonisation. Ils sont là, arbres arrachés, vidés, séparés de la tendresse et du soleil. Le mépris, l'humiliation, la haine les calcinent dans leurs bidonvilles. . . . On transplante des hommes, on les sépare de la vie pour mieux leur extirper leur force de travail, mais on tente aussi d'annuler leur mémoire et d'entraver leur devenir en tant que sujets désirants. (Pp. 56, 12)

> [Those who have known the colonialist rape of their own land and find themselves today expatriated, are undergoing, with few variations, the same domination, the same alienation. The former colonial power pursues its same logic, simply modernizing its appearance. Slavery, the reification of humanity, capitalist exploitation perpetuate themselves with subtlety and demagoguery. In former times colonialists pillaged far-off lands, today in the comfort of home they exploit the men who are driven from their homelands by the need and the underdevelopment that are the aftermath of colonization. They are there, in France, violently uprooted trees, hollowed out, cut off from tenderness and from the sun. Scorn, humiliation, and hatred sear and isolate them in their slum dwellings. . . . Men are transplanted, removed from the harmonies and rhythms of daily traditional life, so as to better extirpate their labor potential, and in the process there is the attempt to void their memory and to block their natural development as subjects of desire.] [15]

The condition of the guest worker in France is one of the social texts that inform *The Sand Child.* The situation of the Maghrebi worker in France as described in this doctoral thesis recalls Ahmed/Zahra's dream to cure herself of the heavy burden of solitude with its invading impotence, where there are "des émotions inversées, venant d'un corps trahi, réduit à une demeure vide, sans âme" (p. 99) ["the inverted emotions that come from a betrayed body reduced to an empty, soulless home"] (p. 73). Later she adds, "Je marche pour me dépouiller, pour me laver, pour me débarrasser d'une question qui me hante et dont je ne parle jamais: le désir. Je suis las de porter en mon corps ses insinuations sans pouvoir ni les repousser ni les faire miennes. Je resterai profondément inconsolé, avec un visage qui n'est pas le mien, et un désir que je ne peux nommer" (p. 88) ["I walk in order to divest myself of things, to cleanse myself, to rid myself of a question that haunts me and of which I never speak—desire. I am tired of carrying its insinuations in my body, without being able either to reject them or to make them mine. I shall remain profoundly unconsoled, with a face that is not mine and a desire that I cannot name"] (p. 164).

The guest workers' lives are turned upside down, and the myth of the Baobab tree imposes itself as paradigm of colonial aggression, violent deracination, status inconsistency, role conflict, and survival.

Patriarchies

The overlay of the Islamic patriarchy and the colonial patriarchal civilizing mission is most resonant in the father's speech from beyond the grave:

> Avant l'Islam, les pères arabes jetaient une naissance femelle dans un trou et la recouvraient de terre jusqu'à la mort. Ils avaient raison. Ils se débarrassaient ainsi du malheur. C'était une sagesse, une douleur brève, une logique implacable. J'ai toujours été fasciné par le courage de ces pères; un courage que je n'ai jamais eu. Toutes les filles que ta mère a déposées méritaient ce sort. Je ne les ai pas enterrées parce qu'elles n'existaient pas pour moi. Toi, ce fut différent. Toi, ce fut un défi. Mais tu as trahi. Je te poursuivrai jusqu'à la mort. Tu n'auras point de paix. La terre humide tombera tôt ou tard sur ton visage, s'introduira dans ta bouche ou-

verte, dans tes narines, dans tes poumons. Tu retourneras à la terre et tu n'auras jamais existé. Je reviendrai, et de mes mains j'entasserai la terre sur ton corps . . . . Ahmed, mon fils, l'homme que j'ai formé, est mort, et toi tu n'es qu'usurpatrice. Tu voles la vie de cet homme; tu mourras de ce vol . . . . Du fond de mon exil, je ne cesse de prier, avec les paupières déjà lourdes, avec les pensées déjà figées, arrêtées en cet instant où tu abandonnes la demeure et le corps, où tu oublies l'amour et le destin, la passion de ce destin que ma volonté a forgé, mais tu n'en fus pas digne. (Pp. 129–30)

[Before Islam, Arab fathers threw an unwanted female infant into a hole and covered her until she died. They were right. In this way they rid themselves of misfortune. It was an act of wisdom, a brief pain, an implacable logic. I have always been fascinated by the courage of those fathers—a courage I never had. All the daughters your mother gave birth to deserved such a fate. I did not bury them, because they did not exist for me. You were different; you were a challenge. But you betrayed me. I shall pursue you until your dying day. You will find no peace. Sooner or later the damp earth will fall into your gaping mouth, your nostrils, your lungs. You will return to earth and it will be as if you never existed. I shall come back and with my hand pile earth upon your body. . . . Ahmed, my son, the man I formed, is dead. You, woman, are merely a usurper. You are stealing that man's life; you will die for the theft. . . . From the depths of my exile, I never cease to pray, my eyelids already heavy, my thoughts already frozen, arrested at the moment when you abandoned your home and body, when you forgot the love and destiny that my will forged, but of which you were not worthy.] (P. 98)

Earlier, I pointed to the overlay of patriarchies. I believe that three levels of patriarchy are discernible in the father's pronouncements from beyond the grave. Level 1 is the real father, a potter by profession, who as creative urge considers his children to be ever so much clay molded to varying degrees of imperfection and perfection. Level 2 embraces the dynamics of the Islamic patriarchy with its principle of male superiority and indisputable authority. Level 3, however, allows one to glimpse, in the interstices of the father's pronouncements, the paternalistic dynamics implicit in the relationship between the colonizer and the colonized that is modeled on the family image, with the colonizer as Father/Mother–King/Queen and the colonized as ever so many ungrateful and indeed unworthy children. The dynamics of none of these patriarchies allow the child's desire for independence, self-determination, or personal sovereignty to go unchecked.

Obviously, I do not consider *The Sand Child* to be a failure; rather, I read it as an elaborately but *not* heavily veiled act of social criticism. It seems designed in part to draw attention to the *lived* experience of the Maghrebi male and female. De-un- and cross-gendering is related to de-un- and cross-territorialization. The blurring of sexual identities, status, and roles parallels the borderization of cultures, the blurring of frontiers, the shifting shape of populations in the global economy. The novel is a significant contribution to the study of ideology and sexuality in its successful effort to redefine the frontiers and problematics of such a study. By examining the extravagant dilemma of the psycho-social-sexual identity of Ahmed/Zahra, Tahar ben Jelloun succeeds in humanizing the North African. Displacement often means exile. Jelloun confronts our consciousness with the complexities of the situation of those condemned to live in exile abroad, in exile at home in the heart of their own culture, alienated in the midst of their own family. Jelloun dramatizes the extent to which one can live as a stranger, an outsider, a foreigner to others as well as to oneself. In this novel we are presented with desert people, a nomadic culture, and a poetics of the multinational nomad. The problems and the challenge of this nomadic condition are grasped in the single prayerful, plaintive query of Ahmed/Zahra: "Ressembler à soi-même, n'est-ce pas devenir différent? Ainsi, je pars pour quelque temps. Je m'éloigne de vous et me rapproche de moi-même. Je suis réduit à une solitude absolue. Étranger au sein de ma famille, je suis négligeable, absolument négligeable. Singulier et isolé" (p. 104) ["Does to resemble oneself not mean to become something different? I go away for a time. I move away from you and come closer to myself. I am reduced to absolute solitude. An alien within my own family, I am negligible. Odd and isolated"] (p. 77).

The previously described Baobab myth, with its emphasis on survival, also carried a warning, for the hollowed-out tree on occasion collapses upon a devouring elephant, crushing it to death. *The Sand Child* is a subversive text in its questioning of the very foundations of Moroccan society and in its depiction of the growing frustration, anger, and determination of Zahra to do something because she has nothing further to lose. From the desire for independence, self-determination, and personal sovereignty, we move to the stirrings of revolt as Zahra assumes herself:

> Etre femme est une infirmité naturelle dont tout le monde s'accommode. Etre homme est une illusion et une violence que tout justifie et privilégie. Etre tout simplement est un défi. Je suis las et lasse. (P. 94)
>
> La violence de mon pays est aussi dans ces yeux fermés, dans ces regards détournés, dans ces silences faits plus de résignation que d'indifférence.
>
> Aujourd'hui je suis une femme seule. Une vieille femme seule. Avec mes vingt-cinq ans révolus, je considère que ma vieillesse a au moins un demi-siècle. Deux vies avec deux perceptions et deux visages mais les mêmes rêves, la même et profonde solitude. Je ne pense pas être innocente. Je crois même que je suis devenue dangereuse. Je n'ai plus rien à perdre et j'ai tellement de dégâts à réparer. . . . Je soupçonne ma capacité de rage, de colère et aussi de haine destructrice. Plus rien ne me retient, j'ai juste un petit peu peur de ce que je vais entreprendre; j'ai peur parce que je ne sais pas exactement ce que je vais faire, mais je suis décidée à le faire. (P. 155)

> [To be a woman is a natural infirmity and every woman gets used to it. To be a man is an illusion, an act of violence that requires no justification. Simply to be is a challenge. I am tired. (P. 69)
>
> My country's violence is also to be found in those closed eyes, in those diverted looks, in those silences, which stem from resignation rather than indifference.
>
> Today I am a single woman. An old single woman. Now at the age of twenty-five, I consider that my old age has at least half a century to run. Two lives with two perceptions and two faces, but the same dreams, the same profound solitude. I do not think that I am innocent. I even think that I have become a little dangerous. I no longer have anything to lose, and there is so much in me to repair. . . . I am suspicious of my capacity for anger and destructive hatred. Nothing can hold me back anymore. I am just a little afraid of what I might do, but I have made up my mind to do it.] (P. 119)

The "two lives with two perceptions and two faces . . . the same dreams, the same profound solitude" addresses not only the situation of *The Sand Child* and the Moroccan context but also the larger francophone question of cultural hybridity. Hybridization involves a recognition of difference and a confrontation of the incommensurables of cultures in contact, in contestation, and in transition. This form of double consciousness seems to carry with it more ambiguity than resolution, more indecision than solution, more displacement than stability. These issues raised in Jelloun's text permeate the novel *The Abandoned Baobab* by the Senegalese author Ken Bugul.

7

The Blossoming of the Undefined Self

Ken Bugul and *Le Baobab fou*

Knowing neither exactly where she is going, nor exactly from whence she comes, torn between a Europe that rejects her and an Africa she has abandoned, Ken Bugul finds herself deprived of her own culture and acculturated into a civilization that either holds her in contempt or values her only as an exotic object of consumption. Ken's mind wanders, becomes diasporic, and reflects the heterogeneity of the colonized and postindependence spaces where competing sets of expectations and cultural values contend for the mind and body. Mariam Mariétou, the Senegalese woman author, writes under the pen name of Ken Bugul, the protagonist of her autobiographical novel *The Abandoned Baobab*.[1] Ken Bugul is caught in the slipknot, in the circular trap, of self-aversion and mimetic desire.

> Mais l'indépendance m'avait déçue.
> Je croyais que l'indépendance allait me sauver.
> Je ne constatais aucune acquisition d'identité propre,
> aucun souffle. L'indépendance était comme
> la reconnaissance et l'officialisation de la dépendance. (Pp. 144–45)

> [But independence disappointed me.
> I had thought independence would save me.
> It was not an acquiring of my own identity at all,
> not a breath of it. Independence was rather
> a recognition of dependence and making it official.] (P. 125)

The original French title, *Le Baobab fou,* is extraordinarily evocative. The two elements comprising it, the substantive and its adjective, signify foreignness (Baobab) and maladjustment (fou). The myth and reality of the Baobab tree have been previously presented in chapter 3. The details of this myth are incorporated into the first two sections of the novel, the "Pre-history" and the "History of Ken." The title in translation, *The Abandoned Baobab,* with its legitimate insistence on abandonment, suggests a move from the original site of colonial violence, the diasporic condition, and a migrant journey *and* narrative. The *fou* of the French title orients the text toward the split self and humanizes the vegetal and the floral.

A Black girl is the central character, inhabiting the rim of the in-between place at the contingent moment of articulating the recognition of similitude and the intimacy of difference. Violent uprooting and wrenching separation from places as well as the from self are the sensations that orient Ken's basic preoccupation with attachment and loss, which are part of the etiology of schizophrenia. A close reading of *The Abandoned Baobab* strongly suggests that (1) there is a specific colonial cultural schizophrenia; (2) its narrative history is inscribed in the thematic and semiotic "errancy" of the text; and (3) the major tropes of the process are contained in the transformation (translation) of the vegetal and cultural. The point is not to pathologize Ken's condition,[2] but to recognize the extent to which certain behavioral and psychological processes reflect the dynamics of the social processes, political issues, and cultural dynamics confronting the people represented by Ken's character. Ken's story is concerned with dislocation, with colonial, diasporic, and migrant subjectivity, and with the consequent risks of *cultural* schizophrenia.

The Rooted and Uprooted Self

Ken Bugul is in effect a lost body. *Moi laminaire* (The Laminarian Self) and *Corps perdu* (Lost Body) are titles of volumes of poetry by Aimé Césaire in which he explores a poetics and a psychology of migrancy, loss, and attachment for the colonized subject. The *laminaire* refers to seaweed that can stretch for miles into the ocean and yet remain attached to the original rock formation on which it grew. The images are fundamentally vegetal, marine, and floral and speak directly to Ken Bugul's longings. Her body is the incarnation of loss: alienated, exiled, shipwrecked, uprooted, she wanders psychologically and sociologically, searching for a place to rest, to anchor herself, to fix herself, to put down roots and to blossom fully. A complex of the uprooted self organizes her obsessions and also the network of images in this work. Her sensations of violent uprooting and wrenching separation are questions of psychic as well as spatial dislocation.

> Après avoir roulé pendant quelques minutes sur la piste, l'avion s'était immobilisé. Je ne comprenais pas pourquoi et c'est à ce moment-là que mes tympans furent crevés par le vrai départ.
> S'arracher
> L'appareil quitta le soleil dans une rage enivrante et presque douloureuse. J'en avais le souffle coupé et instinctivement je me retenais aux accoudoirs du fauteuil. J'avais l'impression d'être arraché à moi-même. (P. 35)

> [After we had been taxiing down the runway for a few minutes, the plane stopped. I didn't understand why and it was then, at that very moment, that my eardrums were punctured by the actual departure.
> Tearing yourself away
> The plane left the sun in an intoxicating and almost painful rage. It took my breath away and instinctively I clutched the armrests. I felt as if I were being torn away from myself.] (P. 25)

Ken is obsessed with vegetation, flowering, and roots. None of that is gratuitous, for it is all related to her situation as a Black woman living in a state of exile from her original homeland. The natural vegetal processes are the opposite of the social and psychological processes that Ken undergoes. The dream of the Baobab tree firmly rooted in the soil is the longing for the integration of the self, and of humankind in harmony with the self, as much as it is the nostalgic dream of a paradise lost. Ken makes it clear that *The Abandoned Baobab* is a story about inhospitality and unhomeliness when she asserts, " 'Chez moi,' cela m'avait manqué toute la vie" (p. 79) [" 'Home' was what I had missed all my life"] (p. 64).

This complex of the uprooted self is closely linked to Ken's meditations on the practice of colonialism in Africa and the role of the

French school in this process. According to Ken, the French school turned everything "upside down," shook up everything, and hurled Africans into a perpetual state of alienation. In place of education, the French politics of assimilation has turned Africans into illogical beings in conflict with themselves and their traditions through the agency of the French school.

> L'école française qui allait bouleverser mille mondes et mille croyances qui se cachaient derrière les baobabs médusés en prenant des formes humaines. (P. 115)
>
> [The French school that was to upset a thousand worlds, and a thousand beliefs hidden behind the baobab trees, paralyzed into taking human forms.] (P. 98)

From the village to the French school, from the south to the north, from apartment to apartment, from street to street, the experience is that of lost illusions. This constant cycle of dislocation/relocation is the experience of transculturation for Ken that leaves her in a state, not of happy "métissage culturel," but a graver state, that of cultural schizophrenia.

> Le colonialisme avait tout ébranlé. Et la conscience s'était noyée dans l'aliénation d'une troisième dimension fascinante et atroce. Mais je ne voulais pas être consciente de tout cela et réagir. Je refusais de croire que le colonialisme en était la seule cause. (P. 64)
>
> [Colonialism had shattered everything. And consciousness had drowned itself in the alienation of a third dimension, both fascinating and hideous. But I did not want to be aware of all of that and have to react. I refused to believe that colonialism was its only cause.] (P. 51)
>
> J'avais une famille sans structures réelles. J'étais née trois jours avant le départ du frère. La première fois que je le vis j'avais dix-sept ans. La communication dont on pouvait tirer la conscience de l'instinct ne s'établissait que par références anodines. Alors le rêve commençait, imbibé d'irréel. Mais aussi surtout, le colonialisme, qui avait créé la distorsion des esprits pour engendrer la race des sans repères. Le colonialisme avait fait de la plupart de nous des illogiques. Je ne voulais pas l'accepter. (P. 85)

[I had a family without any real structure. I was born three days before the brother's departure. The first time I saw him, I was seventeen years old. The kind of communication from which an awareness of one's instinct can be drawn was established by harmless, painless references. And so the dream began, imbued with the unreal. But also and above all else, colonialism had created a distortion of the spirit necessary to enslave a race of people, leaving them no frame of reference. Colonialism had made inconsequential people of most of us. I didn't want to accept that.] (P. 71)

The Fallen Seed and the Lost Bead

The "Pre-history of Ken" and the "History of Ken" are two distinct preambles to the autobiography proper in *The Abandoned Baobab.* At first glance, the "Pre-history of Ken" appears to be merely a childhood idyll describing the joys of a sister and her brother as they conspire to steal sugar from an authoritarian mother in order to sweeten and eat the luscious, rare, ripe, yellow fruit of the Baobab tree. The "Pre-history" can be characterized as an epic, for the story represents an epoch in African civilization—traced from precolonial times to colonial times, its peaceful times, its destruction by fire, the miraculous survival of the Baobab tree at the center of the village, the renewal of the civilization by an extraordinary stranger on an extraordinary steed, the reconstruction of the civilization around the Baobab tree, the introduction of train tracks and trains as well as goods transported on them, such as factory-made shoes. The poetic crafting of the two parts alerts the reader to the themes of continuity and survival. There is the mysterious old man, an ageless immortal creature who is the only one left in "the village of disaster." It is through this character that the first connections with the title of the book are established, for like the baobab, he is characterized as "fou" or mad, and it is he who remembers the former inhabitants who "abandoned" the village and the Baobab tree after a great conflagration.

Il ne restait dans le village sinistré qu'une créature sans âge. Nul ne savait d'où il venait. Il n'avait au monde que le soleil, les baobabs et l'infini de chaleur. Il ne connaissait rien d'autre, à ce qu'il semblait. . . . "Je ne mourrai jamais," disait-il souvent. "C'est un fou" avaient décidé ceux qui avaient émigré plus loin . . . "Salut les jeunes, j'avais déjà rêvé que vous viendriez vous installer ici. J'ai toujours vécu, et croyez-moi, je suis immortel. Après le feu, ils sont partis et je suis resté. Dans mille ans je serai encore-là. Une chose me préoccupe, c'est ce jeune baobab: il est sorti de terre comme planté par ces dieux d'autres mondes. Je fais des recherches et un jour je percerai le secret, ce baobab est lié à un événement qui va bouleverser une génération entière." (P. 21)

[The only one left in the village of disaster was an ageless creature. No one knew from where he had come. All he had in the world was the sun and the infinite heat. It seemed that he had no knowledge of anything else. . . . "I shall never die," he often said. "He is mad," decided those who had left for farther distances.

"Greetings my people," he said, "I had already dreamed that you would come and settle here. . . . I have always been alive and believe me, I am immortal. After the fire, they left and I remained. In another thousand years I'll still be here. One thing only is on my mind, and that is this young baobab tree: one morning it came out of the soil as if it had been planted by gods of another world. I am doing research, and one day I shall pierce its secret; this baobab is linked to an event that will shake an entire generation."] (P. 13)

It is observed in the pre-history that "the newborn was always a reincarnation." The continuity-survival theme is further reinforced by the resemblance between two daughters of different generations, Ken and the pre-history daughter, Codou, who is merely a source of exasperation for the mother. Codou, as Ken will be, is a sensuous, contemplative dreamer. Both girls' worlds will be destroyed:

Perdue dans ses rêves de jeune fille, elle pensait au jour où elle se marierait avec le fils du berger dont la haute stature et la carrure athlétique la faisait frissonner chaque fois qu'elle le voyait. L'huile prit feu. . . . En une minute, tout le village était un brasier attisé par le vent qu'un mauvais esprit avait envoyé pour en détruire l'harmonie. (P. 18)

[Lost in her young girl's dream, she was thinking of the day she would marry the shepherd's son, whose tall stature and athletic carriage made her tremble every time she saw him. The oil caught fire. . . . In one minute the entire village was ablaze, fanned by the wind that an evil spirit had sent to destroy its harmony.] (P. 11)

The theme of survival is reinforced as well by events that bind the two respective mothers. The original mother portentously shatters her water jug at the well, spilling water onto a fallen baobab seed just prior to the conflagration; the new founding mother loses an amber bead of her shattered necklace by the little baobab tree that has begun to sprout. The narrative subsequently develops the complementarity and interchangeability of the baobab seed and the amber bead:

> Le noyau du fruit du baobab n'avait pas bougé car il était fixé à la terre par l'eau que la mère avait renversée. Une semaine après, le début de l'hivernage, le noyau germa à nu: on vit une petite tige portant précieusement une feuille. Les averses, les pas des êtres humains et les sabots des animaux l'épargnèrent miraculeusement et bientôt une jeune plante frêle se réveillait avec le soleil et se couchait avec lui. (P. 17)
>
> Le plus jeune des enfants s'était réfugié dans les cuisses chaudes de la mère en se serrant très fort. Cherchant à accrocher un de ses bras au cou de la mère, il avait cassé le collier d'ambre qu'elle avait porté pour le voyage. Le collier s'éparpilla comme cette chaleur qui embaumait cet univers fantastique qu'était la savane, le pays du soleil et de la lumière. . . . une des perles avait trouvé dans ce sable, sous ce baobab, dans ce village désert un abri qui l'accueillit en silence. (P. 20)
>
> [The pit of the baobab fruit had not budged, for it had been rooted in the soil by the water the mother had spilled. One week later, the rainy season began, the seed germinated: a tiny stalk with a delicate leaf could be seen. Steps of human beings and animal hooves miraculously spared it, and soon a frail young plant would rise and go to sleep with the sun. (P. 10)
>
> The youngest of the children took refuge between the mother's warm thighs holding on to himself very tightly. While trying to put one arm around the mother's neck, he had broken the amber necklace she had worn for the trip. The beads scattered like the heat that embalms the fantastic universe that was the savannah . . . the land of sun and of light. . . . one of the beads had found shelter in the sand, under the baobab, a shelter that silently bade it welcome.] (Pp. 12–13)

One floral, the other mineral, both seed and bead get lost in the earth to reemerge, replicating, thus, the cycle of Persephone, the maternal goddess of fecundity, who must spend a season in the underworld to return in spring. The bead, in particular, is an amber bead of solidified sap that duplicates the golden yellow of the baobab fruit and reflects the village chromatics forged by the relentless sun at its zenith: "Nous étions à la veille de la saison des pluies. . . . Le village de Gouye avait revêtu une couleur diaphane. Les cases étaient jaunes, le sable jaune, les animaux jaunes, les êtres humains jaunes. Il faisait très sec et le soleil craquait sourdement tant il faisait chaud" (p. 15) ["It was just before the rainy season. . . . The village of Gouye had taken on a diaphanous color. . . . The huts were yellow, the sand yellow, the animals yellow, the humans yellow. It was very dry and the sun crackled soundlessly—it was that hot"] (p. 8).

The amber bead, lost by the mother of the first family to resettle in the village after the great fire, is found generations later under the Baobab tree by the two-year-old girl, Ken. Inspired by the women of her village who wear beads on diaper pins in their *pierced* ears, Ken pushes the amber bead deeper and deeper into her ear canal. The auricular piercing shifts very quickly to piercing vocalics of the scream. The history observes: "The labyrinthine depths of a child's thinking and of its imagination are so completely unknown!" The piercing dimension of the Persephone sign (see conclusion) is phonologically suggested in the first half of her name (*percer* in French means "to pierce" and *perce-oreille,* "earwig"—ear-piercing insect). Ken's history ends with: "Comme je voudrais dire à la mère qu'elle ne devait pas me laisser seule à deux ans jouer sous le baobab. . . . l'harmonie était brisée. Ce cri perçant, sous ce baobab dénudé dans ce village!" (pp. 30–31) ["How I wanted to tell the mother that she should not leave me alone at age two under the baobab tree. . . . The harmony was shattered. That piercing scream under the denuded baobab in the village"] (p. 22).

The scene is prepared by a description of the silence that reigns in the village. Both in the pre-history and in the history silence is a prelude to trauma, understanding, awareness, and "piercing" first consciousness. The pre-history has as its major motifs shattering, scattering, the loss of culture, and the loss of *balance* (the inner ear). The depth of significance behind the scream is what the autobiography proper will "remember" and analyze: abandonment by the mother, attachment and loss, the sense of having been born without having been conceived, colonialism, independence, a philosophy of migrancy, and "the double-edged blade of consciousness."

I turn now to a discussion of the madness that the American translation of the title elides. During great moments of political transition, economic catastrophe, and social upheaval that characterize decolonization, independence, and postcolonialism, insanity is often a sign of the disorder, incoherence, and excess of the historical moment. In 1951, in an essay entitled "The Man of Culture and His Responsibilities," Aimé Césaire makes the point:

> Notre devoir d'hommes de culture, notre double devoir est là: il est de hâter la décolonisation, et il est, au sein même du présent, de préparer la bonne décolonisation, une décolonisation sans séquelles.[3]
>
> [Our duty as men of culture, our double duty lies therein: it is to hasten decolonization, and it is, within the immediate context of the present, to begin to prepare a solid decolonization, a decolonization without serious aftereffects.]

The *séquelles,* or aftereffects, can also be translated as "postsurgical scars," "posttraumatic syndromes," or "residual effects." In the context of Césaire's statement, *séquelles* implies an awareness of the potential insanity of the postindependence moment during which, subsequent to the nation, the mind must be decolonized. Césaire's position as a man of culture has always been that the artist has moral and social responsibilities and should be the most useful citizen of his "tribe." Through the 1950s, the artist's duty was to hasten not only the decolonization of the old French colonies but also to promote the disalienation of the mind of the formerly colonized subject who had internalized the systematic ideological devaluation of Black humanity and culture. Césaire's agenda has been the reconstruction of Black nations after independence as well as the development of new concepts of the self and self-esteem. In the postindependence moment, artists were to become inventors of being, propagators of a new spirit, engineers of souls, multipliers of new men and women.

In *The Abandoned Baobab* there is a leitmotiv of burning, scorching, and scarring. The autobiography is concerned with the postsurgical scars, the aftereffects, the traumas, the complexes, the psychoses and neuroses that the man of culture would have spared the decolonized subject. Ken bears the scars of her mental colonization. Remembering her French education, Ken muses, "J'étudiais avec rage. Quand malgré moi je me couchais, je continuais à analyser dans ma tête le Discours de la Méthode." ["I studied furiously. . . . and when I'd go to bed, against my will, I would continue to analyze the *Discourse on Method* in my head."] From its beginnings, francophone literature has sought refuge from the constraints of the French Cartesianism, rationalism, and logic that informed the colonial system of domination and exploitation. Fanon states: "Pour le colonisé, l'objectivité est toujours dirigée contre lui"[4] [For the native, objectivity is always directed against him]. Before Fanon, Aimé Césaire had declared his opposition to the paralyzing grip of colonial logic upon the mind and existence of the colonized subject. To free herself of the grip of rationalist categories upon her consciousness that seem to have left her in a state of radical divorce from the rich life of her other African self, Ken discovers the liberating effects of intoxication and insanity, in which there is a certain phoenicism, or promise of rebirth, through suicide:

> Grisée par le champagne, j'étais aussi grisée par mon autre moi-même qui jouissait de ces moments qu'on voudrait vrais, où l'être se suicide littéralement dans l'illusion. . . . la conscience de ce moment-là le rejet total de tout équation de la raison, du réel. Je me sentais comme sortie d'un gouffre qui m'étais autre que mes réalités et celles de la vie. (Pp. 126–70)

> [Befuddled by the champagne, I was equally intoxicated by my other self, which enjoyed these moments I would so much want to be true, moments in which one literally commits suicide in illusion. . . . my consciousness of that moment was the total rejection of all equations of reason, of what is real. I felt as if I had come out of the pit that was nothing other than my and life's realities.] (Pp. 107–8)

The Madness That Remembers, Sees, and Frees

Embedded in the poetics of Aimé Césaire is a ritualized performance of madness, intoxication, and phoenicism—as inherent risks of the kind of thinking necessary to bridge the gap between those languages, cultures, ideologies, and discourses that, because of their respective politics and worldview, appear incommensurably and irreconcilably at odds with one another. Madness in Césaire is related to the disorientation and dislocation that are the consequences of cultural uprooting and the consciousness of being systematically alienated from one's virtuality and thwarted in one's fundamental desires for self-realization. In therapeutic terms, madness in Césaire is a potent space of release from foreign cultural sanctions and judgments. It is a rich space of shame and blasphemy, of acting up and acting one's way out of assigned invisibility or stereotypical roles:

Parce que nous vous haïssons vous
et votre raison, nous nous réclamons
de la démence précoce de la folie flamboyante
du cannibalisme tenace
Trésor comptons:
la folie qui se souvient
la folie qui hurle
la folie qui voit
la folie qui se déchaine
(*Cahier,* 48)

[Because we hate you you
and your reason, we claim kinship with dementia praecox
with flaming madness
of persistent cannibalism
treasure let's count
madness that remembers
madness that howls
madness that sees
madness that is unleashed
(*Notebook,* 49)

Je déclare mes crimes et il n'y a rien à dire pour ma
défense
Danses. Idoles. Relaps. Moi aussi
J'ai assassiné Dieu de ma paresse
de mes paroles de mes gestes
de mes chansons obscènes
J'ai porté des plumes de perroquets des

dépouilles de chat musqué
J'ai lassé la patience des missionnaires
insulté les bienfaiteurs de l'humanité
Défié Tyr. Défié Sidon. Adoré le Zambèze
L'étendue de ma perversité me confond!
(*Cahier,* 52)

[I declare my crimes and that there is nothing
to say in my defense
Dances. Idols. An apostate. I too
I have assassinated God with my laziness
with my words with my gestures
with my obscene songs
I have worn parrot plumes
musk cat skins
I have exhausted the missionaries' patience
insulted the benefactors of mankind.
Defied Tyre. Defied Sidon.
Worshipped the Zambezi
the extent of my perversity overwhelms me!]
(*Notebook,* 53)

In these passages, Césaire uncovers the value of the salutary, "saving," and therapeutic madness that allows the subject to accuse, expose lies, and evacuate frustrations, rage, resentments, and outrage. Césairian madness is, for the colonized person, a process of disalienation and decolonization of the mind. After realizing the futility of nativist mimicry or chic *ap*propriations of the dominant culture, madness is a strategy for the production of meaning, being, and action. This emancipatory madness begins with Caliban's cursing and evolves into *ex*propriative gestures that deconstruct, decenter, destabilize, renew, and expand the embrace of language, culture, ideology, and discourse so that they yield to the expression of the colonized person's worth, genius, and worldview. Neologisms abound, such as the celebrated *négritude* from *Notebook of a Return to the Native Land:* "Haiti, where négritude stood up for the first time and declared its humanity." Etymologically, *négritude* contains in its semes the suggestions of a new Black attitude, beatitude, pulchritude, lassitude, and study (*étude*) of Black people, civilizations, and history. In the *Note-*

book, as speech-act performativity, the neologism *négritude* effects a parturition of self:

> Je force la membrane vitelline qui me
> sépare de moi-même
> je force les grandes eaux qui me ceinturent de sang.
>
> ASSEZ DE CE SCANDALE!
>
> Accommodez-vous de moi. Je ne m'accommode pas de vous! (*Cahier,* p. 56)
>
> [I am forcing the vitelline membrane that separates
> me from myself,
> I am forcing the great waters which girdle me with
> blood.
>
> ENOUGH OF THIS OUTRAGE!
>
> Put up with me. I won't put up with you! (*Notebook,* p. 57)

> car il n'est point vrai que l'œuvre de l'homme est finie
> que nous n'avons rien à faire au monde
> que nous parasitons le monde
> qu'il suffit que nous nous mettions au pas du monde
> mais l'œuvre de l'homme vient seulement de commencer
> et il reste à l'homme à conquérir toute interdiction
> immobilisé au coin de sa ferveur et aucune race ne
> possède le monopole de la beauté, de l'intelligence, de la
> force. (*Cahier,* p. 76)
>
> [for it is not true that the work of man is done
> that we have no business being on earth
> that we parasite the world
> that it is enough for us to heel to the world
> whereas the work has only begun
> and man still must overcome all the interdictions wedged
> in the recesses of his fervor and no race has a monopoly
> on beauty, on intelligence, on strength.] (*Notebook,* p. 77)

Ken's thought process takes systematic inventory of the psychoses and neuroses affecting the colonized person as well as the stereotypes of Africans and, in particular, the Black woman in the European collective consciousness. Madness, for Ken, is essentially a problem of thought, that is, confused, tormented thinking. Ken's thinking denounces the practice of French colonialism in Africa and its continuing aftereffects. It is a thinking process that continually questions the effects upon the African psyche of the French politics and process of assimilation, which turns out to be, in fact, a process of alienation. For Ken, madness is nothing more, nothing less, than the state of mind that results from the entanglement (slipknot) of questions and chiastic logic that precipitates the thinking—postindependence—subject into the fulfillment or the emptiness of a double consciousness:

> La conscience constituait tout naturellement la lame à double tranchant. Il ne fallait pas avoir la conscience de l'ambiguïté. (P. 124)

> [Consciousness consisted quite naturally of a double-edged blade. The awareness of ambiguity had no place here.] (P. 106)

It is, however, precisely her awareness of this ambiguity that leads Ken through a crisis of identity, a double-edged experience of alienation, the pain of attachment and loss, cycles of melancholy and elation, feelings of worthlessness and the contemplation of suicide.

As discussed in Part 1, postcolonial countermodernity is a time and space of dream, myth, and madness. Paradoxically, only such phenomena can tolerate and contain the teeming tension of antinomies and the extraordinary "realities" of the experiences of colonialism, the challenges of decolonization, the cultural, ideological, and psychological conflicts of independence and postcolonialism. The pseudonym Ken Bugul in the Wolof language means "the child no one wanted." Indeed, *The Abandoned Baobab* is the story of a child buffeted by circumstances—abandoned by her mother, torn from her native land, assimilated by the French school, wandering in a Europe that rejects her, returning to the Mother Africa she herself had rejected. Ken Bugul writes her madness, alienation, hysteria, and panic.

Ken is a "lost body" who "looses it" in the metropolitan environment. Her early insanity finds refuge, however, in writing as a cure, and in so doing reveals itself to be an eminently philosophical, metaphysical, and existential state of analytic reflection.

> L'arrivée des Blancs avait sapé des fondements sacrés, les avait disloqués pour faire du colonisé un angoissé à perpétuité. Ne pourrions-nous pas nous rassembler et surgir, comme là-bas le soleil sait paraître brusquement! (P. 102)

> Les envahisseurs nous avaient séparés, portés les uns contre les autres et nous n'étions pas arrivés à nous en sortir. Et comment parler d'une lutte noire, d'un pouvoir noir, d'une culture noire, de l'unité africaine, si nous n'avons pas encore résolu ce problème? (P. 107)

> [The arrival of the Whites had undermined sacred foundations, had dismembered them, in order to turn the colonized into an anguished people forever more. Couldn't we reunite ourselves and emerge, just as down there the sun knows how to suddenly appear?] (P. 85)

> [The invaders had separated us, had set us against each other, and we hadn't managed to escape from that. And how can we speak of Black struggle, Black power, Black culture, African unity, if we haven't yet resolved this problem?] (P. 90)

Throughout the text, Ken is referred to in French, English, and Wolof as "folle," "crazy," and "dof." Ken Bugul's "insanity" is not blind, violent indirection. Her madness unfolds as an alternative space of exploration and cogitation as she experiences the splitting of the self through the wrenching experience of exile and cultural interaction peculiar to the postcolonial period. Ken's madness is a phenomenon of thought. She cannot, nor would she know how to, prevent herself from thinking. The novel begins under the sign of the overdetermination of meaning and the emptiness of meaning:

> Il y a des foules de sentiments, de multiples ressentiments que nul ne peut dire, encore moins décrire. Je crois que tout ce qui se passe en nous, nous ne l'exprimons jamais entièrement. Car cela nous dépasse. (P. 51)

> [There are seas of emotions, multiple feelings and resentments that no one can express, much less describe. I believe that nothing of what goes on inside of us is ever entirely expressed. For it is beyond us.] (P. 38)

Ken's dementia arises from a postindependence world in conflict, a world of thoughts and concepts in conflict:

> Les formules se choquent. Perdu, l'être cavale dans la réflexion, la méditation. Les notions initient, les idées foisonnent, les projections s'éparpillent, les comparaisons comparent. Chacun essaie un chemin dans le vide, mais la fuite incite à la création et créer c'est combler le vide, le seul vrai adversaire de l'homme. (P. 22)
>
> [Formulas collide. Lost, human beings roam around inside thoughts, meditations. Notions introduce themselves, ideas are born, plans grow profuse, comparisons compare. Each one tries a new path in emptiness, but flight inspires creation, and to create is to fill the void, humankind's only true enemy.] (P. 15)

Alienation is a mode of experience in which the individual feels out of touch with him/herself. The condition often includes a panoply of uncertainties: role conflict, role reversal, questions about what role the subject is expected to play, doubt about his or her own selfhood, and feelings of dehumanization, helplessness, and futility. The tragedy and grandeur of Ken Bugul's alienation is in its double scope as evidence of her otherness vis-à-vis not only European culture, but also her gradual alienation from African culture. Ken discovers herself a stranger unto herself and to her own culture long before coming to France. She is caught, torn, twisted and split in a crisis of identity: Duboisian double consciousness leads to cultural schizophrenia.

> Dans le village de la mère, je ne parlais qu'en français avec les jeunes gens et les jeunes filles qui fréquentaient l'école française. Ayant trouvé cette même année que dire bonsoir à quelqu'un pouvait signifier aussi au revoir, bonne nuit, je le balançais à tout le monde. Je croyais avoir trouvé un moyen de me rassurer en me faisant "toubab." Toujours les revues de mode de Paris qu'on pouvait acheter de seconde main au marché, toujours bonsoir à tort et à travers, toujours faire un tour dans le village pour me montrer, chaussant des chaussures à talons aiguille qui me donnaient si chaud et m'empêchaient de marcher gracieusement, le jupon que je faisais dépasser exprès pour le montrer. Les décrépages permanents des cheveux, l'imitation des coiffures occidentales qui donnaient des visages déstructurés, le vernis rouge comme du sang qui me coulait des doigts.
>
> Ah Dieu! Que j'étais épuisée de vouloir plus que "ressembler," me déformer. (P. 138)

[In the Mother's village, I spoke only French with the young people who went to the French school. Having just learned that year that saying "Bonsoir" to someone could mean "See you again" as well as "Good night," I threw it out to everyone. I thought I had found a way to feel confident by acting "white." Always with Paris fashion magazines I bought second-hand at the market, always "bonsoir" left and right, always taking walks around the village to be seen, with high-heeled shoes that made me hot and kept me from walking gracefully, the slip that I purposely let show, the straightened hair, the imitation of Western hairdos that brought the face into disarray, the blood-red lacquer that dripped off my fingers.

Oh, God! I became so exhausted from wanting more than to "look like," from deforming myself.] (P. 119)

Je n'avais eu toutes ces explications que quelques années plus tard. J'avais toujours été en dehors des événements de la famille. Les chemins de nos mondes avaient pris de sens différents. Les rapports n'étaient pas scellés. À l'époque, je voyais cette distance avec bonheur. Je fonçais de plus en plus dans la colonisation des temps nouveaux. . . . Les mêmes questions se chevauchaient, les mêmes aspirations vers l'Occident s'amplifiaient de plus en plus. *L'identification était difficile. Je consommais deux réalités d'une façon contradictoire. Parce qu'au fond de moi, la nostalgie du lien me hantait. Déchirée!* Les talons aiguille dans le sable chaud qui m'enveloppait jusqu'aux chevilles, le gras qui dégoulinait de mes cheveux décrêpés jusqu'à la brûlure, marcher en me serrant les fesses. Et parfois l'envie de m'abandonner comme les femmes du village, cette grâce *que j'appréciais et rejetais à la fois.*

J'apprenais par coeur les chansons occidentales et voulais les vivre telles. De plus en plus le fossé se creusait, désespérément. L'Afrique me rappelait à elle par ses élans, ses instants de poésie et ses rites. Mais je tenais bon avec les valeurs apportées par la colonisation. *Je ne pouvais retourner sur mes pas, ni même jeter un coup d'oeil en arrière.* (Pp. 142–43; emphasis added)

[I didn't get all these explanations until several years later. I'd always been on the outside of family events. Our paths had taken different directions. The relationships weren't confirmed. At the time, I saw this distance as something fortunate. I was sinking deeper and deeper into the colonization of the times. . . . The same questions would overlap each

> other the same aspirations toward the West were becoming more and more magnified. *Identification was difficult. I was working to achieve two realities in a contradictory fashion. In my innermost self, the yearning for a bond haunted me. Torn in two.* Spiked heels in the hot sand that enclosed me up to my ankles, grease that dripped down from my straightened hair all the way to my bum, my walk with tightened buttocks. And sometimes the desire to let myself go like the village women, that grace *that I both treasured and rejected at the same time.*
>
> I learned the songs from the West by heart and wanted to live them that way. More and more the gap widened, desperately Africa called me back with her life force, her moments of poetry and her rituals. But I held on tight to the bond I had made with the values that colonialism had brought. *I could not go back anymore, I could not even glance backward.*] (P. 123; emphasis added)

In the extraordinarily rich passages just cited, the evolution of experience is from assimilation to alienation to an early splitting of the mind in the context of the collision of two cultures. They also highlight the difference between imitation and identification. Imitation is the need to be like the Western Other, whereas identification for Ken will be the process of differentiation and the recognition of the intimacy of difference. The dementia praecox claimed in the Césaire passage cited on page 183 is an early insanity, usually a prelude to schizophrenia or the splitting of the mind. As she is "sinking deeper and deeper into the colonization of the times," Ken is aware of a withdrawal or a splitting off from the outside African world and her family. This "mild" schizophrenia will become more conflictual when Ken migrates to Brussels and undergoes a graver pattern of psychological reaction to the stresses of life as she immerses herself "in the depths of self-analysis: to be a woman, a rigid woman, to be a child without any notion of parents, to be Black, and to be colonized" (p. 93). Ken muses further:

> Pourquoi n'avoir pas prévu la réaction de la femme noire au néo-colonialisme? . . . Contenir la sourdeur des pulsions qui assurent en partie l'équilibre. (P. 90)

> [Why had they not foreseen the Black woman's reaction to neo-colonialism? One must absorb the muteness of the drives that partly ensure equilibrium.] (P. 113)

> Cette solitude que j'avais retrouvée durement, avec le choc d'avoir perdu, ici, mes ancêtres les Gaulois. Le reflet dans le miroir, le visage, le regard, cette couleur qui me distinguait en me niant. Cette solitude jusque dans les draps des amants d'un soir; ce besoin lancinant des autres, introuvables. (P. 110)
>
> [To this loneliness, so harshly found again, now was added the shock of having lost my ancestors, the Gauls. The reflection in the mirror, the face, the look, the color that set me apart while negating me. The loneliness that follows one all the way into the sheets of the one-night stand; that throbbing need for other people, who cannot be found.] (P. 93)

The traumatic event in Ken's life is her sense of having been abandoned by her mother. It is in Brussels during late adolescence that Ken obsesses on her ambiguous relationship with the composite Mother, who is the mother, the grandmother, and Mother Africa.

> Oh mère que vous ai-je fait? Qu'avez-vous fait? Ah, si vous me voyiez en ce moment, comme je voudrais mourir! (P. 176).
>
> [Oh, mother what did I do to you? What have you done? Ah, if you were to see me at this moment, oh, how I would want to die!] (P. 153)

> Je n'avais rien et je cherchais toute l'enfance dans toutes les situations que je vivais dans le pays du remplacement où je m'abandonnais dans le tragique depuis le départ de la mère. (P. 177)
>
> [I had nothing and was looking for my entire childhood in every situation in a country that had replaced my own, where I gave myself wholeheartedly to tragedy ever since the mother's departure.] (P. 154)

Ken's anxiety is the consequence of momentous transitions—from a familiar childhood environment characterized by communal care, devotion, and rituals, into a different cultural space filled with great expectations. Later in life, any loss is experienced as a reactivation of the early loss of the mother, the community, and familiar ways.

> Il n'y avait que le désir fondamental et la nécessité de l'affection, de toutes les émotions qui donnaient raison, poésie à la vie. Chacun à sa manière, se jetant dans ces déchirements, ces états où désespérément on

se savait perdant et victime. Il ne fallait pas arracher l'enfant du ventre de la mère. Il ne fallait que la mère parte. (Pp. 178–79)

Qu'avais-je fait? Qu'avait fait la mère? (P. 79)

[All that was left was the basic desire and the necessity for affection, for all the emotions that give life sense and poetry. Each in his own way would throw himself into these heartbreaks, these states in which one knew oneself to be the loser and victim. The child ought not to be pulled out of the mother's belly. The mother ought not to leave.] (P. 156)

[What had I done? What had the mother done?] (P. 157)

Explanations of schizophrenia vary according to the type of society: urban society seems to show a higher incidence than agricultural society. Industrial (postcolonial) societies seem to create a higher predisposition to schizophrenia than do agricultural societies. Further, there is the suggestion that in large, developed urban centers, schizophrenia seems most prevalent among the unmarried, immigrants, those of low social status, and people who belong to ethnic minorities.

There is no recognized single cause of the disorganization of the personality known as schizophrenia. It appears that genetic factors produce a vulnerability to schizophrenia, with environmental factors contributing to different degrees in different individuals. Just as human personality is the result of the interplay of cultural, psychological, biological, and genetic factors, schizophrenia may result from an interplay of genetic factors and environmental stressors that can trigger neuro-psycho-biological mechanisms leading to the disorder.[5] Scientists do not agree on a specific formula that is necessary to produce the disorder: "Symptoms unique to schizophrenia have not been identified. No single symptom can be considered pathognomonic of this disorder. Rather, it is characterized by a polythectic cluster of symptoms, usually expressed in a particular course or pattern."[6]

In other words, no "bad" gene or biochemical defect has been proven responsible for schizophrenia. No one stressful event (such as a death in the family or, in the case of Ken, the departure of the mother and her sense of abandonment) seems sufficient, by itself, to trigger the psychological disintegration of schizophrenia. Scientists concur that, most likely, combinations of these factors produce schizophrenia.[7]

As the etymology (*shizein* and *phrén, phrenos*) suggests, schizophrenia is the manifestation of a split, a break, or a clash in thoughts and thought processes. Ken reflects on the paradox of her alienated condition and of her divided selves: "L'aliénation? Moi qui n'avais jamais connu de milieu, de famille, issue d'une génération condamnée, moi qui n'avais aucun repère, comment pourrais-je m'aliéner? Or, l'ambiguïté *établie, l'impossibilité* de l'aliénation en était peut-être déjà une. Je soufflai un bon coup, comme j'en avais l'habitude après chaque moment de flottement où mon dédoublement prenait cette forme désespérée parce que sans autre issue que soi; mais qui était justement soi et comment l'apprivoiser pour être en paix?" (p. 124). Alienation? I, who had never known a center, a family, born from a condemned generation, I, who had no frame of reference, how could I be alienated? Yet, the *established* ambiguity, the *impossibility* of alienation, was perhaps in and of itself a form of it. I breathed deeply as I always did after every moment of floating, when my divided selves took this desperate form because there was no exit but itself; but who exactly was the self and how could I tame this self in order to be at peace? (p. 105). Formerly known as *dementia praecox,* which Césaire salutes in his denunciation of the limitations, tyrannies, and crimes of reason in *Notebook of a Return to the Native Land,* schizophrenia manifests itself in adolescence or in the early twenties and can take the form of a radical, paradoxical dissonance between a brilliant intellectual life and the breakdown of affective and social relationships. Such a dissonance and breakdown characterize the life of Ken in *The Abandoned Baobab,* where one observes the sociogenesis of Ken's self-aversive reactions and behaviors. The chaotic language of the schizophrenic translates the alterations in perspective and thought that are the consequence of the interplay of psychosocial crises and environmental stresses.[8] Ken's cerebral and linguistic disorganization is Fanonian in the sense that it emerges from "what Fanon recognized was the central role played in our human behaviors by our always linguistically constituted criteria of being (that is, our human *skins,* represented *masks*)."[9]

While schizophrenia is found more frequently among the lowest socioeconomic classes, poverty itself is not a direct cause of schizophrenia. Conditions associated with poverty, however, may be implicated in the disorder.[10] Ken's evolution in social status from international student in Brussels to photographer's model, hatcheck girl, nightclub hostess, masseuse, and prostitute traces a social, moral, and psychological decline that results in a schizophrenic panic and suicide attempt: "A number of studies suggest that schizophrenics are not necessarily born to poverty. Instead, it appears that schizophrenics 'drift downward' in social class *after* they become ill. Thus, like many factors associated with schizophrenia, poverty may be a result rather than a cause of illness."[11]

Ken does not demonstate the positive symptoms of schizophrenia that represent an exaggeration or distortion of normal function, such as hallucinations, delusions, and hearing voices when they are not there. In her social decline, as outlined above, and in the evolution of her personality as she struggles with the challenges of race, assimilation, self-worth, gender, sexuality, self-aversion, and cultural conflicts as they get played out in a European capital in the seventies, Ken succumbs in varying degrees to the negative symptoms of schizophrenia that represent a diminution or loss of normal function. Negative symptoms of schizophrenia include "affective blunting (loss of the ability to express emotions fluently), alogia (impoverished nonfluent speech), avolition (loss of drive), anhedonia (loss of the ability to feel emotional attachment or experience pleasure) and attentional impairment. These negative symptoms account for a great deal of the emotional and social morbidity of schizophrenia, since they lead to social isolation and withdrawal, difficulty in holding a job or remaining in school and impaired ability to relate to others."[12]

Scientists concur that research into the psychosocial factors involved in schizophrenic behavior is related to its etiology and pathogenesis and that consideration must be given to environmental events, personality characteristics, subjective experience, and individual adaptive mechanisms and capabilities.[13]

It is the cultural moment and context that produce Ken's dilemma. Ken's illness is her consciousness of what she is undergoing. Medicalizing social disorders limits the possibility of a cure. What is needed, in addition, is a sociodiagnostic. The point of *cultural* schizophrenia is to transcend pathologizing schizophrenia, to move beyond Ken's example as the bio-ontogenetic problem of an individual woman in order to place her shattering experience, examples of which multiply daily in urban centers from Brussels and Paris to New York and

Montreal, into a broader process of socialization such as Fanonian sociogeny. Sylvia Wynter makes this point in assessing Fanon's contribution to the concept of a sociodiagnostic:

> Fanon noted the extent to which all *native* and colonialized subjects had been conditioned to experience themselves as if they were, in fact, as *genetically inferior* as the hegemonic "learned discourse" of contemporary scholars ostensibly represented them (as obsessively as those of Columbus's times had as negatively represented the torrid zone/antipodes).... Fanon sought to relate the "aberration of affect" that led to these behaviors, to a specific sociosystemic organizing process that had, in turn, induced the "aberration of affect" itself. . . . Freud, said Fanon, had placed the emphasis on the individual. He had therefore based the discipline of psychology on an ontogenetic perspective, but "*besides ontogeny, there is sociogeny,*" [said Fanon]. The problem of the black man and of the colonial native's self-aversive reactions was clearly *not* an individual problem.[14]
>
> In the wake of Fanon, look for the explanation of our human behaviors *not* in the individual psyche of the ostensibly purely bio-ontogenetic subject, but rather *in the process* of socialization that institutes the individual as a human, and therefore, *always* sociogenetic subject.[15]

Ken Bugul, as pointed out earlier, *thinks* constantly about her situation in the world. Her "cogito" does not lead to a logical, stable, and triumphant affirmation of who she is. Ken's cogito is a quest for identity. Very early in her experience she realizes the function of her interactions with others, especially her interactions with white men, through whom she feels valorized and revealed unto herself. The process is the discovery of self through alterity—through one's otherness and through the others who have made you an "Other":

> C'est ainsi qu'avec Louis débuta ma première idylle en Occident. Idylle qui me servait à m'expliquer, à m'intégrer, à montrer que j'étais comme eux: qu'il n'y avait aucune différence entre nous, que eux et moi, nous avions les mêmes ancêtres. (P. 54)
>
> [And so it happened that my first romance in the West was with Louis. The romance served to explain myself, to integrate me, to show that I

> was like them, that there was no difference whatsoever between us, that they and I had the same ancestors.] (P. 42)

The cosmopolitan city of Brussels, with its inhabitants from the four corners of the globe, especially women, contributed to the awakening of Ken's feminist consciousness. It is her decision to abort Louis's child that initiates her contact with women of varied cultural backgrounds who find communion together in the anteroom of the abortionist's office. The scene reveals the functioning of Ken's mind as she is constantly struck by the endless ironies of their condition: the anteroom that strangely resembles a cathouse, the doctor who is a butcher and an opponent of racial mixing, who reveals this as he is probing deep within her flesh, and the realization of her own shame about being pregnant with Louis's child. It is precisely this kind of meditation on her condition that keeps Ken hovering at the edge of lucidity and panic, madness and shame. Such a state is the destructive, disabling potential of life in the culturally hybrid space.

> Il y avait quelque chose qui ressemblait à une salle d'attente, mais on aurait dit plutôt une pièce d'un bureau de recrutement où s'alignaient des femmes de toutes les couleurs, des Arabes, des Africaines, des Antillaises. Chacune avait l'air de vivre une tragédie propre à elle. . . . Elles avaient la même couleur. Nous étions ensemble sans l'être. Nous nous regardions sans nous voir. Nous étions des femmes et nous avions les mêmes cauchemars que ne connaissaient que les femmes. . . .
>
> Aucun homme ne se trouvait dans cette salle d'attente qui ressemblait à une antichambre de maison close. Les femmes, dès qu'elles se trouvent ensemble ont l'air si garces. Mille pensées défilèrent dans mon imagination, de Gouye où je suis né jusqu'au jour où un professeur d'histo-géo me séduisit, mon voyage en Occident, mon contact avec les Occidentaux, mes rencontres et celle qui m'avait mené dans cette salle d'attente où je me rendais compte que les femmes, toutes les femmes, avaient le même destin. (Pp. 55–56)
>
> [Something there resembled a waiting room, but I would sooner have called it a recruitment office where women of all colors were lined up, Arabic, African, Caribbean. Each one looked as if she were living her own private tragedy. . . . They had the same color. We were there together without being together. We were looking at each other without seeing

each other. We were women and surely we had the same nightmares, those that only women know.

There was not a single man in this waiting room, which resembled a brothel. As soon as women are alone together, they seem so much like tarts! A thousand thoughts went through my head, from Gouye where I was born to the day I was seduced by a history and geography teacher, my trip to the West, my contact with Westerners, my encounters generally, and the specific one that had led me to this waiting room, where I realized that women, all women, have the same destiny.] (P. 43)

Ce type était un bourreau. Il exploitait la femme jusque dans ses entrailles. (P. 56)

[This guy was an executioner. He exploited woman all the way to her entrails.] (P. 44)

Le soir, Louis me proposa à nouveau de nous marier, de garder l'enfant, d'aller vivre ailleurs, même en Afrique. Pour moi, il n'en était pas question. J'avais quitté l'Afrique depuis à peine trois mois. Comment pourrais-je y retourner avec une grossesse et un mari blanc? (P. 63)

[That evening, Louis once again proposed that we get married, keep the child, go to live elsewhere, in Africa even. I wouldn't hear of it. I had left Africa just barely three months earlier. How could I go back there, pregnant and with a white husband?] (P. 50)

Dans l'immeuble où nous habitions, il y avait des étudiants africains. Une Italienne venait les voir, ils me la présentèrent juste au moment de mes ennuis. Cette rencontre m'apporta une idée plus nette des rapports entre femmes. Ma conscience feministe était née. (P. 63)

[In our building there were other African students. An Italian woman used to visit them, and they introduced her to me just around the time of my difficulties. That encounter gave me a much clearer idea of the relationships between women. My feminist consciousness was born.] (P. 50)

A se demander si les femmes ne vivaient pas les mêmes choses partout. (P. 65)

[It leads one to wonder whether women don't live through the same things everywhere.] (P. 51)

Ah les femmes! Concevoir, admettre, tolérer, servir! (P. 86)

[Ah, women! Conceive, admit, tolerate, serve!] (P. 72)

Nous parlions des problèmes de la femme en cette seconde moitié du vingtième siècle. Je fréquentais de moins en moins mes compatriotes. J'étais souvent avec les Blancs. (P. 67)

[We would talk about the problems of women in the second half of this twentieth century. I spent a great deal of time with white people.] (P. 53)

Ken's feminist consciousness does not lead her into the trap of leveling universals and containment of a system of correspondences that would blind her to the specificity of her condition. Ken understands very quickly that an espousal of the first-world European feminist agenda simply locked her into the old racial hierarchies, with Black women, at best, simply being ignored. Her feminist consciousness progressively moves toward the contemplation of her situation as a Black woman in Europe, for she recognizes: "je m'identifiais en eux, ils ne s'identifiaient pas en moi" (p. 67) ["I identified myself in them, they did not identify themselves in me"] (p. 53). For "them" Ken remains absolutely an "Other." The "in them" and "in me" emphasizes the extent and the importance of the identification process as a structured relation to what it is in the Other.

The "alterity process," referred to above, leads Ken into the dangerous slipknot of attempting, herself, to exploit the European commodification of the Black woman's body through fashion, exoticism, and sexual commerce.

C'était l'époque où l'Occident s'exotisait. Ce qui nous différenciait, c'était qu'elle était une Blanche, mariée, riche et que j'étais une Noire "déséquilibrée," une aventurière. (P. 73)

[It was the period when the West was becoming enamored of the exotic. What made us different was that she was white, married, and rich, while I was an "unbalanced" Black woman, an adventurer.] (P. 59)

Partout j'étais la seule Noire, certes pas l'ambassadrice du peuple noir, mais à défaut des Pygmées ou de Masai à moitié nus, celle qui délirait avec eux Blancs, dans une peau noire. J'étais celle chez qui chacun voulait laisser sa carte de visite; avec qui chacun voulait parler. J'étais le happening de tout ce monde des arts et des mondanités. Culture occidentale et un éventail de connaissances mémorisées sans méthode et projetées tous azimuts me faisaient apprécier par ces mécènes et philanthropes des temps nouveaux. J'allais donc partout et j'étais partout celle qu'on remarquait. Parce qu'elle était noire, et aussi parce que, par désespoir, elle s'accrochait et osait. Elle osait la transparence, elle osait le déguisement, elle osait rire, elle osait pleurer, mais au fond était amère. (P. 101)

[Everywhere I went I was the only Black woman, and surely not as a lady ambassador of the Black people but, as there were no Pygmies or half-naked Masai, I was the one to carry on with them, the white folks, in my black skin. I was the one to whom everyone gave his calling card, with whom everyone wanted to talk. I was the happening of this whole world of arts and social events. Western culture and a whole range of bits of knowledge, memorized without any order, projected in a helter-skelter fashion, made these Maecenases and modern-day philanthropists appreciate me enormously. And so I went everywhere, and everywhere I was the one they noticed. Because she was Black, and also because she hung on and she was daring, out of sheer despair. She dared to be transparent, she dared to disguise herself, she dared to laugh, she dared to weep, but deep down she was bitter.] (Pp. 84–85)

Ces gens riches étaient libres de faire ce qu'ils voulaient, ils absorbaient la diaspora pour l'originalité. "Nous avons une amie noire, une Africaine" était la phrase la plus "in" dans ces milieux. La Négresse après les lionceaux, et les singes, avec les masques Dogon et d'Ifé. J'étais cette négresse, cette "chez vous autres," cette "toi, en tant que noire, il faudrait que . . . ," cet être supplémentaire, inutile, déplacé, incohérent. (P. 101)

[These rich people were free to do whatever they wanted, they were engrossed in the diaspora because it was something new and original. "We have a Black friend, an African woman" was the most fashionable sentence in those circles. The Negress, after the lion cubs and the monkeys, with the Dogon and Ife masks. I was that Negress, that "down where you live," that "you, as a Black woman, you ought to . . . ," that supplementary being, useless, displaced, incoherent.] (P. 85)

The consumption of Africa reaches absurd and riotously funny proportions in the opening scene of chapter 8 of *The Abandoned Baobab,* when the Brussels' Furriers and Diamond Dealers' Association throws a lavish *African* soirée complete with Ken as a "real" African coat-check girl, an "authentic" African band in exile, and of course all guests in the most lavish furs and diamonds poached and pillaged from the jungles and mines of the Dark Continent. The scene reaches its climax when one of the guests arrives with a leopard on a leash. The leopard is driven crazy by the smell of lamb roasting on a spit. Ken dives for cover under a mound of furs in her care, and the African band members seek a hiding place behind the stage. The Whites are incredulous, for, after all, Africans should be accustomed to wild animals. The exotification-commodification process loses its allure and pushes Ken into profound self-analysis on the relations between Black women and White men, the commercial consumption of the Black woman's body, and her complicity in these processes.

> "Oh, Ken, ne va pas chercher des considérations là où il n'y en a pas, là où il n'en faut pas. Une femme ne peut être rien d'autre que de la consommation." (P. 120)

> ["Oh, Ken, don't start looking for considerations where there aren't any, where there shouldn't be any. A woman can be nothing other than a consumption."] (P. 101)

Ken's thinking leads her to cross-examine herself: she functions as judge and defendant and especially as analyst and analysand:

> Paul et Hélène Denoêl s'en faisaient tant pour moi, à mesure que je plongeais dans les bas-fonds de l'autopsychanalyse: être une femme, une femme rigide, être une enfant sans notion de parents, être noire et être colonisée. (P. 110)

> [Paul and Hélène Denoël were so worried about me that I immersed myself in the depths of self-analysis; to be a woman, a rigid woman, to be a child without any notion of parents, to be Black, to be colonized.] (P. 93)

> Prostituée au Blanc, je manquais une des faces de l'ambiguïté. . . . L'homme blanc et la femme noire, la vie, un enchevêtrement d'histoire et de méta-histoire. (P. 125)

> [Prostitute to the white man, one of the sides of ambiguity missing. . . . The white man and the Black woman, life, a jumble of history and metahistory.] (P. 106)

It is, in fact, Ken's need to share affection that entangles her in social/commercial/sexual relations of all varieties: modeling, nude photography, "hostessing" in nightclubs and saunas, ménages à trois, heterosexuality, bisexuality, and a lesbian relationship. Although Ken aborts, prostitutes herself, does not marry, and is herself an abandoned child, her disposition is generously maternal. The more abandoned people are, the more Ken loves them. She welcomes into her embrace all of the hippies, beatniks, and wandering souls "of the ragtag and dreamy diaspora of the 1970s."

Ken's experiences in the European "Promised Land," as she refers to it, provide her with a revelatory perspective on the African experience. In Ken's thinking processes, there is a constant boomerang effect: as she reflects upon her condition in Europe, she is constantly compelled to compare a European cultural phenomenon with the African cultural values she has abandoned. She observes that "la sexualité est culture et atmosphère" (p. 65) [sexuality is culture and atmosphere] (p. 52), and that "Dans tout exode, il y a altération de l'échelle des valeurs" (p. 65) [In every exodus there is a change in the sets of values] (p. 51). The question of abandonment, the need for affection, and reflection on the sociosexual and contrasting cultural values come together as Ken emerges as a figure of maternity while caring for her former lover, the bisexual Jean Werner, who suffers from a "contagious" viral hepatitis. She warms him and holds him tightly against her breasts:

> Malgré les appréhensions pour moi des gens et du médecin, je dormais avec lui, le serrant très fort contre moi comme pour aspirer toute sa douleur. Je buvais dans son verre, je l'embrassais tout le temps, je ne voulais pas l'abandonner dans la solitude de la maladie et de la souffrance. Ses parents, ses enfants, ses rares amis, se tenaient à distance quand ils venaient le voir.
>
> Dans ce pays, les malades étaient seuls, les handicapés seuls, les enfants seuls, les vieux seuls. Et c'étaient les étapes les plus riches de la vie humaine.
>
> Là-bas tout le monde est intégré, concerné, entouré; tout vit ensemble.

Même l'arbre donne l'ombre et la fraîcheur, a son utilité culinaire, ou thérapeutique, il est un lieu de méditation.

Je ne fus pas contaminée et Jean Wermer ne fut pas abandonné. Il se rétablissait très bien et je n'arrêtais pas de lui jouer du théâtre et de lui raconter des histoires drôles.

Plus les gens étaient abandonnés plus j'aimais m'approcher d'eux. (P. 97)

[Despite the apprehension of most people, including the doctor, I would sleep with him, holding him very close to me as if to inhale all his pain. I drank from his glass, I kissed him all the time, I didn't want to abandon him to the loneliness of illness and suffering. His parents, his children, his rare friends kept their distance when they came to visit him.

In this country, the sick were alone, the handicapped were alone, the children were alone, the elderly were alone. And those were the richest stages in a human life.

Down there, everyone was integrated, concerned, surrounded; everything lived together. Even the trees gave shade and freshness, had their culinary or therapeutic uses, were places for meditation.

I was not contaminated and Jean Werner was not abandoned. He was recuperating very nicely and I wouldn't stop performing for him and telling him funny stories.

The more abandoned people were, the more I enjoyed getting closer to them.] (P. 97)

In *Le Baobab fou,* it becomes increasingly evident that geography, as Hector Bianciotti asserts, "which has primarily to do with surfaces, is the most superficial form of exile."[16] In the text the problematics of exile reveal a succession of separations and losses of harmony along a via dolorosa marked by loss of the mother tongue and cultural fluency, expulsion of the child from the mother's lap, weaning, and loss even of the uterine paradise of the African mother:

C'était la pleine lune, mais endeuilée comme la mère la lune s'était réfugiée dans les nuages qui arboraient une terne couleur jaunâtre. J'avais la tête sur les cuisses de la mère. Ces cuisses chaudes qui me rappelaient celles de ma grand'mère qui m'en voulait parce que j'avais été inscrite à l'école française. Elle me haïssait par la suite et elle me regardait comme une souillure, je la dégoûtais. (P. 59)

[The moon was full, but, in mourning, it had fled into the clouds, which spread a lusterless yellowish color. I had my head on the mother's thighs. Those warm thighs reminded me of the grandmother's, who was angry with me because I registered at the French school. Afterward she hated me, regarded me as a blemish; I disgusted her.] (P. 46)

Je me croyais né sans conception. Je me retrouvais colonisé dans le groupe des "sans giron de la mère sans lieu pour reposer la tête." (P. 128)

[I believed I'd been born without having been conceived. I found myself colonized again in the group of those who have "no mother's lap, no place to rest their head."] (P. 109)

Il ne fallait pas arracher l'enfant du ventre de la mère. Il ne fallait que la mère parte. (Pp. 178–79)

[The child ought not to be pulled out of the mother's belly. The mother ought not to leave.] (Pp. 155–56)

Ken lives in a permanent state of exile—social and political, psychological and emotional, geographic and metaphysical. This exilic form of alienation is fundamentally tied to the maternal imago. Ken's alienation also involves a form of repression:

Je n'avais jamais pu parler de moi. En face de Laure et François, je ne me basais que sur des références. J'écoutais, je suivais, je participais, mais ce n'était pas moi. Ils me dépouillaient, me vidaient, m'étalaient. (P. 102)

[Never had I been able to talk about myself. Faced with Laure and François, I based myself only on references. I would listen, I'd follow along, I'd participate, but it wasn't me. They were stripping me, emptying me out, displaying me.] (P. 85)

Saisir l'autre. Un autre moi-même commençait à se sentir responsable. Je cherchais le refuge depuis la perle d'ambre dans l'oreille, pourtant je savais que ce n'était pas un abri, toute cette enchère. (Pp. 101–2).

[To grasp the other. Another me began to feel responsible. I was looking for refuge ever since the amber bead in my ear, and yet I knew that this, this whole auction block wasn't a shelter.] (P. 85)

> Moi qui avais rêvé d'un foyer, d'un père, d'une mère, d'ancêtres, moi qui voulais être reconnue! J'étais jetée dans la cage des fantasmes inassouvis et des chevauchées dans le rêve surréel. (P. 99)

> [I, who had dreamed of a home, of a father, of a mother, of ancestors, I who wanted to be recognized! I was thrown into the cage of unfulfilled fantasies and was taking wild rides into the world of surreal dream.] (P. 82)

Ken's vague dreams of return to the mother's womb become a thinly disguised death wish. In *The Abandoned Baobab* these preoccupations give rise to a haunting poetry of crossroads, crossings, bridges, and goings and comings. They concretize the desire to cross the footbridge that leads to the Promised Land, to reverse roles, to straddle worldviews, to hurdle the distance between myth, reality, and dream.

> Les larmes coulaient de ce puit de solitude qui était mon âme. Je me laissais pleurer et m'entendais parler de suicide. Suicide? Le terme m'avait toujours effrayé en même temps que fasciné. Le suicide était si rare au village. Je n'y avais jamais connu de suicide.
>
> Le cas de suicide se passait toujours ailleurs. Le motif en était tellement sacré qu'on n'en parlait qu'au grands moments. Si le suicide était tout ce que j'avais trouvé pour remédier à cette angoisse qui semblait s'être installée en moi pour toujours, je ne pouvais pas me permettre d'hypothéquer ma vie à un prétexte. (P. 171)

> [Tears were flowing from the well of solitude that was my soul.
>
> I let myself cry and heard myself talk of suicide. Suicide? It was a term that had always frightened me and fascinated me at the same time. In the village suicide was so rare. I'd never known of one there. Suicide always happened somewhere else. Its motive was so sacred that it would be talked about only at very important moments. If suicide was all I could find to remedy the anguish that seemed to have pervaded me forever, I couldn't afford to mortgage my life to a pretext.] (P. 149)

Ken's depression-melancholia mode can be read as a cultural symptomatology pointing to the problems of imitation, projection, identification, and a sense of loss and mourning. In such a mode, the schizophrenic typically feels hopeless, worthless, and considers life an unbearable torment. There is often the desire to punish oneself by self-destruction, or there is, at least, much evidence of suicidal thinking. Ken's extreme case of alienation leads to temporary madness and to the contemplation of suicide.

> J'étais à l'ultime étape où il n'y avait plus que le suicide pur et simple. Sans analyse. (P. 178)

> [I'd reached the final stage where only suicide was left, pure and simple. Without any analysis.] (P. 155)

It is, however, important to note that Ken's death wish is not so much a desire for self-annihilation as it is an ardent Phoenix-like desire, a surrealist desire, to die in order to better *become*. As self-punishment, Ken considers suicide to be an end as well as a beginning—in short, to be a rebirth.

> La conscience de tout ce qui m'était arrivé si loin du village où je suis née, me faisait prier Dieu de me faire renaître comme si presque un quart de siècle n'avait jamais été. (P. 180)

> [My consciousness of everything that had happened to me so far away from the village where I was born made me pray to God to let me be born again as if almost a quarter of a century hadn't happened.] (P. 157)

The Third Dimension: Cultural Schizophrenia and the Challenges of Translation

Schizophrenia, as I use it here, refers to that reactive schizophrenia typified by Ken's existence. Reactive schizophrenia is precipitated by events in an individual's life and is characterized by relatively mild thought disorders of the schizo-affective manic-depressive type, with recurrent cyclical melancholia and moods of elation and depression.

The Abandoned Baobab by Ken Bugul forces the reader to confront the phenomenon of *cultural* schizophrenia.

Metropolitan centers such as Paris and Brussels are magnets for migrants from the former colonies, the protectorates, and territories who search for improved economic, political, social, and cultural lives. Undeniably, these urban centers are culturally dynamic and stimulating. However, "these rich tapestries of cultural difference" rarely succeed day by day as "big tents," "beautiful cultural mosaics," or "harmonious melting pots." These metaphors of harmony seek to depoliticize the political. Particularly since decolonization, with the forced return of colonials to the homeland and the increased numbers of immigrants and guest workers and their combined competitive entry into the workforce, cosmopolitan centers have become conflictual spaces. Inevitably, because of commerce, trade, treaties, wars, colonialisms, borrowings, prestige, domination or subordination, all cultures undergo hybridizations of some kind. Of the many discussions of *métissage culturel,* transculturation, and cultural braiding, the one I find most interesting is that of the French philosophical thinker Michel Serres. *Le Tiers-Instruit* (*The Third Nature*), with the hermaphrodite-twin-rainbow reverie of Harlequin as the embodiment of métissage, would envision cultural blending as an elevatory, almost ascetic, process of self-instruction and ennoblement leading to cultural harmony and enrichment—the inevitable consequence and benefit of contact, exchange, and marriage with alterity. "Tout apprentissage consiste en un métissage" [Every apprenticeship involves a process of hybridization]; "Aime l'autre qui engendre une troisieme personne en toi, l'esprit" ["Love the other who engenders a third person in you, the spirit"].

For some a vision such as Serres's could be a bit anodyne. Homi Bhabha would insist that the importance of hybridization is the presence of difference at the point of the articulation of alterity. Any claim to an ongoing difference is always surmounted by its displacement; hybridity allows one to confront the incommensurable without solving it. While Serres's vision is utopian, perhaps, his analysis is not simplistic. It is an ethic that does not seek to gloss over, depoliticize, or repress the conflictual dimensions of colonialism, decolonization, postcolonialism, and migrancy. In fact, *Le Tiers-Instruit* can be read both as a recognition of the extraordinary challenges laid down by contact with the Other and as an appeal for harmony, understanding, and mutual growth. In *The Abandoned Baobab,* Ken Bugul is forced to confront the dual cultural forces that have shaped her double consciousness and given rise to her third consciousness.

Serres's and Ken Bugul's texts can be read as meditations on migrancy, the challenges of which are part of the etiology of cultural schizophrenia. Ken's dislocations and relocations will be punctuated by her moves from the tiny bush village of N'doucoumane to the village of the French high school, to Dakar, to Paris, to Brussels, from street to street, from apartment to apartment. Not merely a spatial phenomenon, moving is profoundly psychological and sociological in its implications. As observed in *The Sand Child* by Tahar ben Jelloun, one does not move from one life to another simply by crossing a footbridge. Migrancy entails status inconsistency, role conflict, and shifts in consciousness that, together, constitute a radical learning experience.

> Partir exige un déchirement qui arrache une part du corps à la part qui demeure adhérente à la rive de naissance, au voisinage de la parentèle, à la maison et au village des usages, à la culture de la langue et à la raideur des habitudes. Qui ne bouge n'apprend rien. Oui. Pars, divise-toi en parts. Tes voyages risquent de te condamner comme un frère séparé. Tu étais unique et référé, tu vas devenir plusieurs et parfois incohérent, comme l'univers, qui au début éclata, dit-on, à un grand bruit. Pars, et alors tout commence, au moins toute explosion en mondes à part. Tout commence par ce rien.
>
> Aucun apprentissage n'évite le voyage.[17]
>
> [Leaving is a wrenching experience that tears one part of the body away from the part that remains attached to the shores of one's birth, to the neighborhood of one's family relations, to the house and village of customs, to the culture, to language, and to the straightjacket of habits. He who does not move learns nothing. Yes, leave, divide yourself into parts. Your voyages run the risk of condemning you to the fate of a separated sibling. You were unique and with reference points, you are going to become multiple, at times incoherent, like the universe which in the beginning exploded, we are told, in a big bang. Leave, and everything will begin in a world of explosions into separate worlds. Everything begins with this little effort.
>
> No learning can take place without displacement.]

In *The Abandoned Baobab,* Ken sums up the challenge of migrancy very simply by observing that "one cannot simply replace one consciousness with another." She goes on to analyze her double schizophrenic consciousness as giving rise to a third dimension within the unconscious. The culturally schizophrenic are challenged to make contact with this third dimension of consciousness:

> Contenir la sourdeur des pulsions qui assurent en partie l'équilibre, l'épanouisssement du soi défini. Les jours passaient comme des rêves inavoués. L'être qui devait naître dans le subconscient comme les termites font leurs termitières se dissimulaient dans une tierce dimension. (P. 113)

> [One must absorb the muteness of the drives that partly ensure equilibrium, the blossoming of the undefined self. The days went by like unavowed dreams. The being that was to be born in the unconscious, like termites making their anthills, was hiding inside a third dimension.] (P. 97)

Ken's sense of hope for herself and the African future, as well as her intellectual and mental *competence,* prevent her from committing clinical suicide. She dies unto herself in order to free herself of the mental colonization that has precipitated her into the *destructive* space of cultural schizophrenia. The *equilibrium* of the passage above reminds the reader that Ken's story is concerned with balance and survival in postcolonial societies.

Ken's "epic," as she refers to her life, is an example of what can be referred to as "the challenges of translation," that is, the tremendous struggle involved in negotiating the transit from one culture to another. The struggle involves maintaining one's psychological stamina and equilibrium in *the circulation of ideas* and in *the traffic of desires* between cultures, during inevitable alteration of the values of non-European communities. As a consequence, one is aware of the Echo-Narcissus temptations.

In the Echo phenomenon of assimilation, one surrenders completely, as Ken did, to "becoming" French. Léon Damas's poems "Hiccups" and "Sellout" (see chapter 2) address this pattern, this parodic existential absurdity and the rebellion against it. The Narcissus imperative, in which one retreats into the contemplation of self and, particularly, one's cultural heritage for the purpose of cultural affirmation, is discussed by Aimé Césaire in "Narcisse noir" (see chapter 1). The challenges of the postcolonial global community make either choice unviable. We are obliged to oscillate between the Narcissus position of allegiance to our own culture and the Echo position of assimilation.

It is the challenge of transnational adaptability that can lead to a schizophrenic panic, such as the schizophrenia depicted in Ken's story of transculturation. Resistance to the wrenching life experiences of postcolonial economies involves not simply denunciation, nor the celebration of the past, nor nostalgia for an Edenic return to sources; rather, resistance involves the *study* of emergent problems, of the potentially disabling experiences of cultural hybridity, of the failures of migrancy and transplantation, and of the difficult negotiation of the sociopolitical/psychosexual challenges of the postcolonial period. This, for me, is the merit of such a disturbing text as *Le Baobab fou,* because all of these challenges are "caught" in its web.

Ken returns to Africa at the end of the text in order to rediscover what she abandoned. Like Césaire's laminarian seaweed, Ken discovers herself still attached to the site of her origins. Perhaps, in her search for an *inclusive* transnational fluency, Ken will explore the *constructive* spaces of cultural schizophrenia where Echo, the assimilationist self, and Narcissus, the nativist self, will not vie for the soul and psyche of the postcolonial subject—but where the two will give birth to that third dimension, where the lost *balance of the inner ear,* which she pierced and traumatized as a child, will be recovered, and where healthy survival in the enabling hybridity of a cross-cultural postcolonial global village will be assured. Ken's ability to slip the potentially strangling knot of cultural conflict derives from her ability to understand and internalize the European moves, but then to evacuate the internal field of illusions, complexes, desires, and lies that had led her to the contemplation of suicide. The madness that was initially self-destructive eventually serves as an anticolonialist strategy and hence becomes emancipatory for Ken. The processes of cultural hybridity allow one *to confront* the "incommensurables," "the collision of formulas" in postcolonial contexts, without necessarily solving them. As Ken survives the temptation of suicide, there is abandonment of Europe and a new displacement to the rediscovery of the lost Mother Africa. As she takes up a new life beneath the standing but dead Baobab tree, the reader senses the beginning of a new autobiography of Ken Bugul that will trace "the blossoming of the undefined self."

III

Counterconfession

8

Words Proffered in Pain

Gérard Etienne, Shame, and the Counterconfession

To speak as though tomorrow I will die . . .
Mzwake Mbuli, poet, rock musician, tortured South African political prisoner

In the Denunciatory Tradition

"I was 'a graduate' of the peculiar institution . . . *with my diploma written on my back.*' It did not entirely satisfy me to *narrate* wrongs; I felt like *denouncing* them. I could not always curb my moral indignation for the perpetrators of slaveholding villainy long enough for a circumstantial statement of the facts."[1] Thus spoke Frederick Douglass (1817?–95), the American slave who escaped from Maryland and became an abolitionist lecturer, orator, publisher, politician and, toward the end of his life, United States minister resident and consul general to Haiti. His life's purpose was to "energetically assail the ramparts of Slavery and Prejudice, be they composed of church or state, and seek the destruction of every refuge of lies, under which tyranny may aim to conceal and protect itself."[2] In francophone America and following the tradition of the narrative politics of a Frederick Douglass, Gérard Etienne is one of the most denunciatory, provocative, and aggressive writers from the Haitian diaspora. Born in Cape Haitian, Haiti, he currently lives, writes, and teaches in the heart of Acadia in New Brunswick, Canada, where he is a professor of linguistics and journalism. Throughout his narratives and writings, Douglass drew inspiration and moral indignation from his whip-striped back, the bound wrists, and the bloody cracked feet of the martyred slave body in nineteenth-century America. In his writings, Etienne draws inspiration and moral indignation from the tortured human flesh of his Haitian compatriots. The aggressiveness of his prose and poetry emerges from the repressive sociopolitical realities of Haiti during the 1957–1990 dictatorships of the Duvalier regimes. Etienne's writing is a testimony that denounces the undemocratic Haitian history of social injustice—its exploitation and oppression of the Haitian masses not only by foreign merchants but especially by a succession of feudalist totalitarian Haitian leaders. Etienne's work is intellectually challenging in that it raises questions that assault neat, comfortable conceptions of race and racism, culture and acculturation, sanity and insanity, the nature of forced exile, the representation of the Haitian woman, and the status of Haitian literature, as well as Haitian voodoo and consciousness.

The pivotal text in the career of Gérard Etienne is entitled *Le Nègre crucifié, récit* (The Crucified Black, Narrative).[3] It is, indeed, the text that sketches the breadth of philosophy and psychology contained in Etienne's most recent novel, *La pacotille*.[4] Despite the Christological and Eucharistic suggestions in the title, with its focus on the martyred Black body, the shattered mind and broken speech, the novel is not about the expiatory elevation of a Black host. The crucifixion of this Haitian political prisoner does not lead to redemption. Unlike the death of Christ, the crucifixion of a Black man has never saved the world and led to the regeneration of the human spirit. The narrative is preoccupied with the psychological shifts provoked by pain of all kinds—physical, psychic, political, and moral. All of these forms of pain are sharpened and brought to the surface of consciousness through the actual experience of torture during the last forty-eight hours of the prisoner's life. The narrative succeeds in moving beyond the specificity of one detainee in the confines of a tropical prison to embrace the daily martyrdom of the Haitian people. Under the successive metamorphoses of Duvalier regimes, the entire country has seemed a vast dungeon, with the entire populace as political prisoners and the bourgeois capitalist elite as an army of torturers. *Le Nègre crucifié, récit* marks a turning point in the career of Gérard Etienne, not only because of the vehemence of the language and the social critique contained therein but also because this text—with its seeming automatic writing, obsessions, flashbacks, and flashforwards—maps the moral, political, symbolic, and affective universe of Gérard Etienne. In his writings there is a renunciation of the patriarchal, a Jungian, Bachelardian embrace of the feminine within the man, and a feminist critique of the Black Haitian woman's condition. There is also in this work an elaborate meditation on the diverse experiences of exile from one's country while living abroad, as well as the peculiar sense of foreignness one can experience within one's country, one's family, and the self. As my analysis will demonstrate, for me *Le Nègre crucifié, récit* functions as the *unconscious* of Etienne's literary corpus. It is the intertext that informs all other Etienne texts and upon which these texts—novels and poems—all converge. In all of his works, Gérard Etienne bears witness to the paradoxes of the history of the "First Black Republic" and the immiserization of the Haitian people. Etienne dreams of a future of democracy in Haiti while documenting the atrocities of Haitian life under a Black totalitarian kleptocracy. The fundamental narrative force in francophone literary culture is counterstorytelling and its related, dependent genre, the counterconfession, of which Etienne's work is a fundamental example. For the subjugated, the counterconfession is a form of survival through a linguistic project and productivity outside of the confessional scenes of the prescribed and coercive spaces of the church confessional, the courtroom, or the torture chamber.

Torture

The question of torture[5] is a constant in Francophone literary culture, and yet in some ways, beyond the "rememory" of the brutality of the slave experience, torture is repressed and is a part of the "unspeakable." The irony is mordant as Aimé Césaire, in *Discourse on Colonialism,* confronts the brutality, savagery, and beastliness of the "European civilizing mission":

> The conclusion is inescapable: compared to the cannibals, the dismemberers, and other lesser breeds, Europe and the West are the incarnation of respect for human dignity.
>
> But let us move on, and quickly, lest our thoughts wander to Algiers, Morocco, and other places where, as I write these very words, so many valiant sons of the West, in the semi-darkness of dungeons, are lavishing upon their inferior African brothers, with such tireless attention those authentic marks of respect for human dignity which are called, in technical terms, "electricity," "the bathtub," and "the bottleneck."[6]

Césaire specifically evokes the case of Algiers in the *Discourse on Colonialism.* In the 1966 film *Battle of Algiers,* directed by Gillo Pontecorvo, the colonel in charge of putting down the unrest is interviewed by the world press, particularly concerning the use of torture by the French as a means of domination, control, and extortion of information about the rebel underground. An American journalist raises the question of the "methods used by paratroopers" to gather information once they have arrested suspects. A French journalist dismisses the discreet circumlocutions of the American and says directly, "Let's talk about torture." Colonel Mathieu, the commanding officer, rejects the term *torture,* preferring the concept of "interrogation" as a valid "method" against clandestine organizations. Mathieu explains that the "problem" is simple: The Algerian National Liberation Front (FLN) wants to expel the French from Algeria and the French want to remain. When FLN activists are arrested, they maintain silence according to their strict code of behavior for at least twenty-four hours in order to allow the FLN time to reorganize its strategies, safe houses, and meeting places. The "question" according to Mathieu becomes: "Is France to remain in Algeria? If your answer is still 'yes,' you must accept all the consequences." The consequences seem to be the inevitability of torture.

The interview segment is a moment of moral questioning and justification of the violence and the use of torture in the French campaign to maintain its colonial domination in Algeria. It is also a sublimated version of the "confession scene" in political torture, and Mathieu refuses the role of the interrogated, transforming his interrogators into collaborators. This segment is followed by a torture sequence that recalls the opening scene of the film in which an emaciated Algerian traitor succumbs to the pain of torture. The opening scene features only slaps to the face. The room, however, is full of the tools of the torture trade: water, shower nozzles, rubber hoses, electroshock equipment, and tape recorders to document "confessions." The sequence following the interview has an eerie religiosity. Organ dirges accompany scenes featuring a succession of prisoners and different means of torture, which follow one another like a string of prayer beads. There is suffocation, water torture, the burning of flesh with a blowtorch, and electroshock while French policemen, either fascinated or indifferent to the human suffering, smoke, laugh, and engage in conversation. Some prisoners are trussed up and suspended from the ceiling, to be subjected to all manner of corporal invasion. Other prisoners hang as though from a crucifix, with heads rolled back and eyes gazing questioningly like so many images of Christ on the cross. A woman with a single tear streaming down her face gazes unblinkingly at the broken bodies, like a Mother Mary staring at the crucified body of Christ. The film sequence complements the reading of Etienne's *Nègre crucifié, récit.*

The challenge to nations who have successfully thrown off the colonial yoke is to guard against replacing the old domination with a new one. Césaire's theater of decolonization deals with the challenges that face the newly independent nation and the legacy of the dehumanizing process of colonialization that Césaire explicates in his *Discourse on Colonialism:*

> For my part, if I have recalled a few details of these hideous butcheries, it is by no means because I take a morbid delight in them, but because I think that these heads of men, these collections of ears, these burned houses, these Gothic invasions, this steaming blood, these cities that evaporate at the edge of the sword, are not to be so easily disposed of. They prove that colonization, I repeat, dehumanizes even the most *civilized man;* that colonial activity, colonial enterprise, colonial conquest, which is based on contempt for the native and justified by that contempt, inevitably tends to change him who undertakes it; that the colonizer, who in order to ease his conscience gets into the habit of seeing the other man as an animal, accustoms himself to treating him like an animal, and tends objectively to transform himself into an animal. It is this result, this boomerang effect of colonization, that I wanted to point out. (P. 19)

In particular, Césaire's plays indict the excesses and pitfalls of national consciousness and postindependence leadership. All too often, the revolutionary leaders become dictators, as in the case of Mobutu of Zaire, as exposed in the play *A Season in the Congo,* or earlier in history, King Henri Christophe of Haiti, whose mad and impossible dreams for the Haitian people are dramatized in *The Tragedy of King Christophe.* For Gérard Etienne, the Haitian author of *Cri pour ne pas crever de honte* (*Scream to Keep from Dying of Shame*),[7] part of the shame is due to his disappointment in the legacy of the Haitian revolution of 1804, the betrayal of the Haitian people by a succession of despots as bloodthirsty as the former colonial leaders, and the treachery of Black-on-Black criminal domination and exploitation.

The Political Prisoner

In this century of Gandhi, Angela Davis, Malcolm X, Martin Luther King, Andrey Sakharov, Alexandr Solzhenitsyn, Dennis Brutus, Nelson and Winnie Mandela, and Mzwake Mbuli, the words of the political prisoner often have been the thorn in the side of society, its conscience and moral gadfly. The limbo status of the political prisoner, the physical and psychological abuse of the detainee, and the daunting apparatus of a legal system are but signs of the times. Testifying, testimony, and moral testament are three of the driving narrative principles of francophone literary culture. Testifying, testimony, and testament are secular and nonsecular phenomena. To testify is to bear witness, to give evidence as a witness, to make a solemn oath or affirmation in a judicial inquiry for the purpose of proving or establishing some fact. Testimony properly means only such evidence as is delivered by a witness, either orally or in the form of affidavits or depositions, in the trial of a cause. Testament refers to the disposition of one's real and personal property.[8] In the religious, musical, and literary contexts, testifying, testimony, and testament overlap. Testifying is to bear witness in church, to stand and make personal testimony, an avowal of faith and belief in God. In many Black churches, before the services commence, there is a period in which all members who so desire are permitted to stand and make verbal proclamations and avowals of their belief in God and confess their foibles and sins. Confession of one's sins, bad deeds, and life story originally took place in church, but it now also takes place in music and literature and through other forms of art.[9] In Etienne, the reader witnesses the autodiegetic narrator challenging the self to remember every horrific detail of past political sufferings and social indignities, thus placing the self and society on trial. Those in attendance, the reader-narratees, are witnesses.

It is particularly in the writing of the tortured political prisoner that these phenomena—testifying, testimony, and moral testament—emerge in greatest relief to become a genre. For the dominated outgroup, the torture chamber and the courtroom, the torturer and the cross-examiner, are flip sides of the same fundamental experience. In colonial situations, both the torture chamber with its sadomasochistic rules of the game and the courtroom with its ponderous, suppressive rules of evidence and procedure extract certain coerced, led, or limited statements. This observation leads to an expansion of the discussion of counterstorytelling (see chapter 4) with the dynamics of what might be a subgenre. Such narratives might properly be called *counterconfessions*. This genre would include the statements that are either prevented from inscription into the courtroom or the torture scene or are withheld intentionally by the victim. Counterconfessions are the voluntary narratives existing outside of, but in direct counterpoint to, torture-chamber confessions and courtroom testimony. These narratives reveal the experiences, thoughts, intentions, driving emotions, moral dilemmas, and the "irrelevant" and "inadmissible" evidence that the participants feel compelled to relate once freed from the coercion or gag of the torturer or the cross-examiner. It is a counteroffensive to the interrogation (*une contre-offensive à l'interrogation;* see *La pacotille,* p. 253). In its content and tone, Gérard Etienne's writing is a model of the counterconfession, as the following example from *La pacotille* suggests:

> Refus de mon bon ange de céder aux rugissements des loups-garous. Plutôt la mort que la honte, le suicide que l'humiliation, le débordement d'un fleuve que le bouillonnement d'une source. (P. 21)

> [Refusal of my good angel to yield to the roars of the werewolves. Rather death than shame, suicide than humiliation, the overflow of a river rather than the boiling of a spring.]

The passage cited points to an interior monologue that refuses inscription into the scene of torture and that is part of the language of counterconfession:

> Si seulement on écrivait un seul poème qui dirait un corps mutilé. (P. 207)
>
> [Ah . . . if only one could write a poem that could express a mutilated body.]

The experiences of physical torture, exile, cultural schizophrenia, and the grand dream of a woman liberator are the organizing obsessions in the work of Gérard Etienne. His novel *La pacotille* is driven, in a word, by the concept of dislocation. The text is structured in narrative blocks that alternate between the past and the present, the loss of will and the recovery of psychological stamina, and the changes in locale and decor that reflect the contemporary psychic and geographic dislocation of the Haitian diasporic experience, particularly between the United States, Canada, and Haiti. The narrative is driven from obsession to obsession, shifting among reflections on the moral condition of *La pacotille,* on the torture by the *beast,* and the painfully ravishing dream of a female opposite who is redeemer, mediator, and liberator. The feminine obsession is completed by the protagonist's tyrannical, carnal love for the lost mother and the complexity of his sense of abandonment and exile. Historical documentation, firsthand testimony, journalistic reporting, inventories, statistics, poetry, confessions, dreams, visions, songs, rhythms, and screams: the full range of verbal expression is exploited in *La pacotille.*

La pacotille*: The Title*

Gérard Etienne does not forge neologisms, as do many francophone writers, but he invests his vocabulary, nouns especially, with a polysemy that confers on the word all of its multicultural and historical force. The novel title is an example. A definition of *la pacotille* that embraces the different contexts in which it is used in the novel as well as its usage in plantation societies might read as follows:

Pacotille: *noun.* Term used to designate the inauthenticity of objects such as jewelry, furniture; the poor quality of a house, such as a shack; cheap goods often of local or regional manufacture; in certain former highly racially mixed colonial societies, e.g., Brazil, term used (*pacotilha*) especially to designate Mulattoes or those Blacks who approached the ideal of humanity, beauty, and intelligence but who, nonetheless, would never attain it according to the racial assimilationist mythology of the dominant society, which unceasingly reminded them of their inferiority; term of subordination, contempt, and wretchedness; term of pity, affection and self love, a term of value, therefore, with ontological, social, and racial dimensions; a child, a dispossessed being, buffeted by life's tragedies, an uprooted wandering person; in Creole, old clothing and metonymically the wearer of such; nothing, a nothing (person), a person who has nothing and is considered less than human by the ruling elite, the wretched of the earth; a person whom another can use, treat, and mistreat as an object, slave, or prey.[10]

La pacotille and the Beast

The precise identity of *la bête,* the dehumanized despot, the animal or the beast in *La pacotille,* evolves in relation and according to the circumstances and experiences of the *pacotille,* identified as a crucified, tortured Haitian Black, a Haitian immigrant and/or the protagonist named Ben Chalom, all of whom are sons of peace. The beast is a terrible patriarch, a father, the storm-trooper secret police, the corrupt in the service of the grand beast, the monster, the president of the nation that is a "pigsty." Most often the beast has the identity of the political leader according precisely, in my opinion, to the meaning that Frantz Fanon gives this term: The leader or *Le leader,* is, more often than not, a son of the people who, once elected by the people and enjoying full electoral and presidential powers, betrays the people by imposing a dictatorship that is nothing less than a transformation of the old colonialism into a new intraracial colonialization. The leader replaces the former colonial officer and himself becomes a beast using the same arsenal of control as the former colonial power in order to expand and consolidate his personal wealth and power. The beast resorts to forced labor, slavery, repression, terror, massacres, deportations, the police, the domination of one ethnic group by another, and torture. The beast seems to have the fantastic or uncanny power to change forms and to be omnipresent through time and space. The beast is the old colonizer, as Césaire describes him in *Discourse on Colonialism,* the new leader in the person of François Duvalier, President-for-Life, "the most ferocious of beasts in the Caribbean," (*La pacotille,* p. 143) the ton-tons Macoutes or secret police, the Canadian, French, or American immigration officer. This latter figure is a milder incarnation of the beast, but Ben Chalom's encounters with the various immigration officials also reveal the acceleration of his neurosis. In the shape of a shadow or an alter ego, the beast can insinuate himself into the psyche in the form of the madness that inhabits the will and mind of the oppressed:

> Quoique je fasse, je demeure un zombi de la bête. Où que je sois, la bête est sur mes traces. (*La pacotille,* P. 224)
>
> [Whatever I do, I remain a zombie of the beast. Wherever I am, the beast is on my trail.]

> N'être qu'un bourreau, toute sa vie, sans un seul moment de bonheur où le cœur vibrerait aux douleurs des autres. Arracher les ongles d'un prisonnier, le transporter dans un cercueil d'un endroit à l'autre. Briser ses os à coups de pierres. Suivre les préceptes des intemporels. Demeurer enfermé dans la haine, la peau du faible, l'envie de la solitude du faible, ceci jusqu'à la vieillesse, voilà la bête. (P. 56)
>
> [To be only an executioner, all of one's life, without a single moment of the kind of happiness where one's heart vibrates in sympathy with the pain of others. Tearing out the fingernails of the prisoner, transporting him in a casket from one place to another. Breaking his bones under the crushing blows of rocks. Following the rituals of the demonic. To remain shut up in hatred, the skin of the weak, the envy of the solitude of the weak, and all of this up through old age—that is the beast.]

> J'avais prononcé le nom de la bête. Une seule fois. Dans une métaphore. Voilà qu'il s'en souvient. . . . il a pu identifier le parasite qui m'a fait connaître tant de nuits blanches. (P. 253)

[I had pronounced the name of the beast. One single time. In a metaphor. And there he remembers it. . . . He has been able to identify the parasite that has caused me to know so many sleepless nights.]

D'être la chienne de la bête. (P. 254)

[To be the she-dog bitch of the beast.]

A travers vos confidences, j'ai cru comprendre que cette bête-là a été produite par votre peuple. (P. 254)

[According to your revelations I believe I understood that this beast has been produced by your people.]

Obsession quotidienne, l'Immigration canadienne. Permettez monsieur que je vous étrangle, que j'incendie votre ville, que je marche sur votre cadavre. Permettez monsieur l'Officier qu'avec mon baton magique je vous transporte dans mon écurie pour faire mon chemin de croix, de la même façon que votre Christ sous les griffes d'une bête, sous les bottes d'un bourreau. . . . Je vous rends un grand service en vous etranglant. Je vous débarrasse de la plus cruelle maladie qui détruit votre race, la haine d'une espèce. (P. 148)

[Daily obsession, Canadian immigration. Allow me, Sir Officer, to strangle you, to burn down your city and walk on your corpse. Permit me, Mister Officer, with my magic wand to transport you into my stable so that you might redo my road of the cross in the same way as your Christ under the claws of the beast, under the boots of an executioner. . . . I am doing you a great service by strangling you. I am ridding you of the cruelest affliction that is destroying your race, the hatred of another race.]

This last passage constitutes a multiple allusive redescription of the colonizer's various incarnations through history. The following passage exposes Ben Chalom's awareness of the damage also done to him by his experiences, obsessions, and neuroses.

On trouvait au début une explication à mes troubles de personnalité. L'exil forcé. Le dépaysement qui rend la vie amère. Encore plus amère pour ceux qui ne reverront jamais leur coin de terre. On le comprend.

> Ce qu'on ne comprend pas, c'est la destruction de la personne par la personne, c'est le plaisir de se saigner dans son cercle, de succomber au moindre repli de la conscience. (P. 167)
>
> [In the beginning they found an explanation for my personality disorders. Forced exiles. Homesickness which makes life bitter. Still more bitter for those who will never ever again see their corner of the earth. It is understandable. What is not understandable is the destruction of the self by the self, it is the pleasure of bleeding oneself in one's circle, of withdrawing to the innermost regions of the mind.]

Shattered Consciousness: From the Dynamics of Torture Toward an Aesthetics of Pain

Le Nègre crucifié and *La pacotille* are exposés of the dynamics of the torture of political prisoners in Haiti. In their literariness, these texts elaborate an aesthetics of pain. The silent scream, as depicted in paintings such as the *Guernica* of Pablo Picasso and as seen on innumerable posters from countries dominated by totalitarian regimes, is universally recognized as a symbol of torture. The gaping mouth of the scream, such as the one figured on the cover of the second edition of *Le Nègre crucifié,* draws attention to the two fundamental aspects of the torture process—the physical and the verbal. The ensemble of physical and verbal relations between the torturer and the prisoner always comes down to relations of domination and subordination. The verbal relations include the interrogation, the confession, the screams, and the voice both of the torturer and the prisoner. The physical relations include the torture, the voice and shouts of the torturer as instruments of command, the voice and screams of the prisoner as expression of compliance, the body of the torturer which inflicts pain, and finally, the flesh of the prisoner, the site of pain in the extreme where the body as flesh becomes a carnal knowledge of the point of intersection between life and death.

The torturer, on one elementary level, is seeking "information" or "confessions." In the grander scheme of domination, what is sought is the recognition by the prisoner of the power of the torturer and the omnipotence of the political regime he or she represents. In Etienne's words, the aim of torture is "the pulverization of the mind" (*La pacotille,* p. 51). The task of the torturer is to break the prisoner's will, first by isolating him from the world so as to better expose the prisoner to his own constitutional fragility by inflicting upon him physical, psychological, and spiritual pain. Nothing is eliminated as a potential weapon in the torturer's arsenal of pain. He of course uses the instruments traditionally associated with torture, such as those that figure on the aforementioned cover of the second edition of *Le Nègre crucifié:* handcuffs, eye bandages, whips, branding irons, shackles, the boot, the rack, the head screw, the spiked iron collar, the cippus, the stock, and so on. One learns from Etienne's works that torture, as an institution, perverts the function of the most banal objects and uses them to inflict pain. The comforts of civilization such as water, electricity, furniture, walls, doors, windows, the dog, and cigarettes become enemies. State-sponsored torture, totalitarianism, and brutal repression of the kind seen in Haiti result in a contamination of everything that is the norm. The law, the court, judges, medicine, and the hospital and doctors are accomplices that align themselves against the political prisoner. The most intimate experiences become experiences of terror: sleep, sexuality, and the prisoner's body and physiology are turned against him in order to humiliate him in the extreme. Everything is perverted, but, especially, everything is deconstructed so as to contribute to the disintegration of the mind of the prisoner. While the emphasis seems to be on the physical torture of the body, the ultimate goal is the destruction of the mind. This process of destruction of the mind is dramatically documented in an example taken from recent history outside of the Haitian context. Under the Fascist regime of Mussolini, at the trial in 1928 of the Italian political prisoner Antonio Gramsci (1891–1937), the state prosecutor declared, "We must stop the workings of this man's brain for the next twenty years."[11]

From the example of Gramsci one can conceive of the torture of a political prisoner as the resolution on the part of authorities to shut down and destroy the functioning of the political prisoner's mind. One learns from the fate of Etienne's pacotille:

La bête veut recommencer à zéro.

La seule chose, dira-t-elle à la milicienne, c'est la pulvérisation de la pacotille jusqu'à ce qu'il fasse nuit dans ses yeux, que ses cendres soient répandues sur les perrons de la cathédrale, qu'il reconnaisse l'erreur de sa mère pour l'avoir poussée. (P. 51)

[The Beast wants to start all over again.

The only thing that matters, it said to the woman soldier, is to smash this pacotille to pieces until there is nothing but night in his eyes, until his ashes are spread on the grand steps of the cathedral, until he recognizes the mistake his mother made in giving birth to him.]

J'ai cessé de compter les coups de fouet, de matraque, de coups de pied. Elle n'arrêtera jamais de frapper malgré les consignes du Chef des tortionnaires avant le supplice. Décapiter la pacotille en se foutant du cri des femmes, des bêtes dociles, des oiseaux migrateurs. La décapitation d'un corps humain, du genre humain, d'un membre de la race. La décapitation. Plus une seule compensation à la laideur de la bête, aux gaz qui lui pètent le ventre, aux ulcères qui la font déparler durant les cérémonies aux esprits. Saigner La pacotille, décapiter un garçon, rompu aux idées d'égalité, de justice, d'amour-propre.

Toujours sous les griffes de la bête. (P. 51)

[I stopped counting the lashes of the whip, the blows of the club and the repeated kicks. The woman soldier will never stop hitting despite the orders of the chief of torturers before the flogging. The only thing that matters is decapitating the *pacotille,* not giving a shit about the screams of the women, those docile beasts, those migratory birds. The decapitation of a human body, of the human species, of a member of the race. No further illusions about the ugliness of the beast, with the gases that explode from his belly, the ulcers that make him speak in tongues during dark ceremonies with the spirits. Stick and bleed the *pacotille,* decapitate this boy filled with ideas of equality, justice, and personal dignity. Always under the claws of the beast.]

One notices the tenacity with which the pacotille cultivates his attachment to the homeland and to the memory of his innocence as weapons against the beast.

Je ne veux pas me tenir pour battu en me laissant absorber par un nouveau pays. (P. 101)

[I don't want to simply give up as beaten by allowing myself to become comfortably assimilated in a new country.]

> Oh non. Je ne dois pas du tout me sentir à l'aise à la caféteria du Centre social. Je ne renoncerais à la corde qui me relie au pays. (P. 218)

> [Oh no. I must not allow myself to feel comfortable in the cafeteria of the social center. I would never break the cord that ties me to my country.]

> Avec tout ce qui peut rendre à un gosse sa virginité, ses fantaisies lumineuses, ses soirs légers, ses jeux à la marelle, ses mots d'amour au cœur des demoiselles. (P. 176)

> [With the wish for everything that can give back to a child his virginity, his shining fantasies, his light airy evenings, his hopscotch games, his sweet words of love spoken to the heart of innocent young maidens.]

> Si je pouvais m'oublier un seul instant afin de retrouver ma virginité, quelle victoire sur la bête, quel triomphe en ce bas monde. (P. 242)

> [If I could forget myself just for an instant in order to recover my virginity, what a victory over the beast, what a triumph in this low and rotten world.]

The Narratology of the Counterconfession

The question of form imposes itself because *Le Nègre crucifié* has as its subtitle the word *récit,* or *narrative.* Normally, *narrative* refers to "the history," to the diachronic, and one has recourse to speaking of a referential text and a chronology. In textual semiotics, however, the narrative refers to the structure underlying the discursive manifestations.[12] In Etienne's texts, most often the narrator is autodiegetic, that is, inside the narrative and also the main character. I repeat a point made earlier that in Etiennian narrative, the reader witnesses the autodiegetic narrator challenging the self to remember every horrific detail of past political sufferings and social indignities, thereby placing the self and society on trial. Those in attendance, the reader-narratees, are witnesses. The subtitle underscores the literary act of witnessing. This literary act is perhaps the most powerful form of witnessing. Both *Le Nègre crucifié* and *La pacotille* are narratives. Here the literary act of witnessing is a fictional narrative illustrating, with the effect of facticity through documentation, the seemingly fantastic and unspeakable truths of political detention and physical torture. The narrative is crafted to provoke a reaction of outrage in the reader. The Nègre crucifié or the protagonist in *La pacotille* is, himself, author, witness, actor, participant-in-history, observer-journalist, narrator, and survivor. The closer le nègre or la pacotille is to death, the more determined he is not to lose his memory, the more sensitive he is to the possibility of the loss of memory, and the more determined he is to recount, recite, narrate, document, and write his memoir, or counterconfession.

When one understands the struggle on the part of the political prisoner to maintain a measure of coherence in his consciousness, which has been shattered by the experience of torture, the characteristics of this narrative of the Nègre crucifié are more understandable: fragments, a chorus of "characters" as foils of the self; a thought process that moves forward in fits and starts; thoughts and speech interrupted most likely by the physical and verbal interventions of the torturer; flashbacks; reappearing thoughts, seemingly unmotivated observations, zigzags in the narrative sequence; and temporary unintelligibility. These phenomena, along with the tone of urgency and an orality in the writing style, raise the question of whether or not this narrative can be called automatic writing. I think not. What matters, however, is that there is an impression of automaticity. As the semiotician Michael Riffaterre would say:

> La différence définitoire, c'est que le texte automatique fait fi de toute logique, bouleverse les séquences temporelles, ignore la référentialité. . . . Qu'elle soit spontanée ou imitée, je l'appellerai effet d'automatisme. Tout texte où cet effet est observable appartient au genre dit "écriture automatique." . . . Sa littérarité ne consiste pas à être une dictée du subconscient, mais à en avoir l'air. Les incompatibilités qui ont cet effet sont de véritables agrammaticalités. . . . L'absurde, le non-sens, par le fait

même qu'ils gênent le décodage, contraignent le lecteur à une lecture directe des structures.[13]

[The defining difference, is that the automatic text dismisses any concern for logic. . . . upsets temporal sequences, ignores referentiality. . . . Be it spontaneous or feigned, I shall call it an impression of automaticity. Every text where this effect is observable belongs to the genre called "automatic writing." Its literariness does not consist of being a dictation of the unconscious but of appearing to be such. The incompatibilities that have this effect are true agrammaticalities. . . . The absurd, nonsense, in that they disturb easy deciphering, force the reader to do a direct reading of the structures.]

Le Nègre crucifié as a narrative is an act of survival *through linguistic productivity.* In *Le Nègre crucifié, récit* the reader falls upon the phrase "to think by a juxtaposition of images." A cogito of torture is being elaborated: I am in deep pain, I am dying, I am going "to think," be it only "by a juxtaposition of images" (p. 83) and therefore I shall survive. The narrative as a notation of the thoughts that coursed through the pulverized mind of the prisoner is "reproductive." According to Julia Kristeva, there is productivity when the text (*récit*/narrative) makes work of language.[14] In maintaining the tension between the physical and the verbal dimensions in the torture of the political prisoner, the narrative can be conceived of as a defense against the destruction of the flesh, against the disintegration of the mind, and against the invasion especially of the *silence* of death. This is talking for survival and talking in order to testify, to bear witness and testimony, and to leave a moral testament. The writing is, indeed, to quote from a title of a volume of Etienne's poetry, *Le Cri pour ne pas crever,* the scream as a defense against succumbing to death. After escape, writing becomes a victory over oblivion. One of the overwhelming experiences of the political prisoner is the fear that no one knows what is happening, that he or she has been forgotten, and this fear is reinforced by the torturers. The counterconfessional testimony of the surviving political prisoner becomes therefore a triple victory over shame, personal and collective amnesia, and the intimidation tactics of torture and human rights abuse. The need to testify is clearly articulated in *La pacotille:*

> Il faudra raconter, oui, raconter aux dieux absents de mes tribulations, si je sors du cauchemar. . . .
>
> Même dans un long cauchemar. Contre de nouvelles formes de microbes, ces tueurs aux dents longues, ces démons au menton carré qui détraquent ma parole, mes mots, mon feu, ma poésie. Oui. Il faudra raconter la fuite des esprits sous la mitraille, raconter, raconter mon nègre, sans tricherie, avec le souci de la vérité, la vérité de ma dépossession, de mon impuissance devant la verge du major Romain, raconter, Seigneur, jusqu'à ce que se libère l'oiseau de l'espoir de la masse de poussière couvrant mon cimetière tropical. (P. 21)
>
> [I must recount all of this, yes, tell the absent gods of my tribulations, if I come out of this nighmare. . . .
>
> Even in a long nightmare. Against new forms of germs, against these killers with long fangs, these square-jawed demons who unhinge my speech, unsettle my words, stir up my fire, shake up my poetry. Yes. I will have to tell of the flight of the spirits under machine gun fire, recount, tell, my black brother, without deception, with the scruples of truthfulness, the truth of my dispossession, of my impotence in front of the penis of Major Romain, tell it all, dear Lord, until the day comes when the sweet bird of hope will rise from the deep dust that covers my tropical cemetery.]

Language as work and project allows the prisoner to regain control, be it but momentarily, of his body and even allows him to give orders to his torturer: a perverse and defiant kind of masochistic contract develops between the torturer and tortured.

> Une flamme sort de ma bouche. Je la lance en haut des châteaux qui sont des siècles de typhoïde d'un peuple dépossédé de sa matrice et de ses champs de bananes.
>
> Fornique-moi, Chef, jusqu'au coucher du soleil. Fornique-moi. Parce que j'écris ton nom sur mes excréments, fornique-moi pour ça. Je sais qu'à ce moment on est en train d'écrire une histoire semblable aux histoires des Révolutionnaires cacos qu'on raconte, les soirs à la chandelle celle d'un condamné à mort, aux oreilles de bourrique, d'écrire mon enfance sur des feuilles de cocotier, sur le sang, sur le mensonge. (P. 35)

[A flame shoots out of my mouth. I hurl it above the castles that are the centuries of typhoid of a people dislocated from its matrix and its banana plantations.

Fuck me, Boss, until the sun goes down. Because I am writing your name on my excrement. Fuck me for that. I know that at this time a story is being written similar to the stories told about the peasant "Caco" Revolutionaries at night by candlelight the story of a man condemned to die, with the ears of a donkey, writing my childhood on coconut palm leaves, on blood, on the lie.]

As a narrative, *Le Nègre crucifié* is written in incomplete phrases and fragments that express the broken, fractured body parts that litter the tropical cemetery of Haiti. One might be tempted to speak of Etienne's orality, when in fact his narrative is more stream-of-consciousness interior monologue that is experimenting with novelistic form and music—the gamut of human expressivity, including and especially writing itself (labels often obscure more than they illuminate). One must be cautious and clear when describing orality in a text by a Black writer, because, unfortunately, as Eileen Julien has underscored, "orality" has become a metonymy for "African."[15] An urgency and a certain *orality* in the highly wrought *writing* style of this narrative underscore the rich semantic field signified by the term *parole* or *word.* This text is parole in that it is a plea. It is parole evidence, as the record of a life lived and as eyewitness testimony; as a conditional release from prison, as in "on parole"; as "*parole d'honneur,*" word of honor, in which the individual swears to maintain silence concerning the details of a dread event. The irony is that *Le Nègre crucifié,* as a narrative, is consciousness *transcribed* in words, parole, and honor *written.* Etienne writes the "unspeakable."

Gérard Etienne's fragmented style is perfectly illustrated in the following paragraphs, which expand my sense of the orality of his writing. There are blocks and angles of expression that isolate events and emotions or give temporal, spatial, and affective perspective to events and emotions. The result is the effect of a certain geometry and calculus in the seeming dementia of language. In terms of *ekphrasis,* his style approaches that of cubism and expressionism, as is seen in the painting *Davertige,* which appears on the cover of *La pacotille.* If I have insisted on the word (parole), I can emphasize equally the rhythm of the Etiennian paragraph as being imposed by recurring syntactic structures in the initial position. These rhetorical parallelisms punctuate the fragments, or writing blocks, with melodic, semantic, or pausal rhythms that contribute to the text's orality.

> Obsession quotidienne, l'Immigration canadienne. Si au moins on connaissait l'officier qui va vous recevoir, si au moins on connaissait le fondé de pouvoir à qui on a affaire, on pourrait lui faire des yeux doux, vanter sa beauté, son intelligence, la supériorité de son pays par rapport à la France; on pourrait jouer à l'ange, à l'enfant de chœur de l'oratoire Saint-Joseph, au nègre qui consent à baisser la tête devant monsieur Blanc, à se faire traiter en esclave, en perpétuel garçon de cour; on pourrait reconnaître son infériorité, l'avilissement de sa race, l'humiliation de ses ancêtres pendant quatre cents ans d'esclavage; on pourrait jouer à la victime de méchants loups de la même manière que le Président qui, en assassinant, crie pourtant au secours; au garçon qui a perdu sa virginité avant même l'âge de la croissance; on pourrait offrir une sœur en victime expiatoire, jurer sur la tête de sa mère qu'on se montrerait reconnaissant, qu'on accepterait même d'être une fois par semaine le valet de chambre de celui qui vous a sorti du pétrin. (P. 142)
>
> [Daily obsession, Canadian immigration. If at least one knew the officer who was going to receive you, if at least one knew the power exercised by the person one is dealing with, one could flatter him, praise his beauty, his intelligence, the superiority of his country compared to France: one could play the angel, the choir boy from St. Joseph's, play the nigger who consents to bow his head before Mr. Whitey, who allows himself to be treated as a slave, as a perpetual boy: one could recognize his inferiority, the vileness of his race, the humiliation of his ancestors during four hundred years of slavery; one could play the victim of treachery . . . in the same way as the President who while assassinating someone screams for help; one could play the boy who has lost his virginity well before adolescence; one could offer a sister as a sacrificial victim, could swear on the head of one's mother that one would show oneself to be grateful, that one would accept being the valet once a week of the person who would get you out of this mess.]

Rarely binary, the structure is most faithfully a compound three-part jazz harmony: /__/__/__/. Still more rhythmic and marked by reiteration is the following example, in which Etienne himself seems to be addressing the question of counterstorytelling, that is, the history of colonization from the perspective of the colonialized:

> Dans les brousses africaines où il nous apprenait le péché en nous faisant découvrir la nudité des femmes. Dans les cases de nos ancêtres où le génie nègre sauva le Blanc des maladies qu'il ne connaissait pas. Dans les bois du pays où le nègre entra sa langue dans le cul du Blanc afin de le débarrasser des vers qui le rongeaient, des parasites qu'il attrapait pendant sa longue traversée du désert. Deux mille ans, monsieur l'Officier. Deux mille ans l'ont vu avec sa flèche abattant des animaux pour le festin des rois, pour les ciboires en ivoire, en cuivre, en argent. Cela ne s'est jamais dit. On ne l'a jamais appris, monsieur l'Officier. On détruirait la civilisation si on disait aux enfants blancs qu'autrefois, dans une colonie française, le nègre apprenait tout seul à lire au milieu de Blancs analphabètes, si on enseignait l'histoire, la vraie, celle de la race qui, même décimée dans les négriers, pouvait quand même trouver le courage pour construire des villes où sa présence donne maintenant la trouille aux mêmes vagabonds qui n'ont jamais voulu que le soleil engendre d'autres espèces que la leur. (P. 147)
>
> [In the African bushes where he taught us of sin by explaining to us the nudity of our women. In the huts of our ancestors where black genius saved the white colonizer from the illnesses he did not understand. In the woods of the country where the black stuck his tongue up the white man's ass in order to rid the European of the worms that ate at his insides, and the parasites he caught during his long trek across the desert. Two thousand years, Mr. Officer. Two thousand years saw him with his bow and arrow bringing down animals for the feast of kings, for the platters in ivory, copper, and silver. That was never spoken of. We never learned about that, Mr. Officer. Civilization would be destroyed if one told the white children that before, in a French colony, Blacks learned to read all by themselves among illiterate Whites, if one were to teach all of the history, the full and complete one, that of the race who even after having been decimated by the slave traders could just the same find the courage to construct cities where their presence instilled fear in the same vaga-

bonds who had never wanted the sun to give rise to any species other than their own.]

In these typical Etiennian paragraphs, one notes an urgency that is linguistically realized by (1) regular syntactic breaks, as in: *In the African bushes where* he . . . *In the huts of our ancestors where* black genius . . . *In the woods of the country where* the black; (2) a language stripped of all unnecessary or nonfunctional grammatical elements; (3) an elimination of introductory elements or presentations: one enters directly into the heart of the subject without preparation or transitions as in *Daily obsession, Canadian immigration;* (4) a preference for nouns or nominalization; and (5) the suppression of conjunctions, verbs, and predicate forms. The result would be a movement or structure such as the following: Cœur battant. Souffles. Elle marche. Pas de voitures sur la route. Heart beating. Huffing and puffing / She walks / No cars in the street.

Gérard Etienne, or the Theology of Exile

Particularly in *Nègre* and in the long poem *Cri* Etienne elaborates the problematics of modern exile. At the time of the publication of the first edition of *Le Nègre crucifié, récit,* Claude Roy wrote: "I received *Le Nègre crucifié, récit* like a wave so violent sweeping over me that, still today, I remain stunned from it."[16] With such responses, how then can one explain the relative silence that surrounds Etienne's work, which can only be described as extraordinary? Absent from most anthologies and most of the so-called panoramas of francophone literature, Etienne's work is nonetheless noted by the great curator and critic of Haitian literature, Léon-François Hoffman. Writing about the novels of Haitian exiles who attacked the Duvalier regimes, Hoffman reflects,

> Je pense . . . au *Nègre crucifié* de Gérard Étienne. . . . La chose n'a rien d'inusité en soi, nous avons vu que la politique est une préoccupation constante des romanciers haïtiens, et ce dès les origines. Ce qui est nouveau, c'est l'extrême violence et l'obsession de la torture qui se retrouvent dans les romans publiés dans les vingt dernières années . . . pour autant toutefois que ce soit vraiment un roman: l'auteur a sous-titré son oeuvre: "récit." Il s'agit en fait du long monologue halluciné d'un

prisonnier politique à la veille de son exécution, qui se voit et se dit crucifié, "cloué au Carrefour du Cimetière, exactement à l'angle des rues Monseigneur Guilloux et Alerte." Cette litanie insoutenable dénonce les tortures et les exécutions, la misère, la saleté, la maladie et la famine du peuple, les plus sadiques perversions sexuelles et le gouvernement des Américains par Haïtiens interposés. D'une façon qui mériterait une analyse détaillée, Gérard Étienne disloque la syntaxe pour la recréer selon une nouvelle logique, désarticule le temps et, à coups d'images inusitées, se forge un langage personnel.
. . . la recherche non pas tant de nouveaux thèmes que d'un enrichissement des thèmes existants par une nouvelle expression.[17]

[I think of *Le Nègre crucifié, récit,* by Gerard Etienne. In and of itself the theme is not unusual, we have seen that politics are the constant preoccupation of Haitian novelists, and this from the beginning. What is new is the extreme violence and the obsession with torture that is repeated in the novels published in the last twenty years. To the extent that it can be called really a novel, the author has subtitled his work "Narrative." It is in effect a long hallucinatory monologue by a political prisoner on the eve of his execution who sees himself and declares himself crucified, "nailed at the Crossroads of the Cemetery, exactly at the intersection of the streets Monseigneur Guilloux and Alerte." This unbearable litany denounces the torturings and executions, the misery, the filth, the sickness and the famine of the people, the most sadistic sexual perversions and the government of the Americans through Haitian intermediaries. In a way that would merit a detailed analysis, Gérard Etienne dislocates syntax in order to recreate it according to a new logic, disarticulates time and tenses and with strokes of unusual imagery, forges for himself a personal language. . . . There is not so much the search for new themes as there is an enrichment of existing themes through the expression of a new language.]

Although the sense of impotence weighs upon the exiled writer, there exists in Gérard Etienne an awareness of the power of the word that proclaims the truth as well as the necessity of breaking the silence, as this excerpt from *Cri* indicates:

Ah! vous seriez contents
si je me taisais
Alors crevez crevez avec ma vérité

Mourez avec mes cris
avec mes laideurs
Je vous force à vomir votre portrait
cette plate littérature
où dans la boue vous roulez
oubliant l'esclavage et votre ami le Chef
Crevez vous m'entendez
Et quand ils auront porté les murs du palais
sur leurs épaules d'esclaves
Vous resterez seuls avec Michaux
et ses dieux grecs
Car bouffons mes amis nous voilà rassurés
car leur logique formelle pourrit notre poésie (P. 62)

[Ah! You would be very happy
If I were to shut up
Well then, burst, explode with my truthfulness
Die with my screams
With my uglinesses
I am forcing you to throw up from your own self-portrait
This flat literature
Where you wallow in the mud
Forgetting slavery and your friend the Leader
Die, do you hear me?
And when they will have carried the walls of the palace
Upon their shoulders of slaves
You will be left alone with Michaux
And his Greek gods
Because my friends, you buffoons,
Here we are reassured
For their classical logic rots our poetry.]

Is this a manifesto for a more engaged literature? Etienne seems to be responding to the silence, hesitation, and uneasiness that have for so long surrounded his name and the reception of his work. What is the explanation for this silence? Is it the shock—indeed, the scandal—of his uncompromising style, his indefatigable attention to detail in the description of torture, the horrors, and sexual cruelty, his unleashed subjectivity in a state of psycholinguistic delirium that no longer recognizes the proprieties of good taste? Is it his strident, staccato tone? His *vox clamantis in deserto* John-the-Baptist style? Bearing witness is more than memory; it involves the integration of memory and recollection and the analysis of past events for the benefit of the community. Etienne's work is, above all, a bearing witness to everything that has befallen him, and especially everything that has happened in Haiti under the Duvaliers.

> ô mémoire accrochee au passé douloureux des esclaves . . .
> par-dessus mon silence et mon analphabétisme . . . (P. 23)
> Maître de mes souffrances bourreau de mes amours
> donne-moi la force d'escamoter le mal. . . .
>
> Et ne me demande pas de poétiser mes langages. Je suis
> de la race des voleurs, des assassins. . . . (P. 24)
>
> J'ai besoin de ta colère . . .
> J'ai besoin de ta haine pour . . .
> J'ai besoin de mon passé, papa. (P. 35)
>
> Rends-moi ma mémoire pour inscrire dans ma poésie chaque geste du puissant, mon ennemi, pour que je n'oublie rien, pas même les cadavres de mes amis sur lesquels dansaient les valets du Chef, pas même les orgies de Rochambeau qui invitait les femmes à venir assister à l'égorgement de leurs maris, pas même le refus d'une négresse de s'asseoir près de moi pendant que des bandes de carnavals noyaient dans le clairin les douleurs d'un peuple de mendiants
>
> Le passé est à moi. . . .
> Je veux l'assumer, papa. . . . l'assumer (P. 36)

> [O memory clinging to the painful slave past.
> Over and above my silence and my illiteracy . . .
> Master of my sufferings executioner of my loves
> Give me the strength to overcome the pain. . . .
> And please do not ask me to poeticize my language.
> I am of the race of thieves, of assassins. . . .
> I need your anger. . . .
> I need your hatred in order to . . .
> I need my past, man.

> Give me back my memory in order to inscribe into my poetry every gesture of the powerful one, my enemy, so that I will forget nothing, not even the corpses of my friends upon whom the leader's valets danced, not even the orgies of Rochambeau, who used to invite wives to come so that they might attend the slaughter of their husbands, not even the refusal of a black girl to sit next to me while carnival gangs drowned the pain of a people of beggars in cheap rum
>
> The past is mine. . . . I want to assume it, man. . . . assume it.]

The existence of this Haitian voice is a perpetual state of exile—social and political, psychological and emotional, linguistic, geographic, and metaphysical. Although he uses the word *exile* often, the word, the sensation, or, rather, the experience that is most Etiennian is that of "*la déchirure,*" the tear, the rip, the tearing away, the rending, or the wrenching. "La déchirure" is the sense of the deep wound suffered and the gap created by the wrenching experience of the separation of the self from a preferred place, milieu, persons—even from a favored self. These breaks are paradoxical in that they are at one and the same time a devastating blow to the emotions and an awakening of consciousness. The loss of harmony leads to the recovery of the native land and the lost self through the work of the imagination, language, and "poetic creativity." Rather than poetic creation, Gérard Etienne might say "poetic escape," although the language in the text is not so much escapist reverie as it is revolutionary protest, rage, and outrage. As the crucified Black tells us in *Le Nègre:*

> Il y en a qui font avec leurs ongles des bateaux sur les murs de leurs cellules pour se sauver de la prison. (P. 85)
>
> [There are those who with their fingernails on the walls of their cells make little boats in order to escape from prison.]

> du mendiant mon ami mon double mon déchirement
> J'écris mon exil. (*Cri,* p. 11)
>
> [From the beggar my friend, my double, my unbearable pain
> I write my exile.]

les bras en croix . . . . (*Cri,* p. 12)

Je ne sais comment étudier ton absence
Je veux te dire ma déchirure
Je veux te dire ma typhoïde
la vie me saigne
la vie me tue
J'irai chercher un peu de pluie
pour prolonger un poème de mer (P. 13)

J'écrirai grand dieu mon premier testament
avec une forte douleur au ventre et à l'esprit
avec un rien d'amour dans ma vie d'exilé (*Cri,* p. 15)

[My arms crossed
I do not know how to study your absence
I want to tell you of my deep wound
I want to tell you of my typhoid
Life is bleeding me
Life is killing me
I shall have to search for a bit of rain
To prolong my poem of the sea

I shall write great god my first testament
With a tremendous pain in the belly
And in the spirit
With not a sprig of love in my life as an exile]

l'image se développe sous l'acide et l'amour
lance ta vie par-dessus l'impuissance (*Cri,* p. 16)

[The poetic image is developed out of acid and love
Raise your life over and above this impotence]

The prisoner is confronted with the need to write and, at the same time, the impossibility of writing, which forces him to use the very elements of his incarceration as writing tools: the walls of the prison, his excrement, his blood, or coconut leaves, and especially the tablet of his mind.

In *Le Nègre crucifié,* exile[18] reveals itself to be a succession of experiences of separations and losses of harmony along a via dolorosa. This way of the cross leads back to the Haitian mother. Forced departure from the mother country, the loss of the mother tongue, expulsion of the child from the knees of the mother, weaning, and, finally, birth are experienced as a series of falls from paradise. A perfect example of survival through linguistic productivity is the letter the death-row prisoner writes in his mind to his mother.

> Si j'écris à ma mère, pense mon personnage, pour lui dire qu'elle a eu tort de m'avoir mis bas!
>
> Chère maman, je t'écris une lettre. Ne t'occupe pas des mots. Dans cette lettre, ils ont des pattes de mouches. Chaque phrase va te faire vomir. Tu sais que la langue des Blancs de France n'est pas faite pour ma cervelle. C'est une langue de taureau à dix cornes, chère mère.
>
> Je t'écris pour te dire que j'ai mal de vivre loin de toi, que depuis ton dernier voyage, je mets mon pigeon dans la derrière des poules. Mon père me laisse courir dans le quartier avec des pantalons déchirés. Il me fouette le matin, le midi et le soir.
>
> La domestique de Madame Rodriguez vient de faire un bébé sans jarrets. Les zombis de cette femme sont responsables de ce malheur. Je ne sais si tu as une radio dans le pays des Dominicains. Mais tu dois savoir qu'il y a d'autres figures après le massacre des Roinègres d'Haïti, d'autres coquillages aussi. Je fais le serment de te mordre et de te faire crier. Ce sera ma façon de te remercier de m'avoir mis bas, un jour de noirceur. Je te demande pardon. J'ai besoin de rentrer encore dans ton ventre pour sortir vingt ans après.
>
> Je dis ce qui est dans ma tête. Je n'aime pas mentir. Il faut me faire confiance, car je perds chaque jour la dignité de la parole. Il me faut aussi des livres de dépotoirs. Les nègres d'Haïti n'ont pas de livres de dépotoirs. Ni des journaux où l'on montre aux enfants l'électricité.
>
> En écrivant cette lettre, je te fais mal, beaucoup de mal. Ce n'est pas bien d'aimer sa mère, comme je t'aime. Cela me rends de plus en plus nègre.
>
> Si tu savais comment on est en Haïti: un zombi sous les bottes du Chef.
>
> Maintenant, d'autres détails. Les bâteaux des Américains sont dans la rade de Port-au-Prince. Deux tontons devant moi crachent la tuberculose. Il y a aussi les enfants d'Eloïse, tu t'en rappelles? Ils ont toujours des pians de la tête aux pieds. Ensuite, il y a mon ventre qui me fait mal.

Je ne sais pas ce que j'ai dedans. Il est comme un ballon dirigeable qui risque de péter un jour.

Aujourd'hui, j'ai dit beaucoup de choses. Je n'ai pas d'amis, maman. Tu comprends ça, toi.

Mon personnage lit et relit la lettre. Pour lui c'est une faiblesse d'écrire comme ça. Il déchire la lettre et la mange.

On le regarde faire. La foule est enragée. Il faut t'accepter comme tu es, pense-t-il. (P. 41)

[What if I write to my mother, thinks my character, in order to tell her that she was wrong to have dropped me into this world!

Dear Mother, I am writing a letter to you. Don't worry about the words. In this letter they have a spidery scrawl. Each sentence is going to make you throw up. You know that the language of the whites from France is not made for my brains. It's a language of a bull with ten horns, dear mother.

I am writing to you in order to tell you that I suffer from living far from you, that since your last trip home, I stick my bird into chickens. My father lets me run about the neighborhood in torn pants. He beats me morning, noon, and night.

Madame Rodriguez's servant has just given birth to a baby without legs. The zombies of this woman are responsible for this misfortune. I don't know whether you have a radio in the country of the Dominicans. But you must know that there are more problems after the massacre of certain prominent men in Haiti, more political mess as well. I swear when you return that I am going to bite you and make you cry out for having given birth to me. It will be my way of thanking you for having dropped me one black day. I'm sorry, please forgive me. I just want to go back inside your belly and not be born until twenty years from now.

I am saying what is in my head. I don't like to lie. You have to believe in me, because every day I am losing the dignity of speech. I also need schoolbooks. Blacks in Haiti don't have schoolbooks. Nor even newspapers where one can show electricity to the children.

I know I am causing you pain, great pain. It's not good to love one's mother the way I love you. It just makes me more and more a weak Black man.

If you only knew how we exist in Haiti: a zombie under the heel of the Leader.

Now, more details. The ships of the Americans are in the harbor of Port-au-Prince. Two secret policemen in front of me are spitting up from tuberculosis. There are also Eloise's children, do you remember them? They still have yaws from head to toe. And then, there is my belly that aches. I don't know what's inside of me there. It's like a dirigible balloon that runs the risk of exploding one day.

Today, I have said lots of things. I have no friends, mother. Do you understand that?

My character reads and rereads the letter. For him it is a weakness to write like that. He rips up the letter and eats it.

We watch him. The crowd is outraged. You must accept yourself the way you are, he thought.]

Without any real action in terms of plot development *Le Nègre crucifié* is composed of shouts, screams, memories, desires, projects, and projections into the future while the prisoner-narrator awaits death, at times longing for it. This situation of imminent death and dreams of the future is the crucial contradiction that opens the door onto literary creation, that is, onto the subtitle, the *récit,* or narrative. This tortured Black man, detained in one of the leader's infamous prisons, most often in a state of delirium from physical pain, dialogues with himself or with his double, whom he addresses as "my character," "you," "my portrait," "my shadow," and "the beggar." As foils of the self, they possess "a disturbing strangeness and yet a strange familiarity." The above-cited letter to the mother exemplifies elaboration of the different dimensions of exile and alienation. It posits these experiences as being fundamentally related to the maternal image and obsession. In canto 7 of *Cri,* Etienne writes:

L'absence de toi dans mes brûlures
l'absence de toi dans mon désir
. . . .
la télévision–corde ombilicale le reliant à la terre
mère. (P. 37)

[The absence of you in my burning sensations
The absence of you in my desire . . .
The television–umbilical cord tying him to the
motherland.]

In the letter to his mother, the prisoner outlines the problems of his *déchirure,* or gaping, deep wound. The overwhelming sensation is one of abandonment, of a tearing away and expulsion, which has as a consequence at least five different levels of alienation. Birth is recalled as a fall and exile from the uterine garden of the mother, with the two successive expulsions from the mother's breast and knee. The prisoner's exile is typically modern in that it is a marginalized state of one who lives as an outsider in the heart of his most intimate community. This alienation is spatial, linguistic, social, and political. The mother is absent. Absence is always experienced as a longing for the maternal, the motherland, the mother tongue, the family, the community. In Etienne's universe, the coordinates of his space will be marked by Port-au-Prince, Haiti, France, Canada, Quebec, Montreal, New Brunswick, and Moncton. The fifth dimension of the prisoner's alienation takes the form of psychological repression. After the expressive release of pent-up emotions—the composition of the letter—"his character," as the text indicates, eats the letter—an act that signals the return of the psychological mechanism of repression. The eating of the letter represents the unwillingness or inability to let go of his emotional pain. Etienne's counterconfession is the transcription of the enduring effects of torture and the daily pain of life under a dictator.

pour cette torture que je traine à mon réveil et
pour toutes les amours interdites à ma race d'esclaves
L'Espoir est une route, une rue:
. . . cette route vers la terre natale (P. 17)

[For this torture that I drag with me during my
every waking hour and for all of the loves forbidden to
my race of slaves
Hope is a way, a street:
. . . This road toward the native land]

je t'écris aujourd'hui mon premier testament
dans un cri de honte étranger à mon sang
Je te l'écris avec la même haine dans la prison
les mêmes accords lyriques qui terrassent mes ennemis
J'ai dit les bêtes et ma légende

la honte et ma faiblesse
J'ai mis les doigts dans ma gorge
où s'inscrivent des clameurs gonflées de révoltes. (P. 64)

[I write for you today my first testament
In a scream of shame foreign to my blood
I write it for you with the same hatred as in prison
The same lyrical harmonies that brought down my
enemies
I have told of the beasts and my legend
The shame and my weakness
I have dug fingers into my throat
Where the swollen clamorings of revolt inscribe
themselves.]

There is in Etienne's work a poetics of desire and projections, silence and shouting. In *Le Nègre crucifié* and *Cri,* anguish and the implosions of potential, frustrated desires are most often concretized as a sensation of swelling from within: the aching stomach, the belly bloated, "comme un ballon dirigeable qui risque de peter un jour" [like a dirigible hot-air balloon that runs the risk of exploding one day, the long-dormant volcano]. The locus of loss and lack seems to nurture a desire to break out of the state of negation, to leap forth, and to hurdle obstacles, as well as a will to open, to puncture, to pierce the sky with one's will, presence, and witness.

lance ta vie par-dessus l'impuissance . . . (*Cri,* P. 16)

[Raise your life above this impotence.]

Je me suis mis à chanter, à danser, à trouer le ciel, à perforer mon estomac, comme si ma souffrance était à l'origine du monde, que j'étais fait pour porter des cathédrales sur mes épaules et retrouver mon équilibre après chaque regard de pitié. (P. 27)

[I began to sing, to dance, to pierce the sky, to puncture my stomach, as if my suffering were at the origin of the world, as if I had been made to carry cathedrals on my shoulders and regain my equilibrium after each look of pity.]

Voici que mes voiles se déploient lentement . . .
et je ne regrette pas que tu m'aies façonné
O ma noirceur mon génie . . . (P. 43)

[And so now my sails unfold slowly
and I do not regret that you have fashioned me
Oh my blackness my genius]

Shame

The primal scream in Etienne's work seems to me at one and the same time a compensatory gesture, an exorcism, an affirmation of life, a bearing witness, and finally silence and solitude broken. It is a gesture of protest "against a world of torturings, tears, cries, injustices, against the drought that persists in Haiti despite the rain that ravages the countryside" (*Nègre,* p. 105). The primal scream is also the recognition of and deliverance from shame. The shame evoked in the letter to the mother and in *Cri pour ne pas crever de honte* is developed later in *Le Nègre crucifié.*

J'ai honte d'être un demi-homme à qui on refuse un peu d'eau. Même l'eau des morgues. Honte de sentir monter en moi tant de haines. De voir des bras tendus, d'entendre des discours dont chaque mot est un crime commis à minuit. Honte des nègres qui se cachent le jour pour sortir la nuit enlevant aux mères de famille leurs fils, leurs filles, leurs oncles, leurs tantes, leur papa, leurs domestiques. Honte de ma figure noire. Honte de cette décomposition de moi en mille consciences, en noms sans histoire qui pulvérisent le peu de Révolutions qu'on veut encore laisser à mon cœur. (P. 83)

Mon vocabulaire a des bornes. Le seul mot de misère est déjà pour moi un livre de philosophie. (P. 87)

[I am ashamed of being half a man to whom they refuse to give a little water. Not even the water of stagnant ponds. Ashamed of feeling rise within me so many hatreds. Of seeing my arms hang down helplessly, of hearing speeches whose every word is a crime committed at midnight. Ashamed of those Black men who hide during the day only to come out at night kidnapping from mothers their sons, their daughters, their uncles, their aunts, their fathers, their servants. Ashamed of my Black face. Ashamed of this decomposition of myself into a thousand consciousnesses, into names without stories that crush the few revolutionary thoughts that still remain in my heart.

My vocabulary has some limits. The word *misery* alone is already for me a book of philosophy.]

This is *panopticism,* in the most horrific Foucauldian sense, of the universal widespread techniques of coercion of all the forces and the bodies of a given society made to submit to the sovereignty of the dictator. The omnipresent *gaze* of the beast also has, as a consequence for Etienne, *shame* in a Sartrean sense.

Shame implies the recognition of what one has become, in particular the recognition that one is as the Other sees one—as a nothing, as less than human, as a *pacotille*. Shame is also the awareness of oneself as simultaneously invisible, yet visible, that is, of one's status as an object fixed by the Other's gaze, and knowledge that one's individual freedom and self-determination have been engulfed and denied by the intrusive, coercive freedom of an omnipotent Other. In the passage above, Etienne transcends his objectified, humiliated, and atrophied status to accede to an awareness of the self as full of possibilities in a humanistic, economically democratic society.[19]

Etienne undeniably writes for a Haitian public. The experience of the Haitian diaspora, however, expands the space from the island to the Americas, Europe, and Africa. At the end of *Le Nègre crucifié,* the prisoner can only state:

Tout ce que je sais, c'est que je ne suis pas un nègre d'Haïti, mais un homme du monde. (P. 146)

[All that I know is that I am not a nigger from Haiti but a man of the world.]

Etienne's position reminds us of the original context in which the word *négritude* was originally used by Césaire in the *Notebook of a Return to the Native Land:* "Haïti où la négritude se mit debout pour la première fois et dit qu'elle croyait à son humanité" [Haiti where negritude stood up for the first time and stated that it believed in its own humanity]. Further, Etienne's declaration recalls the centuries-old affirmation by the freed Carthaginian slave Terence, who declared his feelings of solidarity with humanity in the phrase from his play *Héautontimoroumenos* (*The Man Who Punishes Himself*): "Homo sum: humani a me nihil alienum puto" [I am a man: therefore nothing that is human is strange to me]. Etienne acknowledges his affinities with Quebecois, Acadian, and American culture. His vision addresses what is fundamentally human, but through the lens of his very particular Haitian experiences. For Etienne, torture and exile are experiences of expansions, bridges, borders, and crossroads.

The letter to the mother is for me the key microtext that summarizes the knot of tensions present throughout Etienne's work and that reveals the complexity of his exilic state. The nostalgia for a return to the prenatal paradise, a vague death wish, the mystical vision of an affective union, the desire for an integration of the split, fragmented self, the drive to become something other, and utopian dreams of a universal harmony are the preoccupations that give rise to Etienne's poetics of crosses, crossings, and crossroads. Hermes-Saint Peter-Legba, all guardians of crossroads, twins, Gemini and Marassa, the voodoo twin demigods—all make their presence felt in Etienne's discourse. They are figures of differentiation, frontiers, endings, and initiations. As embodiments of the crossroads, they express the desire to be free of the limbo state, to cross the bridges that lead to the promising beyond, to move beyond the present to make the transitions, and to transcend the distance between history and myth, reality, and dream. They dramatize a Janus vision that is simultaneously retrospective and prospective.

For Gérard Etienne, language and exile are passions in the religious sense of suffering and exaltation, asceticism and elevation; and yet, the crucified Black prisoner is not a figure of realized redemption, ecstasy, or fulfillment. The Christological symbolism is ironic and disturbing. This tortured Black prisoner is often what not only Terence but also Charles Baudelaire would call *l'Héautontimoroumenos,* the man who punishes himself through his own personal pain. "Je suis donc mon propre bourreau" (*Nègre,* p. 79) [I am therefore my own executioner]. It is this personal suffering that expands the consciousness of the prisoner to an all-embracing human compassion.

Gérard Etienne, creolophone, francophone, anglophone, professor of linguistics at the University of Moncton, New Brunswick, is a man of the world. He is indeed a man of the crossroads, a nomad, a Black wandering Jew, an uprooted man solicited by many voices, by many demons, by many languages. The subtitle of the preceding section—*A Theology of Exile*—is inspired by the complexity of the ironized Christological experience of Etienne's work. Hector Bianciotti's description of a linguistic adventure grasps the ambiguous adventure of the passionate, linguistic exile of Gérard Etienne (see chap. 1, pp. 52–53).

Gladys or the Etiennian Woman

> O toi mon compagnon, mon double imaginaire,
> nous avons franchi les ronces, les volcans
> et la peur. Nous avons accompagné nos morts au
> purgatoire et fait pivoter le ciel autour de l'amour.
> Arbre tordu de ma raison pour qui j'écris
> la vie à conquérir, laisse ta mélopée pour mes
> peuplades en deuil. Car je crie et je veux mourir
> sans tes nuits de fraîcheur qui frissonnent en moi
> comme une brise de mai.[20]
>
> [Oh you, my companion, my imaginary double,
> we have crossed over the brambles, the volcanoes
> and the fear. We have accompanied our dead to
> purgatory and made the sky pivot around our love.
> Twisted tree of my reason for whom I am writing of
> the life to be conquered, leave your recitative for my
> tribes in mourning. For I cry out and I want to die
> deprived of your nights of freshness which shiver
> through me like a breeze in the month of May.]

As the above excerpt suggests, in Gérard Étienne's texts the projection and doubling of the self lead to a complementary *récit* or counterconfession that analyzes the paradoxes, torturous temptation, and difficulties of love under racist and totalitarian conditions. The following excerpt from an interview-discussion of his novel *Une Femme muette* is one of the most condensed illustrations of the functioning of Etienne's analyses and literary creation:

Lorsque Gros Zo annonce à Penny une blonde de Toronto, qu'il est marié, Penny qui sort avec Gros Zo lui dit: "T'es un menteur, T'es un hypocrite . . ." Alors Gros Zo lui réplique: "Mais non, la femme dont il s'agit est un esprit." Penny lui dit: "Mais ce n'est pas possible. Si c'était un esprit tu n'en aurais pas parlé avec tant de chaleur." Et elle décide d'aller en Haïti rencontrer Maîtresse Erzulie. Toutes les filles de l'hôpital sont d'accord avec elle, s'il y a une Maîtresse Erzulie dans la vie de Gros Zo il faut que tu ailles la rencontrer. Mais Penny, craintive, demande à Gros Zo: "Bon, Napoléon, et si Maîtresse Erzulie refuse l'autorisation?" Et Gros Zo de répondre: "C'est pas possible. Elle l'aurait fait pour une négresse mais pas pour toi. Parce qu'au fond, Maîtresse Erzulie est une blonde aux yeux bleus, elle a de longs cheveux, elle est svelte comme toi. Donc tu comprends, pour toi Maîtresse Erzulie ne refuserait pas son autorisation pour que je t'épouse." C'est comme ça dans la vie réele des nègres haïtiens: Maîtresse Erzulie, c'est notre femme en premières noces. Je me rappelle, à ce moment j'avais des problèmes en Haïti, et mes parents sont allés voir un hougan, la première qu'il leur a dit: "Écoutez, il est temps que Gérard épouse Maîtresse Erzulie.

Donc voilà, toute ta vie, à partir de quatorze ou quinze ans, on t'apprend à coucher avec une femme blanche, une blonde aux yeux bleus. Toute ta vie, tes fantasmes, tes psychoses, tes névroses, tout ça passe par Maîtresse Erzulie. Parfois tu te couches sur ton lit, tu éjacules, en pleine adolescence, et on te dit le lendemain matin: Tu as fait l'amour avec la Maîtresse." Ou encore: tu vas au lit le soir, tu mets du parfum sur ton lit, espérant que Maîtresse Erzulie vienne coucher avec toi. Mais c'est triste ça dans la vie d'un peuple. Ainsi quand Gros Zo dit à Anne-Marie que "T'es une négresse. Je ne t'aime pas," ou bien "Ma femme rêvée est une blonde." Qu'est-ce que tu veux? C'est ancré même dans notre subconscient. Voilà ce que le vodou fait de nous aujourd'hui. Mais attention, je ne dis pas qu'il n'y a pas là une richesse extraordinaire. . . . C'est extraordinaire ce que tout ce fantastique vodouesque peut nous apporter au niveau même de notre esthétique. Et ça, je l'exploite systématiquement dans mon œuvre.[21]

[When Gros Zo announces to Penny, a blond from Toronto, that he is married, Penny, who is dating Gros Zo, says to him, "You are a liar, you're a hypocrite." Then Gros Zo responds to her, "No, no, the woman in question is a spirit." Penny says, "But that's not possible. If it were a spirit, you would not have spoken of her with such passion." And she decides to go to Haiti to meet her. All the girls at the hospital agree with her, if there is a Mistress Erzulie in Gros Zo's life you have to go and meet her. But Penny, fearful, asks Gros Zo: "Well, little Napoleon, and if Mistress Erzulie does not give her permission?" To which Gros Zo responds, "That is not possible. She would have acted that way for a negress, but not for you. Because basically Mistress Erzulie is a blond with blue eyes, she has long hair, she is svelte like you. So you can understand, for you Mistress Erzulie would not refuse to give her permission for me to marry you." It is that way in the real life of Black Haitians: Erzulie is our first wife. I remember, at a time when I had some problems in Haiti, and my parents went to see a voodoo priest, the first thing he said to them: "Listen, it is time for Gérard to wed Mistress Erzulie."

So there your entire life, from about fourteen or fifteen years of age, you are taught to sleep with a white woman, a blond with blue eyes. Your entire life, your fantasies, your psychoses, your neuroses, all of that is filtered through Mistress Erzulie. Sometimes, in the bloom of adolescence, you go to sleep in your bed, you ejaculate, and you are told the next morning, "You made love with the Mistress." Or what is more, you go to bed at night and you perfume your bed, hoping that Mistress Erzulie might come sleep with you. But that is sad in the practical life of a people. Thus, when Gros Zo says to Anne-Marie, "You are a negress. I can't love you" or "My dream woman is a blond," what can one do? It is anchored in our subconscious. That's where we are currently in our historicity. But, hold on, I am not saying that there is not in all of that an extraordinary richness. . . . It is quite extraordinary what the voodoo fantastic can bring to us on the level of our aesthetics. And all of that, I draw on systematically in my work.]

This remarkable statement condenses in its texture certain analytical categories at work in Etienne's project, such as the analysis of the fantasmatic doubling of the Haitian woman. Through his characters and in interviews, Etienne reveals his appreciation of the richness of Haitian voodoo, which he accepts and assumes as an undeniable ontological variable in the collective consciousness of the Haitian people. For Etienne, Haitian voodoo is a resource, a rich source of poetic excitement. Nonetheless, he questions the effect of voodoo upon the psyche of the Haitian people, particularly with regard to the Haitian woman and the figure of Erzulie, the voodoo goddess of the waters, beauty, and love. This analysis illustrates the provocative nature of Etienne's work.

Gérard Etienne's analysis of Mistress Erzulie, the voodoo goddess of the waters, beauty, and love, and the effect her depiction has upon the collective psyche, is intimately related to his concern about the depiction of the Haitian woman in literature. I have already discussed the functioning of the mother image in relation to the exilic mode in Etienne. In considering the woman in the discourse of Gérard Etienne, I have limited the choice of text to *Gladys* (1963), *Dialogue avec mon ombre* (1972), *Le Nègre crucifié* (1974), and the essay "La Femme noire dans le discours littéraire haïtien" (1979; The Black Woman in Haitian Literary Discourse). These are the texts in which the first portraits of women in Etienne are sketched. There are few critics of the representation of women in Haitian discourse as severe or as generous as Gérard Etienne. Etienne seems to escape the traps of Haitian literary tradition that inadvertently (perhaps) established a tradition of humiliating "binary fantasmatization" of the Haitian woman. This inherited system of symbolic values constructs, according to Etienne, a binary opposition between the black-skinned woman and the lighter-skinned mulatto. The opposition perpetuates a racist, feudal, and colonial vision reinforced by a low romanticism that exploits antitheses based on a set of assigned values of lightness and darkness. The character portrayals of the Black and Mulatto women systematically oppose Black and White, the savage and the civilized, the peasant and the bourgeois, the servant and the lady, night and day, filth and cleanliness, impropriety and propriety, voodoo and rationality, excess and moderation, consumption and veneration, secrecy and openness, dishonesty and honesty. It is a tradition that, according to Etienne, closes off our imagination to the existential value of the Haitian woman, and in which the construction of Black female figures rests upon a series of distortions and negations that run the risk of perpetuating the myths and stereotypes that have distorted the image of the Black woman's humanity and denigrated and even denied her importance in Haitian history.[22]

La pacotille laments: "Pas moyen d'avoir de la bonté dans un pays où il faut s'endurcir pour aimer, rester bouche bée devant un coucher du soleil, une onde de rivière. . . . dans un pays où un regard de tendresse se transforme automatiquement en provocation de la force milicienne" (p. 96) [There is no place for kindness in a country where you must harden yourself in order to love, remain spellbound before a sunset, before the scintillating waters of a river. . . . in a country where a look of tenderness is automatically seen as a provocation by the military force]. Gérard Etienne wishes to hide nothing. Thus his universe is of necessity violent: the violence of torture, of the social and political misery in Haiti; the violence of a man who understands, firsthand, what it means to be raped; the violence of the living conditions, the truths, and emotions he exposes. Let us take, for example, *Le Nègre crucifié,* in which Etienne protests the violence of his countrymen.

> Mon personnage pleure. L'amour est impossible. . . . Que tu es lâche, papa, plus lâche qu'un homme qui maltraite sa femme après l'avoir prise toute la nuit.
>
> te battre comme un soûlard qui bat sa femme. Histoire de vengeance ou d'impuissance. Comme un papa prêté qui fouette à mort son fils prêté. Histoire encore d'impuissance. Comme tes soldats qui me fouettent à mort, Chef. Histoire d'un peuple de démons.
>
> L'amour est une faiblesse en Haïti. (P. 111)
>
> [My character is crying. Love is impossible. . . . How cowardly you are, brother, more cowardly than a man who mistreats his wife after having had her all night long.
>
> You should be beaten like a drunkard who beats his wife. A story of vengeance or impotence. Like a tit-for-tat father who beats his son to death tit for tat. Another story of impotence. Like your soldiers who beat me to death, Leader. The story of a people of demons.
>
> Love is a weakness in Haiti.]

> Et puis, il n'est pas question de penser au futur, dit-il à la fille. Il n'est pas question de penser aux temps qui viennent. Ils se rendent compte de leurs précipices, les vérités qu'ils voudraient se dire. Entre eux, c'est l'ombre éternelle. Comme si un nègre devait se séparer de son âme et couper ses doigts qu'il jetterait après aux chiens affamés. (P. 101)

> Je lui dis qu'en Haïti, l'amour est impossible. . . .
> Je lui dis qu'en Haïti, l'amour est un os jeté aux chiens, qu'il n'est pas question d'aimer. (P. 102)

Cette lâcheté en moi, en toi, la paresse qui nous tue, nous empêche de vivre loin d'ici, dans un coin au fond de la mer, dans un château au fond de la mer, toi sirène, moi baleine. (P. 48)

Elle veut le consoler, lui dire que la vie est un combat sans fin. (P. 74)

Nounoune, la remorque de mes pensées (P. 52).

[And then, it is no question of thinking about the future, he says to a girl. There is no question of thinking of times that are coming. They realize from their perches the truths they would love to say to each other. Between them there is the eternal shadow. As if a Black man should separate himself from his soul and cut off his fingers which he would toss to ravenous dogs.

I tell her that in Haiti, love is impossible . . .
I say to her that in Haiti, love is a bone tossed to the dogs, that there is no question of loving in Haiti.

This cowardice in me, in you, the laziness that kills us, that prevents us from living far from here, in a corner at the bottom of the sea, in a castle at the bottom of the sea, with you as a mermaid, I as a whale.

She wants to console him, tell him that life is not an endless combat. . . . Nounoune, the towline of my thoughts.]

There is violence, yes, but in Etienne there is also tenderness, and especially gratefulness, for and to the woman who is "the towline of his thoughts"—lifting him from the daily miasma of life to the reverie of utopian spaces. Etienne constructs a nontraditional portrait of the Black Haitian woman that attempts to grasp this woman in her existential complexity, particularly in relation to the excesses, abuses, and weaknesses of the colonial, military, bourgeois, feudal, patriarchal Haitian male.

A systematic reading of Etienne's works reveals lexical constants that point to certain obsessions that "chart" a psyche. The trajectory of emotions and experiences relating to the woman is: violence, pain, wandering; thirst, water, rest; dreams, daydreams, intimacies, expansion of the soul, the grand dream of return (union and reconciliation with the woman), mother, the mother tongue, and the mother country. Daydreams in which the protagonist lives out the present in happy images are always, in Etienne's works, luminous projections of the feminine. What manner of woman is Etienne's female character?

The Etiennian woman is fleeting in all senses of the term. She is running away, disappearing and unseizable. *She* is many disjointed traits: a sketch and a minimalist, cubist, at times surrealist portrait. For the protagonist *she* is an object of desire who seems unattainable. *She* can inspire fear, especially the fear of abandonment. *She* is a being dreamed of and constructed from a matrix of maternal conflicts and affiliations. *She* is a tangle of contradictions, kindred spirit, imaginary double, sister. *She* is the being in whom all the contradictions of the soul and the unconscious seem resolved.

For the Etiennian feminine, the gender of nouns in French is important when one considers the preponderance of feminine phenomena with which *She* is associated: consciousness, conscience, consolation, tenderness, fear, poetry, strength, imagination, inspiration, contradiction, elevation, and shadow are all feminine nouns and entities in Etienne's work. *She* is the reflection and the likeness of the universe.

She is also the reflecting mirror and, as such, the reflection as well as the opposite, a repetition and a difference. Together, *He* and *She* form a chiasmus or a repetition through reversal. She is the feminine projection of certain aspects of his unconscious, his tenderness, his potential, and his wounded self, as well as the incarnation of strength when he is weak. She is his opposite in that she is the embodiment of the questions and psychological torments that plague him according to the demands of life. As a mediating spirit she is his guide toward full self-realization. She is the guide to love, the guide through life, through shadows toward revolution, to death. At times, she has a name —Gladys, Nounoune, Josette, Evelyn, Deborah, Natania, Michaella, Guilene, and, especially, Mother, the true mother, the mother tongue, the mother country.

The water imagery offers Etienne's characters, as dreamers, the intoxicating escape into the intimate realm of the maternal feminine. The escapist and utopian visions are expressed in the structure and strength of the lyric. When the imagination idealizes the masculine and the feminine, they become values and, as such, allegorical, thereby conferring upon the lyric the grandeur of the epic. *Gladys* becomes "A Song of the Haitian People." This poetry was written by Etienne in his youth and prior to *Le Nègre crucifié*. The tone, language, and style are relatively classical, if not precolonial, in their Edenic qualities. A selective reading of verses from this long poem illustrates the transformation in which, through the "marvelous" simultaneity of the poetic process, the singular embraces the plural and the personal lyric expands to embrace the national epic, and in which the idealized composite woman is the incarnation of an all-embracing, positively totalitarian, utopian vision of Haitian society.

> C'est l'heure de cueillir les roses de la lune
> Lève-toi Bien Aimée LE GRAND RÊVE arrive. . . .
> J'ai fait le tour de moi pour trouver ton image. . . .
> Le souffle de mon message fraternel . . .
> cette éternelle chanson de l'Homme errant . . .
> je ne sais et ne sens qui je suis. . . .
> Gladys mon immaculée . . .
> Jusques à quand resteras-tu sourde à mon appel. . . .
> O femme venue parmi deux pensées parallèles, Femme
> que je mettrai sur les étages d'une vision qui prend
> aujourd'hui la forme d'un monde recréé, j'habiterai tes
> lots de terre encore mal défrichés, ton espace et ta
> physionomie, ton Univers et ta substance, se parlant
> gentiment. . . .
> ton ombre . . . un ange . . . mon double . . .
> Passe et repasse belle Hirondelle
> Mon PEUPLE attend l'eau pure des mornes
> et l'unisson des lèvres blasées
> fera germer l'humain de l'or. . . .
> Je te salue magique vision
> qui te fais chair dans ma poésie. . . .
> Mais toi mon double dans l'illusion
> dis-moi veux-tu l'essaim des songes
> pour qu'à la vie j'apporte des grottes
> où nous ferons l'indivisible. . . .
> Femme muette suspendue au fil de l'azur
> filets graduels du froid et savane brûlante
> Femme demi-rose accrochée au sommeil
> Espace compris entre le songe et la matière
> Femme envahie de nuages familiers . . .

quand sur la route de la PAIX
la main dans la main . . .
Nous irons le front chargé de fruits
pour que soit faite chair l'idée d'un monde réel. . . .
O GLADYS ma chambre inondée de contraires
je t'ai chantée et te chanterai dans l'hosanna des songes
Un jour peut-être nous couperons ensemble
de petites tranches de vie
quand l'espèce aura jailli de l'union des coeurs. . . .
je t'attendrai mon UNIVERS
de mon SOURIRE
toute orné de lumière que nos bras auront forgé pour
de meilleures récoltes. . . .[23]

[It is the hour to gather the roses of the moon. . . .
Stand up Beloved THE GRAND DREAM is come. . . .
I have searched my being in order to find your image. . . .
The inspirational breath of my fraternal message . . .
This eternal song of the wandering Man . . .
I do not know and cannot feel who I am. . . .
Gladys, my immaculate conception . . .
Until when, for how long, will you remain deaf to my call. . . .
Oh, woman come from among two parallel thoughts,
Woman whom I shall place on the plateaus of a vision that
takes the shape today of a world re-created, I shall inhabit
your plots of still untilled soil, your space and your
physiognomie, your Universe and your substance,
speaking one to the other with kindness. . . .
your shadow . . . an angel . . . my double . . .
Pass by and pass by again beautiful Sparrow
My PEOPLE await the pure water of the high hills
and the song in unison of indifferent lips
will germinate a golden humanity. . . .
I salute you magical vision
who is made flesh in my poetry. . . .
But you my double in illusion
Tell me won't you of the swarm of dreams
so that to life I might furnish the grottoes

where we shall accomplish the indivisible. . . .
Mute Woman suspended in the azure blue sky
gradual threads of the cold and of burning savanna
Woman half-pink hanging on to sleep
Space caught between reverie and materiality
Woman overtaken by familiar clouds . . .
when on the route toward PEACE
hand in hand . . .
We shall go forth our brows laden with fruits
so that the idea of a real world will be made flesh. . . .
OH GLADYS my chamber flooded with contradictions
I have sung of you and shall continue to sing your praises
in the hosanna of dreams
One day perhaps we shall cut together
small slices of life
when the species will have sprung from the union of hearts. . . .
I shall await you my UNIVERSE
with my SMILE
All adorned with lights
that our arms will have fashioned for better harvests. . . .]

In the so-called "Unnecessary Preface" to *Gladys,* the Haitian poet Léon Laleau underscores the intimate symbolic relationship between man, water, and woman. In *Le Nègre crucifié,* the prisoner suffers a constant thirst, and woman is often portrayed as a figuration of Aquarius, the Water Bearer, the spring, the source, from which emanates a revitalizing energy, courage, strength, and determination. It is in the extraordinary portrait of *the crucified Black woman* that tenderness and pity are seen as acts of insolence and provocation by the military power structure.

Je vois une femme. Elle assiste à la chose et veut me donner une cruche d'eau. Il y a un fusil pointé sur ses seins.

Le chef lance l'ordre de violer toutes les femmes du Pays: femmes corbillards, femmes poules, femmes charognes. Tout cela pour la femme qui a essayé de mettre un peu d'eau dans ma bouche.

Parmi les femmes qui sont là, il y a une qui se distingue des autres. Elle a une robe couleur chadèque. Ses cheveux sont une touffe de bayahondes.

Pitié, dit-elle. On l'entend à peine. Les soldats du chef ronflent. La femme tombe deux fois. Deux fois, elle se relève. (P. 34)

[I see a woman. She attends the event and wants to give me a pitcher of water. There is a rifle pointed at her breasts. The man in charge shouts the order to rape all the women of the countryside: funereal women, chicken women, carcass women. All of that for a woman who tried to put a little bit of water in my mouth. Among the women who are there, there is one who stands out from the rest. She is wearing a dress pale blue in color. Her hair is like a tuft of thistles. Pity, she cries out. She is hardly heard. The commander's soldiers fire. The woman falls two times. Two times she gets back on her feet.]

The dialectical relationship of two kindred spirits implies a reciprocal psychological projection. In *Air and Daydreams* Gaston Bachelard suggests:

L'homme qui aime une femme "projette" sur la femme toutes les valeurs qu'il vénère. Et, de même, la femme "projette" sur l'homme qu'elle aime toutes les valeurs que sa propre psyché voudrait posséder, conquérir.[24]

[The man who loves a woman "projects" onto the woman all of the values and qualities he himself venerates. And, in the same way, woman "projects" onto the man she loves all of the values and qualities that her own psyche would like to conquer and possess.]

In his delirium and his daydreams, the crucified Black man creates numerous characters and doubles. It is thus in *Le Nègre crucifié* that Etienne creates his "dialogue avec [son] ombre":

Je me fais plusieurs personnages. Chaque personnage fait est une idée pourrie, une pile de contradictions depuis vingt-quatre heures. . . . Un [autre] encore trace sur le ciment de ma cellule la figure de ma mère. (P. 12)

[I create for myself several characters. Each character created is a rotten idea, a heap of contradictions piled up since the last twenty-four hours. One [other] of these characters is still tracing on the cement of my cell the face of my mother.]

There is an almost perfect correspondence between the psychological and textual functions and mechanisms of the "shadow" and "double" in Etienne and the discussion of the shadow by Gaston Bachelard:

> Ces dédoublements serait si l'on "pensait," un dédoublement de philosophe: la question où suis-je, qui suis-je? De quel reflet d'être suis-je l'être? Mais ces questions pensent trop. Un philosophe les renforcerait avec des doutes. En fait la rêverie dédouble l'être plus doucement, plus naturellement. Et avec variété! Il y a des rêveries où je suis moins que moi-même. L'ombre est alors un être riche. Elle est une psychologue plus pénétrante que le psychologue de la vie quotidienne. Elle connaît, cette ombre, l'être qui double par la rêverie l'être du rêveur. L'ombre, le double de notre être, connaît en nos rêveries la "psychologie des profondeurs." Et c'est ainsi que l'être projeté par la rêverie—car notre moi rêveur est un être projeté—est double comme nous-mêmes."[25]
>
> [These deconstructions of the self into doubles would be if one "were thinking" a deconstruction of the philosophical type: the question where am I, who am I? As a being, of what am I the reflection? But these questions think too much. A philosopher would reinforce them with doubts. In fact, dreaming and daydreaming deconstruct our being more gently, more naturally. And with such variety. There are reveries in which I am less than myself. The shadow is then a rich being. She is a psychologist more penetrating than the psychologist of everyday life. She knows, the shadow, the being who is the double emerged from a daydream and she knows the dreamer as a being. The shadow, the double of our being, recognizes in our reveries the psychology of our innermost depths and most intimate secrets. And it is thus that the self who is projected through daydreaming—for indeed our dreamed-of self is a projection of the self—is the double of ourselves.]

In *La pacotille,* the woman who is a double is named Guilène. She is an Esther figure representing the female liberator. As a beautiful mulatto woman, Guiléne is a form of Erzulie, the aforementioned goddess of beauty, love, and the waters in Haitian voodoo.

> Je me sentais vraiment mal à l'aise en compagnie d'une mulâtresse qui présentais des traits physiques identiques à ceux de Gladys. La fille qui m'avait tourné la tête à Camp Perrain pour laquelle j'avais écrit quelques vers romantiques. Dans sa porcherie, le petit nègre. Ainsi en avait décidé le père de Gladys ainsi que la femme du monstre. (P. 190)

> [I used to feel truly ill at ease in the company of a mulatto woman who had physical features identical to those of Gladys. The girl who had turned my head at Camp Perrain and for whom I had written some romantic verses. There I was, in her pigpen, the little negro boy. So had Gladys's father decided as well as the wife of the beast.]

The mulatto woman inspires awe, fear, lust, idealism, revolutionary courage, and anxiety in the Black peasant youth:

> J'aurais escamoté ma morale de révolutionnaire si j'avais souillé le corps de Guilène. Un corps qui appartenait d'abord à son peuple. Dans tout ce qu'il contenait de ferveur, de courage, d'électricité. C'était ça. Elle allait m'aimer. Pour de vrai. Plus qu'un camarade de combat, je devenais son double. Son complice. (P. 201)

> [I would have tarnished my revolutionary morality had I sullied the body of Guilène. A body that belonged first of all to her people. With all that it contained of fervor, courage, electricity. That was it. She was going to love me. For real. More than as a comrade in arms, I was becoming her double. Her accomplice.]

The emotions and experiences associated with this Etiennian woman is recalled at this point to measure the importance of the character Nounoune in *Le Nègre crucifié:* violence, pain, wandering; thirst, water, rest; dreams, daydreams, close intimacies, expansion of the soul, the grand dream of return—union and reconciliation with the woman—mother, the mother tongue, and the mother country. This network of associations is magisterially orchestrated by Etienne in the scene of the meeting between "a character" and Nounoune, the woman-refuge-mother-sister-chimera-lover figure:

> Il fait pitié. Nounoune le console. Il tremble de peur. Ouvre-moi ton ventre. Que j'y entre avec mes bras cassés. Donne-moi ton ronflement, ton sourire, tes hanches. Ouvre tes yeux, que j'y voie les fusées du monde. Que je m'assoie sur tes cuisses, pour te donner un peu de mes souffrances. Fais ma conquête, Nounoune, sois ma mère. Je te le demande au nom des enfants bâtards, au nom de ceux que fouette le chef. Je te le demande, Nounoune, au nom des assassins de nos parents. Nous n'avons pas besoin de calendriers, ni d'espace, ni d'horizons. Nous sommes tout cela à la fois. Nounoune l'enserre. Rentre ses dix doigts dans sa gorge.

Elle lui fait vomir un premier vers, puis un deuxième, puis un troisième. Il se sent soulagé. Reprend du souffle, dit à Nounoune des mots qu'elle ne comprend pas. Ils s'embrassent. Deux anolis prennent leur bain de soleil. (P. 48)

[One feels sorry for him. Nounoune consoles him. He trembles with fear. Open your belly to me. Let me enter therein with my arms crossed. Give me your breath, your smile, your hips. Open your eyes that I may see the fireworks of the universe. Let me sit on your thighs, so that I can share with you some of my sufferings. Conquer me, Nounoune, be my mother. I beg this of you in the name of all those bastard children, in the name of those beaten by the beast. I ask this of you, Nounoune, in the name of those who murder our relatives. We don't need any calendars, space, or horizons. We are all of that at one and the same time. Nounoune wraps her arm around him. Sticks her ten fingers down into his throat. She makes him throw up a first thing, then a second. Then a third thing that is troubling him. He feels relieved. Catches his breath again, says to Nounoune words that she cannot understand. They kiss. Two tiny green lizards sun themselves.]

Mon personnage vole. Se retrouve encore avec Nounoune. . . . Nounoune est belle. Il veut la prendre.

Il a envie d'étrangler la fille à cause de sa beauté qui lui fait peur. Je ne peux, dit-il, digérer l'idée d'une beauté avec ma laideur. Il faut te sacrifier pour mon malheur et mon bonheur. Il prend un couteau. Veut couper la gorge de la fille. Elle lui dit: je ne suis pas ton ennemie, malgré les apparences. Je suis le devant-jour, toi la levée de la lune.

Il se jette sur Nounoune, lèche sa peau, mord ses yeux.

Pourquoi ne fait-on pas l'amour dans la bouche. Nounoune avant que les nuages t'enveloppent.

Nounoune

Je dois souffrir pour le salut des paysans

Lui et Nounoune s'entrelaçent.

A côté d'eux, Haïti n'existe pas. (P. 56)

[My character takes wing. Finds itself once again with Nounoune. . . . Nounoune is beautiful. He wants to take her.

Suddenly he wants to strangle the girl because her beauty frightens him. I can't, he says to himself, stomach the idea of such beauty next to my ugliness. You have to sacrifice yourself for my unhappiness and my happiness. He takes a knife. Wants to slit the throat of the girl. She says to him: I am not your enemy, despite appearances. I am daybreak, you the rising of the moon.

He throws himself upon Nounoune, licks her skin, nibbles her eyes.

Why don't people make love through the mouth. Nounoune before the clouds envelop you.

Nounoune

I am a sufferer for the salvation of the peasant.

He and Nounoune wrap themselves around each other.

Next to them, for a moment, Haiti does not exist.]

I have described the Etiennian woman as a *fleeting body.* In this regard, the following is one of the key passages in which the obsessions with the inaccessible woman who appears as a dream, the fear of abandonment, the impossibility of love, and the difficulty of envisioning the future in Haiti all dissolve into one image:

> Il cherche Nounoune, partout dans le ravin, sous la robe des femmes, sous la tonnelle. Il la cherche dans les latrines du quartier, partout où une odeur de femme rappelle la senteur de la fille. Il cherche cette femme qui le comprend. Il vient de la perdre dans un cercueil qui disparaît comme on fait disparaître des hommes. (P. 59)

> [He is searching for Nounoune, everywhere in the ravine, under the dresses of woman, under the arbor. He searches for her in the neighborhood latrines, everywhere where the smell of a woman recalls the fragrance of the girl. He searches for this woman who understands him. He has just lost her in a coffin that is disappearing the way they make people disappear in Haiti.]

With Nounoune in *Le Nègre* and Guilène in *La pacotille,* the prisoner-protagonist finds a female double and accomplice with whom he commits the crime of dreaming a future of democracy, social equality, economic prosperity, humanism, and love. The protagonist is not only a political detainee tortured by the state apparatus, but also a prisoner of love tortured by the social, caste, and political impossibilities of love in Haiti. Paradoxically, in that place of horror, in that "tropical cemetery," in the "pigsty" that is Haiti, Le Nègre and Nounoune,

La pacotille and Guilène, through their political passion, live out the utopian future of love they imagine.

In Etienne's work there is the expression of a deep feminine within the man that is, it seems to me, a compensatory projection of the deeply regretted, missing maternal bond. There is a feminization of his daydreams and a feminization in language of his ambiguous experiences in love and his grand love and emotion for Haiti. In Etienne's work, love, the practice of poetry, the feminization of his dreams and daydreams, exile and his socio-politico-psychological agenda for the liberation of Haiti fuse into a marvelous simultaneity that only the imagination, reverie, and poetic vision can realize. Gérard Etienne's literary project is multi-purposed: to free Haiti *and* the Haitian woman from their respective state of zombification; to effect a reconciliation between the Haitian woman, her history, and her country; to transform the hidden potential of a Haitian Black woman into explosive, expansive, expressive structures; to reveal her existential dimensions; and to steer the imagination of artists and readers toward spaces more open to the liberation of the Haitian woman and her country. Throughout Etienne's work the prestige of the feminine is profound, and the expanding correspondence between the woman, the mother country, and the Haitian future of hope is explicit. Here is an example from *Cri:*

> Déjà ma petite fille Michaëlla court dans le soleil. Il se dessine dans ses yeux un sauvage cavalier dressé entre le ciel et nos rêves de bâtisseurs d'hommes. Déjà les troubadours de la grande plaine forment une colonne autour de nos morts prêts à lancer dans l'air des papillons dans l'attente d'UNE femme révolutionnaire.
>
> Il songe à l'avenir de son pays qu'il maudit mais qu'il considère comme une femme. On l'aime trop pour la détester. On la déteste trop pour l'aimer. C'est un aller-venir entre l'amour d'un pays et la rage de la haïr. On est trop marqué, on a trop de blessures pour que tout cela disparaisse en un seul jour. Il faut prendre du temps, pense-t-il. Un aller-venir entre l'idée de faire disparaître Haïti, de la supprimer de la planète et celle de la rendre prospère. (P. 36)

> [Already my little girl Michaëlla is running in the sunlight. In her eyes a wild horseman is being sketched standing between the sky and all our

dreams of builders of men of the future. Already troubadors of the high plain form a column around our dead ready to release into the air hopeful butterflies while awaiting A revolutionary woman.

He is lost in dreams about the future of his country that he curses but that he considers like a woman. You love her too much to hate her. You detest her too much to love her. It is a constant going and coming between the love of a country and the rage of hating her. One is too marked, one has too many wounds for it all to disappear in one single day. You have to give yourself time, he thinks. A constant going and coming between the idea of making Haiti disappear, of erasing her from the planet and the idea of making her prosper.]

And from *La pacotille:*

> On viole l'histoire. Ton histoire de nègre poupou, de nègre de fruits sauvages. Sans racines depuis plus d'un siècle. On rêve d'une Esther libératrice issue des matrices de la mer qui volerait par-dessus des masses d'air s'ouvrant aux complaintes des vieillards, qui parfumerait les cases des villes, rien qu'avec sa queue de comète, son souffle puissant, sa beauté étincelante. Cette femme-lumière, bardée de lumière à ses flancs, ferait pousser des arbres là où la fertilité de la terre a été violée. On la verrait s'élever dans le ciel, plus haut que chars de feu venus de l'autre monde, baignée de fraîches ondées, de myosotis, de citronnelle. (P. 79)
>
> [One violates history. Your history of a wretched Black man, of the Black man of wild fruits. Without roots for more than a century, one dreams of a liberating Esther risen from the matrixes of the sea who would fly above the masses of air opening herself to the pleas of the old, who would perfume the shacks in the city ghettos, with nothing more than the sweep of her comet train, her powerful breath, her sparkling beauty. This woman of light, clad in light at her flanks would make trees grow there where the fertility of the land had been raped. She would be seen rising in the sky, higher than the chariots of fire, from another world, bathed in cool mists, forget-me-nots, and citronella.]

Nous l'attendons, depuis cinq siècles, cette femme libératrice. Plutôt non. Une marée noire. L'unique signe d'une révolution souterraine, mugissante, bruissant de forces incontrôlables. Nous la voulons pour notre délivrance. Pour montrer au monde notre beauté, notre laideur, la vie qui nous échappe tous les jours, faute d'un arbre qui s'approprierait tout l'oxygène de l'univers afin de protéger nos enfants contre l'étouffement. (P. 79)

[We have been waiting for her, for five centuries, this liberating woman. Rather not. A black tide. The unique sign of an underground revolution, roaring, rumbling with uncontrollable forces. We want her for our deliverance. In order to show to the world our beauty, our ugliness, the life that slips through our fingers every day, for want of a tree that would take in all the oxygen of the universe in order to release it to protect our children from that which suffocates them.]

One wonders if the 1991 novel *La pacotille* marks the end for Etienne of the cycle of torture and the aesthetics of pain, as well as the end of the long dark night of sufferings for the Haitian nation. In the mid-nineteen nineties, Etienne chose the essay as his preferred format of expression and published *La Question raciale et raciste dans le Roman québecois*,[26] a study of race and racism in the Quebecois novel. In *L'Injustice! Désinformation et mépris de la loi* (Injustice! Disinformation and Contempt of the Law),[27] he discusses issues such as free speech, freedom of expression, and civil disobedience. The essay *La femme noire dans le discours littéraire haïtien* (The Black Woman in Haitian Literary Discourse) has become a book-length study of the same title,[28] in which Etienne develops his original "méthode anthroposémiologique," which combines semiotics, anthropology, and sociological research methods to investigate the literary sign beyond the margins of "the self-sufficient text." Etienne believes that the millennium must signal the blossoming of the decolonization of literary criticism and literary theory in the domain of francophone studies.

Conclusion: The Francophone
Coming out from under the Sign of Persephone and "the Dark Night of the Postcolonial African World"

Nous savons nouer les nœuds de la complicité.

[We well know how to tie the knots and tangles of complicity]
—Aimé Césaire, *Une Saison au Congo*

As a semantic matrix, the suffix *phone* in franco*phone* evokes the voice and hearing. The throat and the ear are the channels of voice and hearing that lead to the brain and descend to the "guts," that is, to the most intimate, secret, and mysterious parts of our being, mental space, intellect, and emotions. "In Quest of the Lost Song of Self" and "Silence Broken, Solitude Broken" are titles of essays I have written in the past that represent my continuing effort to come to grips with the "psycho-scripto-auricular vocalics" of francophone literary culture. *Le cri,* the scream, the shout, the primal call, is the voice caught and cut at the threshold between the primal materiality of language and its signifying message. *Le cri* is the voice as a welling forth, a torrent of autochthonous sound from the labyrinthine, cavernous depths of the self. This voice, as original sound, is distinct from echo or, in the context of French assimilation, from the rhetoric of "the hideous leprosy of mimicry" that Césaire lamented in *Notebook of a Return to the Native Land.* As a countervocalics, the cry is the voice's manifestation of the denunciatory tradition.

The seemingly disparate signs of ear and voice, the geological descent and return, the labyrinth, and the floral find their synthesis under the sign of Persephone,[1] the mythical goddess of the fields who is condemned to spend the winter in the underworld as wife to Pluto, god of the underworld. All of the disparate signs related to the Persephone myth were orchestrated transculturally in texts by Aimé Césaire as early as 1939, treated magisterially in the prose poem *The Torrent* by the Québecois writer Anne Hébert in 1945, and set forth in 1982 in all of their psychological complexity in *The Abandoned Baobab* by the Senegalese woman writer Ken Bugul. In Aimé Césaire's work, for example:

> Baobab c'est notre arbre[2]
>
> l'oreille collée au sol
> j'entends passer demain.[3]
>
> C'est au cri que l'on reconnaît l'homme. Au cri fils aîné de la vie, ou plutôt la vie elle-même qui sans dimensions, sans renonciations d'un libre et imprévisible mouvement s'incarne, dans l'immédiateté de la voix. Et voici crier le poète nègre:
> Nous crions parmi les gratte-ciel
> Comme nos ancêtres
> Criaient parmi les palmiers d'Afrique
> Car nous sommes seuls
> Et nous avons peur . . .
> Et sur le fond lourd des angoisses, des indignations rentrées des désespoirs longtemps tus, voici monter et siffler une colère, et l'Amérique, sur le lit ébranlé de ses conformismes, s'inquiète de quelle atroce haine ce cri est la délivrance:
> I speak in the name of the Black millions.[4]
>
> [The Baobab is our tree. . . .
>
> My ear pressed to the ground,
> I can hear tomorrow passing by
>
> It is by the cry that one recognizes man, by the scream, the eldest son of life or rather life itself without dimension, without renunciations in a free and unforeseeable movement that becomes incarnate in the immediacy of the voice. And here cries out the Black poet:

We cry out among the skyscrapers
As our ancestors
used to cry out among the palms of Africa
For we are alone
And we are afraid . . .

And on the heavy base of anguishes, of indignities turned inward, of despairs long held silent, here rises and whistles an anger, and America, on the shaken bed of her conformities, worries about what dreadful hatred this cry is the deliverance:

I speak in the name of the Black millions.]

In Anne Hébert:

> Je possède donc la certitude que je ne conserve aucune maîtrise sur ma voix. (P. 56)
>
> J'entrevis son éclat métallique comme celui d'un éclair s'abattant sur moi. Ma mère me frappe plusieurs fois à la tête. . . . Quand je rouvris les yeux, je me trouvais seul. . . . je ressentais une douleur violente à la tête. J'étais devenu sourd.
>
> Mais les jours épouvantables où je ressassais ma révolte, je percevais le torrent si fort à l'intérieur de mon crâne, contre mon cerveau, que ma mère me frappant avec son trousseau de clefs ne m'avait pas fait plus mal.[5]
>
> [I know now for sure that I have absolutely no control over my voice.
>
> I saw its metallic glimmer like a lightning flash coming down upon me. My mother struck me several times on the head. When I opened my eyes, I found myself alone. I felt a violent pain in my head. I had become deaf.
>
> . . . But on those horrible days when I kept turning over and over again my revolt, I could hear the torrent so intensely inside my skull, against my brain, that my mother's striking me with her key ring had not caused me greater pain.]

And, finally, in Ken Bugul:

> Soudain un cri! Un cri perçant. Un cri venait briser l'harmonie, sous ce baobab dénudé, dans ce village désert. L'enfant s'enfonçait de plus en plus profondément, la perle d'ambre dans l'oreille. (P. 25)

[Suddenly a scream! A piercing scream. A cry from underneath the baobab tree came to shatter the harmony of the deserted village. The child was pushing the amber bead deeper into its ear, deeper and deeper. The cry echoed in a heat of rhythm and dance.]

These passages orient us respectively toward certain preoccupations: the flowering of virtuality, a geology of desire, an auscultation of the future, the liberation of the voice of protest, and difference and release in the scream. Globally, they highlight an awareness that many francophone communities remain depleted natural resources, impotent economies, and vast wastelands of silenced cultural and intellectual potential. Césaire's description of the voiceless, unproductive French West Indies of the 1940s is a disturbingly appropriate description of far too many nations in the postcolonial era:[6]

Terre muette et stérile. C'est de la nôtre que je parle. Et mon ouï mesure par la caraïbe l'effrayant silence de l'homme. Europe. Afrique. Asie. J'entends hurler l'acier le tam-tam parmi la brousse, le temple prier parmi les banians. Et je sais que c'est l'homme qui parle. Encore et toujours j'écoute. Mais ici l'atrophiement monstrueux de la voix, le séculaire accablement, le prodigieux mutisme. Point de ville. Point d'art. Point de poésie. Point de civilisation, la vraie, je veux dire cette projection de l'homme sur le monde; ce modelage du monde par l'homme; cette frappe de l'univers à l'effigie de l'homme.

Une mort plus affreuse que la mort, où dérivent des vivants. Et les Sciences ailleurs progressent, et les philosophies ailleurs se renouvellent, et les esthétiques ailleurs se remplacent. Et vraiment sur cette terre nôtre la main sème des graines.

Point de ville. Point d'art. Point de poésie. Pas un germe. Pas une pousse. Ou bien la lèpre hideuse des contrefaçons. En vérité, terre stérile et muette.[7]

[Land mute and sterile. It is of ours that I speak. And my hearing measures across the Caribbean the frightening silence of man: Europe, Africa, Asia. I hear howling steel, the tom-tom in the jungle, the temple praying among the banyan trees. And I know that it is man who is speaking. Again and always I listen. But here the monstrous atrophy of the voice, the secular prostration, the prodigious mutism. No city. No art.

> No poetry. No civilization, the true. I mean that projection of the world by man onto the world! This shaping of the world by man. This forging of the universe in the effigy of man.
>
> A death more horrible than death where the living drift. And elsewhere the sciences progress; and elsewhere philosophies are renewed and esthetics are replaced. And vainly on this our land the hand sows seeds.
>
> No city. No art. No poetry. Not a sprig. Not a sprout. Or else the hideous leprosy of mimicry. Indeed, land sterile and mute.

The challenges to francophone literary culture have been to cease being the wife, to overcome the deafness, with its attendant silence, in order to step out from the darkness of political dependency and the mutism of disenfranchisement. As an address, the cry emerges with a subject, like Persephone, like Ramatoulaye in *Une si longue lettre,* emerging from the shadows and *the realm of the unacknowledged.* Counterstorytelling entails coming out from under the sign of Persephone, the involuntary *wife,* and like the rebellious deaf son in Anne Hébert's Québecois novel *Le Torrent,* escaping the deafening curse of radically enraged paralyzing consciousness.

The scream of a formerly tortured political prisoner is transformed into a shout for justice and a cry for the liberation of his subjugated, accursed compatriots. In the work of the Haitian writer Gérard Etienne, the voice is the instrument that mediates the articulation of rage, outrage, memory, witnessing, testament, revelation, and the integration of a shattered consciousness. It is the voice of the counterconfession.

If the nineteenth century was the century of colonization, the twentieth century has been the century of decolonization. The end of the twentieth century is a solemn, critical moment in the history of colonialized peoples. Rousseau's *Social Contract* (1762) and *The Declaration of the Rights of Man and the Citizen* (1789) informed the utopian vision of Toussaint-Louverture and the ideals of the Haitian Revolution. The counterhumanism of Aimé Césaire sought to extend these humanistic principles and the 1948 Human Rights Act to include the excluded colonialized masses. The abuse of human rights and the economic pillaging by monocratic regimes in Africa and the Caribbean have left imperfectly decolonized and independent nations in a new state of postcolonial mutism and sterility in which former victims and revolutionaries have become victimizers and the ideals of the French Revolution, the Haitian Revolution, and the decolonizing optimistic goals of the 1960s remain unrealized. As Bernard Zadi Zaourou of the Ivory Coast states, "Le second pillage du continent africain n'est pas un pillage venu d'étranger. Le second pillage est un pillage de nègres par les nègres. Là est le drame"[8] ["The second pillaging of the African continent is not a pillaging come from abroad. The second pillaging is a pillaging of Blacks by Blacks. Therein lies the tragedy."]

The tragedy to which Zaourou refers is foreseen in Césaire's 1967 drama *Une Saison au Congo* (*A Season in the Congo*). As one ponders the postindependence monocratic regimes in Africa and the Caribbean, the words of the nameless archetypal international banker in *A Season* are contemptuously cynical and painfully prophetic, for they envision the slipknot of relations and complicity between the former colonizer and the new African elite in which the masses will be caught.

> *Quatrième Banquier:* Pour rendre traitable le Sauvage, il n'est que deux pratiques:
> La trique, mon cher, ou bien le matabich!
>
> *Premier Banquier:* Eh bien?
>
> *Quatrième Banquier:* Eh bien, je vous croyais plus vifs.
> Suivez l'idée. Que veulent-ils? Des postes, des titres,
> Présidents, députés, sénateurs, ministres!
> Enfin le matabich! Bon! Auto, compte en banque
> Villas, gros traitements, je ne lésine point. Axiome, et c'est là
> l'important; qu'on les gave!
> Résultats: leur cœur s'attendrit, leur humeur devient suave.
> Vous voyez peu à peu où le système nous porte
> Entre leur peuple et nous, se dresse leur cohorte
> Si du moins avec eux, à défaut d'amitié
> En ce siècle ingrat sentiment périmé
> Nous savons nouer les nœuds de la complicité.
>
> *Premier Banquier:* Il suffit; bravo collègue! Accord sans réticence!
>
> *Choeur des Banquiers:* Hurrah! Hurrah! vive l'indépendance!
>
> [*Fifth* (sic) *Banker:* To handle savages, there are two ways:
> One is the club, but that's seen better days.
> The other is the purse.

> *Second Banker:* Go on
>
> *Fifth Banker:* All right, I'll spell it out. Just pay attention.
> What do their leaders want? They want to be
> Presidents, ministers, living in luxury.
> In short, the purse! High-powered cars,
> Villas, high wages, cushy bank accounts.
> Spare no expense. Just grease their palms and stuff
> Them. The investment will pay off.
> You'll see, their hearts will melt. And presently
> Those smirking, smiling politicians will be
> A special class between us and their people.
> They'll hold the people down provided we
> Tie them with bonds—well, maybe not of friendship,
> That's out of date in this sad century—
> But knots and tangles of complicity.
>
> *First Banker:* Bravo! Good man! We're with you.
>
> *Chorus of Bankers:* Hurrah! Hurrah! Three cheers for independence]
> (*Season,* Act I, sc 4)[9]

Later in the action of the play, Lumumba laments not having foreseen and forestalled the emergence of this new caste of African oppressors.

> . . . quand j'ai nommé les premiers officiers noirs, le premier général, le premier colonel noir, je ne pensais pas que plus vite que ne pousse la lave du volcan, une caste serait né, de chiens voraces et insatiables, la caste des colonels et des nouveaux messieurs, et c'est cette caste qui a confisqué à son profit, à son seul profit, les avantages que vous étiez en droit d'attendre de notre révolution congolaise! (*Une Saison,* Acte III, sc. I)
>
> [When I appointed the first Black officers, how could I imagine that quicker than lava spurts from a volcano, a new caste would be born, the caste of colonels and new masters, and that those voracious, insatiable dogs would monopolize all the benefits of Congolese freedom.] (*Season,* Act III, sc. I)

Aimé Césaire's decolonizing discourse remains a valid critique of postcolonial realities in which the bright sun of independence has become the midnight sun of state-sponsored terrorism and torture; where the promised future of liberalization and democratic renewal has become the present immiserization of the masses by the kleptocracy of the one-party state. Césaire's discourse remains valid for this postcolonialism in which the democratic fulfillment of human potential has been betrayed by the forced ecological, economic, and human desertification of African and Caribbean nations. Maryse Condé pondered the difficulties involved in the construction of a new state and summarized the people's deferred postcolonial dreams in her novel's title, *Hérémakhonon*, which in Malinke means "wait for happiness."

The exodus, forced exile, and brain drain of North African, Black African, and Caribbean intellectuals, writers, dissidents, professionals, and skilled technicians from nations with repressive regimes contribute to the nomadism of great numbers of formerly colonialized subjects. For many of them, such as Achille Mbembe, the Cameroonian historian residing in the United States, this end of the twentieth century is "the dark night of the postcolonial African world."

> Nous voici donc en cette fin de siècle, acculés, dans un face à face avec la terrible fermeture postcoloniale et son étourdissante affirmation d'impuissance, et ses pulsions et ses déchaînements démesurés, et ses effrois irraisonnés, et sa force psychotique, grotesque, bouffonne, qui ne respecte plus rien, ni les choses, ni les femmes, ni les hommes, ni les vieux, ni les gamins et les gamines, qui insulte, frappe, méprise, se gave de vin et de nourriture, crache, vomit, s'étrangle d'indigestion, cette démence et cette vénalité, la bestialité, ce qui est vraiment inquiétant, est le pouvoir d'accomplir le mal, juste comme ça, le pouvoir d'infliger le supplice et la mort à midi, l'impunité, mon Dieu, surtout l'impunité au "Togo," au "Zaïre," au "Kenya," au "Cameroun." . . . l'Etat-cannibale qui dévore, se repaît du corps de ses gens, les suicide à petit feu, cette part démoniaque du pouvoir et du commandement, et cette orgie de l'anéantissement qui viennent contredire, chaque soir, chaque midi et chaque matin, le désir qu'à chacun de nous de durer, nous empêchant, tous, de comprendre la nuit du monde africain, et de porter un souci conséquent à notre propre existence. Avoir vécu et continuer de vivre cette corruption et ce trépas au quotidien ne justifie peut-être pas nos pauvres vies de Nègres, Que sont-elles, de toutes les façons, puisque, nés au lever du soleil ou à la tombée du jour, combien d'entre nous meurent

> avant l'aube, dans un lancinant craquement de mâchoires, la course prématurément achevée, le cri strident et inexaucé.[10]
>
> [And so here we are at the end of the century, cornered, in an encounter with the dreadful postcolonial closure, its stunning affirmation of impotence, its irrational fears, and its absurd, grotesque, psychotic strength that no longer respects anything, neither things, nor women, nor men, nor old people, nor little boys, nor little girls, that insults, hits, is contemptuous, gorges itself on food and drink, spits, vomits, chokes from indigestion, this madness and this venality, the bestiality, and what is truly upsetting is the capacity to carry out evil, just like that, the power to inflict torture and death at noon, the impunity, my God, especially the impunity in "Togo," in "Zaire," in "Kenya," in "Cameroon." . . . The cannibalistic state that devours, feeds on the people's body, driving them to commit suicide slowly, this diabolical part of power and command, and this orgy of annihilation of the rights of the individual that comes every evening, every noon, and every morning to crush the desire that each one of us has to hang on, to prevent us all from understanding the dark night of the postcolonial African world, and from bringing to bear any consequential concern of ours about our very own existences. Having lived and continuing to live this day-to-day demise perhaps in no way justifies our miserable Black lives, what are they, at any rate, since born at the rise of the sun or at the falling of night, the race untimely run, how many among us, die before dawn, in a throbbing crunching of jaws, with a strident and unanswered scream.]

In delineating the responsibilities of the man of culture during the anticolonialist period of 1959, Césaire, at the risk of displeasing some of his more optimistic comrades, warned of the conditions that would plunge liberated nations into a "dark night of the postcolonial African world."[11] He feared that certain colonial and colonialist structures would too easily be reconstituted in the very heart of what he called those "imperfectly decolonized nations" where a group or a class of individuals, epigones of colonialism, would develop a hierarchical society with a de facto colonial effect, establish internal colonization of certain ethnic groups, and perpetuate a colonialist exploitation of the masses through the use of instruments of repression identical to those used by European colonial regimes. Césaire notes in *Notebook,*

"Il n'est point vrai que l'oeuvre de l'homme est finie" [12] [It is not true that the work of man is done].

In Césaire's essay "Culture et colonisation" (Culture and colonization),[13] he analyzes the dynamics and psychology of colonialist practices and their effect on the exchange, survival, destruction, and production of culture. The essay refines and expands on the idea of the quality of contact between civilizations, so forcefully presented in the "Discourse on Colonialism." In the period of the cultural chaos of 1956, Césaire called on "colonial, semi-colonial and para-colonial, societies to organize the cultural chaos into a new synthesis worthy of the name culture that would function as a reconciliation and transcendence of the old and the new. One of the continuing challenges in francophone culture is to overcome the cultural and psychological alienation that is the legacy of the colonial experience. Césairian Negritude is above all a cultural affirmation, a reconcilation and transcendence of the old and the new, and a performative process of identity and disalienation. For some, along with the postmodern and the postcolonial, we are in a post-Negritude era. Césaire responds,

> People ask: "Is there still something relevant in Négritude? Isn't it interesting only at a purely historical level?" This is not true at all. I think that as long as you will have Negroes a little bit everywhere, Négritude will be there as a matter of course. The Martinican grievance that we wanted to voice out forcefully is not so much physical misery, economic exploitation, even if this was really the case, as the *aliénation* which as policy has made the Martinican conscience founder. And believe me this fight against aliénation is never totally over.[14]

As for the sociodiagnostic of the "dark night of the postcolonial African world," the imperative, according to Césaire, is to act and to transfigure it. Just as in 1959 Césaire called upon his fellow intellectuals and artists to be "propagators, multipliers and inventors of new souls," in the restructuring of society today Césaire has launched a call to action against stagnation and negation:

> un afro-pessimisme, et même un afro-dénigrement; une insistance sur la part maudite de l'Africain. Une sorte d'hésitation parmi les noirs de la diaspora—les descendants africains. Certains par toute sorte de con-

torsions prennent leur distance de l'Afrique. En Afrique il y a certes la misère, la guerre, la famine, la maladie. Mais il y a autre chose. Il faut une mobilisation, une remobilisation de toutes les énergies—artistes, savants, femmes africains. . . . Il faut continuer et non pas s'endormir dans une sorte d'acceptation et de résignation."[15]

[An afro-pessimism, and even an afro-denigration, an insistence upon the accursed part of the African fate. [There is] a kind of hesitation among Blacks of the diaspora—African descendants. Some, by means of all kinds of contortions, are distancing themselves from Africa. In Africa there are, most certainly, problems of poverty, war, famine, sickness. But there are also other things. What is needed is a mobilization, a remobilization of all energies—African artists, scholars, women. . . . We must continue and not slip into a kind of acceptance and resignation.]

Artists, scholars, men and women, must envision new postcolonial societies in all of their complexity and seeming banality:

Le poète a toujours parcouru sa ville. Le poète, c'est d'abord celui qui crée. C'est la création. C'est la vie continuée. Mais par conséquent ça me parait tout à fait normal qu'un poème débouche sur la création d'une société, d'une école, ou d'une crèche. C'est de la poésie.[16]

[The poet has always roamed his city. The poet is first and foremost the one who creates. The poet is creation. The continuation of life. And so, consequently, it seems quite natural to me that a poem gives rise to the creation of a society, of a school, of a day-care center. All of it is poetry.]

The writers considered in this study understand quite well Mariama Bâ's insight to the effect that what society, fate, tyranny, hatred, fear, and history deny their people, art has the responsibility to imagine and sustain in them: the ravishing dream of equality, justice, and dignity in a humanistic, all-inclusive, economically democratic society.

Notes

Introduction

1 Jack Andrew Yeager, *The Vietnamese Novel: A Literary Response to Colonialism* (Hanover, N.H.: University Press of New England, 1987).

2 Mildred Mortimer, *Journeys through the French African Novel* (Portsmouth, N.H.: Heinemann Educational Books, 1990); Eileen Julien, *African Novels and the Question of Orality* (Bloomington: Indiana University Press, 1992).

3 Mary Jean Green et al., *Beyond the Hexagon: Francophone Women Writers* (Minneapolis: University of Minnesota Press, 1996).

4 Frantz Fanon, "The Negro and Language," in *Black Skin, White Masks* (London: Pluto Press, 1986), p. 11.

5 Valerie Smith, "Black Feminist Theory and the Representation of the 'Other,'" in *Changing Our Own Words,* ed. Cheryl Wall (New Brunswick, N.J.: Rutgers University Press, 1989), p. 47. See Sylvia Wynter, "1492: A New World View," in *Race, Discourse, and the Origin of the Americas: A New World View,* ed. Vera Hiatt and Rex Nettleford (Washington, D.C.: Smithsonian Institution Press, 1995), pp. 5–57.

6 This excerpt is from a paper presented by Mariama Bâ at the conference on the Function of the Modern Literatures of Black Africa, Frankfurt, October 1980. The essay appears in *Ecriture française dans le monde* 3, no. 5 (1981): 3–7 and is cited by Irène D'Almeida, *Francophone African Women Writers: Destroying the Emptiness of Silence* (Gainesville: University Press of Florida, 1994), pp. 28–29.

7 Lionnet, "Métissage, Emancipation, and Female Textuality in Two Francophone Writers," in *Life Lines: Theorizing Women's Autobiography,* ed. Bella Brodzki and Celeste Schenck (Ithaca, N.Y.: Cornell University Press, 1988), pp. 260–78.

8 See Graziella Parati, *Public History, Private Lives: Italian Women's Autobiography* (Minneapolis: University of Minnesota Press, 1996), pp. 10–11.

9 Jean Bernabé, Patrick Chamoiseau, and Raphaël Confiant, *Éloge de la*

Créolité/In Praise of Creoleness (Baltimore: Johns Hopkins University Press, 1990).

10 The Haitian-American writer Edwidge Danticat (in *Krik? Krak!* [New York: Vintage Books, 1996], p. 220) offers a compelling counterbraiding discourse that introduces more of the heterogeneity, "unruliness," tentativeness, and diasporic unpredictability of form, traditions, temporalities, memory, and relationships in francophone texts:

> When you write, it's like braiding your hair. Taking a handful of coarse unruly strands and attempting to bring them unity. Your fingers have still not perfected the task. Some of the braids are long, others are short. Some are thin. Some are heavy. Others are light. Like the diverse women in your family. Those whose fables and metaphors, whose smiles and soliloquies, whose diction and *je ne sais quoi* slip into your survival soup, by way of their fingers.

11 "The great autobiographers are great precisely because they ceased in their 'affectionate seeking after truth,' so have never ceased coming into being, so have never ceased to realize truth" (Olney, *Metaphors of Self: The Meaning of Autobiography* [Princeton, N.J.: Princeton University Press, 1972], p. 325).

12 Ken Bugul, *Le Baobab fou* (Dakar: Les Nouvelles Éditions Africaines, 1984), p. 22; Bugul, *The Abandoned Baobab* (Chicago: Lawrence Hill Books, 1991), p. 15.

13 Aimé Césaire, *Tropiques,* réédition, 1, no. 3 (1978): 7. Unless otherwise indicated, all translations are mine.

14 Bernabé, Chamoiseau, and Confiant, "Éloge de la Creólité," pp. 80–81.

15 Ibid., p. 95.

16 Aimé Césaire, *Notebook of a Return to the Native Land,* trans. Clayton Eshleman and Annette Smith (Berkeley: University of California Press, 1983). Further citations of this work will appear in the text.

17 See Aimé Césaire, "L'Homme de culture et ses responsabilités," *Présence africaine* 24–25 (1959): 66.

18 See Aimé Césaire's Address to the American Association of Teachers of French (AATF), Miami, 1989.

19 Césaire, "L'Homme de culture et ses responsabilités": 66.

20 Aimé Césaire, *Moi laminaire* (Paris: Seuil 1982).

21 Aimé Césaire, *Discourse on Colonialism,* trans. Joan Pinkham (New York: Monthly Press Review, 1972), p. 31.

22 The most far-reaching study of the works of Damas is contained in "Léon Gontran Damas," papers presented in Paris in 1988 and published in *Actes du colloque Léon Gontran Damas,* ed. Jacqueline Leiner (Paris: Editions Présence africaine), 1989.

23 Germaine Brée, "Preface," in *Life Lines: Theorizing Women's Autobiogra-*

phy, ed. Bella Brodzki and Celeste Schenck (Ithaca: Cornell University Press, 1988), p. ix.

1 *The Game of Slipknot*

The aptness of Mariama Bâ's formulation that "Books knit generations" reasserts itself as one takes up the pen to write about francophone literature and recalls foundational texts and their filiations with one's own work. Lilyan Kesteloot's work has inspired successive generations of students of francophone studies, including myself. Kesteloot begins her study with René Maran and establishes the facts surrounding the Goncourt Prize, the reception of the novel, and the controversy surrounding the preface to *Batouala.* I do the same, very briefly, with the knowledge that to many specialists it could appear repetitive. I remain concerned that the beginnings of francophone literature are increasingly given less attention in curricula and that many students are unaware of this extraordinary inauguration of francophone literature. I begin with Maran not simply because *Batouala* is of inaugural importance, but especially because Maran and his work are instructive lenses through which to foresee many of the fundamental preoccupations of francophone literary culture and of this study. Claude Wauthier's study, a monumental description and exhaustive panorama of early African and Caribbean francophone literature with lengthy illustrative excerpts, is an indispensable reference. The English translations are most useful, some of which will be used in this study. See Lilyan Kesteloot, *Les écrivains noirs de langue française* (Bruxelles: Institut de Sociologie, Université Libre de Bruxelles, 1963); Kesteloot, *Black Writers in French: A Literary History of Negritude,* trans. Ellen Conroy Kennedy (Washington, D.C.: Howard University Press, 1991); and Claude Wauthier, *L'Afrique des Africains* (Paris: Editions du Seuil, 1964); Wauthier, *The Literature and Thought of Modern Africa,* 2d ed. (London: Heinemann Educational Books, 1978).

Certain original French texts will not be cited when an established English translation exists, as in the case of *Batouala,* translated by Alexandre Mboukou; the bilingual edition of *Notebook of a Return to the Native Land,* translated by Clayton Eshleman and Annette Smith; *Discourse on Colonialism,* translated by Joan Pinkham; and the works of Frantz Fanon.

1 René Maran, *Batouala, véritable roman nègre* (Paris: Albin Michel, 1921).

2 Tahar ben Jelloun, *La Nuit sacrée* (Paris: Editions du Seuil, 1987); Jelloun, *L'Enfant de sable* (Paris: Editions du Seuil, 1985); Jelloun, *The*

Sand Child, trans. Alan Sheridan (New York: Ballantine Books, Harcourt, Brace, Jovanovich, 1987).

3 Anténor Firmin, *De l'égalité des races humaines* (Port-au-Prince: Editions Estève, 1885). Further citations of this work are in the text.

4 Comte Joseph-Arthur de Gobineau, *L'Essai sur l'inégalité des races humaines* (Paris: Belfond, 1967).

5 Ernest Renan, *Philosophical Dialogues,* quoted in Firmin, *De l'égalité des races humaines,* p. 480.

6 Caryl Phillips, "The Legacy of Othello," in *Frontiers of Caribbean Literature in English,* ed. Frank Birbalsingh (New York: St. Martin's Press, 1996).

7 This dilemma of identity is more elaborately pondered by René Maran in a novel variously titled *Roman d'un nègre, Jean Veneuse,* and, finally, *Un homme pareil aux autres* (Paris: Editions Arc-en-ciel, 1947).

8 René Maran, *Batouala, An African Love Story,* trans. Alexandre Mboukou (Washington, D.C.: Black Orpheus Press, 1972).

9 In the chapter "Faith and Exile: Cheik Hamidou Kane and the Theme of Alienation," Abiola Irele analyzes the predicament of the protagonist Samba Diallo in terms that mirror the situation of René Maran: "a conflict between two sets of impulses: on the one hand . . . an instinctive allegiance to a way of life that has shaped his very being . . . on the other . . . respect and admiration for the metaphysical courage involved in the European position and his horror at the historical result it has engendered" (Irele, *The African Experience in Literature and Ideology* [London: Heinemann, 1981], p. 171).

In particular for Maran, one should emphasize not only the "historical result" but especially his horror before the spectacle of the *human* result. Also, while Irele does not refer to DuBois, his analysis reflects the kind of dynamic and "tensions" that emerge from the DuBoisian double-consciousness paradigm.

The work of Irele that is most pertinent to the issues in this study and to which I refer in several places is his 1992 essay entitled "In Praise of Alienation." See my remarks, in particular p. 289, note 2. Irele's essay articulates the mechanisms of alienation and ambiguity in broader terms that have implications for the analysis of African women's writing, Caribbean writing, and African American literature.

10 See Tahar ben Jelloun, *La Nuit sacrée;* Kourouma, *Les Soleils des Indépendences* (Paris: 1970); and Diabaté, *Comme une piqûre de guêpe* (Paris, 1980).

11 René Maran, *Un homme pareil aux autres* (Paris: Editions Albin Michel, 1947).

12 Joseph Zobel, *La Rue Cases-Nègres* (Paris: Editions Jean Froissart, 1950).

13 Unless otherwise stated, excerpts from the works of Aimé Césaire are quoted from the three-volume *Œuvres complètes,* the first of which is titled *Poèmes,* the second *Théatre,* and the third *Œuvres historiques et politiques: Discours et communications* (Fort-de-France, Martinique: Editions Desormeaux, 1976).

14 For a succinct overview of the development of francophone literature see Christopher Miller, "Francophonie and Independence," in *A New History of French Literature* (Cambridge, Mass.: Harvard University Press, 1989), pp. 1028–34. See also Christopher Miller, *Blank Darkness: Africanist Discourse in French* (Chicago: University of Chicago Press, 1985).

15 Cheik Hamidou Kane, *L'Aventure ambigüe* (Paris: Julliard, 1961), p. 137.

16 On suspicion, see "l'ère du soupçon linguistique" (the age of linguistic suspicion), as used by Jacqueline Leiner in *Imaginaire-Langage-Identité culturelle* (Tübingen: G. Narr, 1980), p. 4.

17 The relevance of the experiences of status inconsistency, role conflict, and consciousness to francophone literary culture in general will be discussed at the end of this section, and their particular relevance to the work of Tahar ben Jelloun will be discussed in chapter 3.

18 Frantz Fanon, *The Wretched of the Earth* (New York: Grove Press, 1968), p. 224. Homi Bhabha cites "culture abhors simplification" in *Nation and Narration* (London: Routledge, 1990), p. 303.

19 Kai Erikson, *Everything in Its Path* (New York: Simon and Schuster, 1976).

20 See Homi Bhabha's discussion of the phrase "zone of occult stability" in *Nation and Narration,* p. 303.

21 Charles Baudelaire, *Œuvres complètes* (Paris: Bibliotheque de la Pléiade, 1975–76), p. 81.

22 *Aimé Césaire,* ed. Lilyan Kesteloot (Paris: Editions Séghers, 1962), p. 181.

23 Aimé Césaire, "Lettre à Maurice Thorez," *Œuvres complètes,* 3:472.

24 Césaire, *Tropiques* 1, no. 3 (1978): 7.

25 See Michael Riffaterre, *The Semiotics of Poetry* (Bloomington: Indiana University Press, 1984), and especially Riffaterre's discussion of the function of syllepsis in *Fictional Truth* (Baltimore: Johns Hopkins University Press, 1990), pp. 77–83, 103–10, 131.

26 Léon Gontran Damas, *Pigments: Névralgies* (Paris: Editions Présence Africaine, 1972), p. 43.

27 Ellen Conroy Kennedy, *The Negritude Poets: An Anthology of Translations from the French* (New York: Viking Press, 1975), p. 52.

28 W. E. B. DuBois, *The Souls of Black Folk,* in *Writings* (New York: The Library of America, 1986), pp. 384–85.

29 Jacques Lacan, *The Language of the Self: The Foundation of Language*

in Psychoanalysis, trans. Anthony Wilden (Baltimore: Johns Hopkins Press, 1968).

30 Fanon, "The Negro and Language," pp. 37–38.

31 The title of a slender volume published in June 1932, *Légitime défense,* was an intellectually radical manifesto written by a group of Black students in Paris featuring a notice concerning scholarships and financial aid entitled "Nœud coulant" (Slipknot). See *Légitime défense* (rpt.; Paris: Jean-Michel Place, 1979), p. 15.

32 See Wauthier, p. 145: "Francesco Nditsouna expressed this militant concern in one sentence: 'I am not a poet, I want to be a fighter,' he said at the beginning of his collection, *Fleur de latérite.*"

33 Léon Gontran Damas, *Poètes d'expression française* (Paris: Seuil, 1947), p. 13.

34 Wauthier, p. 145.

35 Fanon, *Wretched of the Earth,* p. 47.

36 Césaire, *Discourse on Colonialism,* p. 23.

37 My analysis converges with that of Frantz Fanon, Julia Kristeva on exile, Homi Bhabha on cultural hybridity, Edward Said on writing and worldliness, Michael Seidel on exile and narrative, Léopold Sédar Senghor on *métissage culturel,* and especially Aimé Césaire in his writings on the nature of language and the act of writing for the linguistically colonized.

38 Léon Laleau, *Musique Nègre* (Editions Parville, 1931).

39 Kennedy, pp. 50–51.

40 Jelloun, "Letter from Europe," *New Yorker,* 22 February 1988, p. 92.

41 Louis Morpeau, *Anthologie d'un siècle de poésie haitienne 1817–1925* (Paris: Editions Bossard, 1924), p. 218.

42 Fanon, "The Negro and Language," pp. 17–18.

43 In *Writing "Race" and the Difference It Makes,* Henry Louis Gates Jr. cites the example of Laforest and the trap of language to which he succumbed (*Critical Inquiry* 12 [autumn 1985]: 13).

44 Césaire, "De Forlonge," in *Corps perdu, Œuvres complètes,* 1:276.

45 Césaire, "Le cristal automatique," in *Les Armes miraculeuses, Œuvres complètes,* 1:110.

46 Césaire, "Entretien avec Aimé Césaire," interview by Jacqueline Sieger, *Afrique* 5 (October 1961): 66.

47 Césaire, interview with author, November 1982.

48 Hector Bianciotti, *Sans la miséricorde du Christ* (Paris: Gallimard, 1985), p. 42.

49 T. S. Eliot, *The Complete Poems and Plays, 1909–1950* (New York: Harcourt Brace Jovanovich, 1930). From "Little Gidding" in *Four Quartets* (ll. 118–20), p. 141.

50 Ibid., *The Waste Land* (ll. 20–24), p. 38.

51 Ibid., *The Waste Land* (ll. 141), p. 50.

52 Césaire, cited by Georges Ngal, in "Le Théâtre d'Aimé Césaire: Une dramaturgie de la décolonisation," *Revue des sciences humaines* 35 (1970): 619.

53 Césaire, *Et les chiens se taisaient,* in *Œuvres complètes,* 2:71.

54 Césaire, "Les pur-sang," in *Les Armes miraculeuses, Œuvres complètes,* 1:90.

55 Césaire, *Et les chiens se taisaient,* in *Œuvres complètes,* 2:60.

56 Césaire, interview by René Depestre, 1967 Cultural Congress of Havana, in *Poesias* (Casa de las Americas, n.d.). Reprinted in Césaire, *Discourse on Colonialism,* p. 66.

57 Suzanne Césaire, "Misère d'une poésie," *Tropiques* 4 (January 1942): 50.

58 Césaire, "L'Homme de culture," p. 117.

59 Césaire, *Notebook,* p. 47.

60 Aimé Césaire, *A Tempest,* trans. Richard Miller (New York: Ubu Repertory Theater Publications, 1992).

61 Marianne Wichmann Bailey, *The Ritual Theater of Aimé Césaire* (Tübingen: G. Narr, 1992), p. 35.

62 Césaire, cited by Rob Nixon, in "Caribbean and African Appropriations of the Tempest," *Critical Inquiry* 13, no. 5 (spring 1987): 557–78.

63 For a mapping of the polemics involved in the discussion of Négritude, see Abiola Irele, "In Praise of Alienation," in V. Y. Mudimbe, *The Surreptitious Speech* (Chicago: University of Chicago Press, 1992), p. 206, nn. 4, 5.

64 Françoise Pfaff, *Conversations with Maryse Condé* (Lincoln: University of Nebraska Press, 1996), p. 114.

65 Césaire, "Et les chiens se taisaient," *Œuvres complètes,* 2: p. 59.

66 Césaire, cited by François Beloux in "Un poète-politique, Aimé Césaire," *Magazine littéraire* 31 (August 1969): 32.

67 Césaire, *Notebook,* pp. 43, 57.

68 Césaire, *Discourse on Colonialism,* p. 68.

69 Césaire, "L'Homme de culture," p. 66.

70 Césaire, *Notebook,* p. 69.

2 *Toward a Sociology of Humor*
Léon Gontran Damas and Body Talk

1 Kennedy, pp. 39–60. Kennedy has translated sixteen Damas poems from the most well-known volume, *Pigments.* Where possible I have used her translations; such translations hereafter will be cited to Kennedy. All other translations of Damas are my own. Kennedy's excellent volume on the Negritude poets is out of print.

2 Fanon, *Wretched of the Earth,* p. 43.

3 Léon Gontran Damas, *Veillées noires* (Paris: Stock, 1943), p. 13.

4 Baudelaire, *Le Peintre de la vie moderne: Le Dandy,* in *Œvres complètes,* pp. 1177–80.

5 Paul Laurence Dunbar, *The Poet,* in *The Collected Poetry* (Charlottesville: University Press of Virginia, 1993), p. 191.

6 Dunbar, *We Wear the Mask,* in *The Collected Poetry,* p. 71.

7 Ludwig Wittgenstein, *Tractatus Logico-Philosophicus* (London: Routledge and Kegan Paul, 1962), fragment 5.6, p. 149.

8 Aimé Césaire, *Une Tempête,* Act 3, sc. 5.

9 Sigmund Freud, *Wit and Its Relation to the Unconscious,* in *The Basic Writings of Sigmund Freud,* ed. A. A. Brill (New York: Random House, 1938), p. 802.

10 Langston Hughes, *The Book of Negro Humor* (New York: Dodd, Mead, 1966), p. vii.

11 Léon Gontran Damas, *Black-Label* (Paris: Gallimard, 1956), pp. 9, 61.

12 Freud, *Wit and Its Relation to the Unconscious,* p. 803.

13 Césaire, "Isidore Ducasse comte de Lautréamont," *Tropiques,* 6–7 (February 1943): 13.

14 Freud, *Wit and Its Relation to the Unconscious,* pp. 720–21.

15 Rimbaud, *Lettre du 13 mai 1871,* in *Œuvres complètes* (Paris: Gallimard, 1972), p. 268.

3 *Counterexertions*

Theorizing the Francophone Condition

1 Fanon, "The Negro and Language," p. 21.

2 On this subject of the racially mixed woman it is interesting to compare two francophone novels: *La Négresse blanche* (1950), by the Martinican female writer Mayotte Capécia, and *Métisse blanche* (1989), by the Vietnamese mixed-blood female writer Kim Lefèvre.

3 For a discussion of Rimbaud's phrase and his use of the "modern," see Henri Meschonnic, *Modernité Modernité, "Il faut être absolument moderne": Un slogan en moins pour la modernité* (Paris: Editions Verdier, 1988), pp. 123–27.

4 Aimé Césaire, "Naissances," in *Œuvres complètes,* 1:283.

5 Aimé Césaire, "Chevelure," in *Œuvres complètes,* 1:232.

6 Aimé Césaire, "Au-delà," in *Œuvres complètes,* 1:102.

7 Aimé Césaire, interview with Keith Walker, Fort-de-France, Martinique, June 1976.

4 *Colonialism, Literary Tradition, and Counterstorytelling*

1 Fanon, *The Wretched of the Earth,* p. 236.

2 For an extended discussion of the etymology of the terms *colonialism, decolonialization,* and *decolonization,* see the following texts, which have provided the historical documentation upon which *Countermodernism and Francophone Literary Culture* is based: Raoul Girardet, *L'idée coloniale en France 1871–1962* (Paris: Editions de la Table Ronde, 1972); Guy Pervillé, *De l'empire français à la Décolonisation.* (Paris: Hachette, 1991); Charles-Robert Ageron, *La Décolonisation française* (Paris: Armand Colin, 1991).

3 Wauthier, p. 131; Pervillé, p. 9.

4 Ageron, p. 133–34.

5 Ibid., p. 136.

6 Ibid., p. 135.

7 Ibid., p. 137.

8 Ibid., p. 147.

9 Léopold Sédar Senghor, "Prière de Paix," in *Hosties noires* (Paris: Seuil, 1948).

10 Wauthier, p. 156.

11 My approach is directly influenced, informed, and shaped by Edward Said's thinking on colonialism as articulated in his lectures on culture and imperialism at Dartmouth College and his instruction in a seminar at the School of Criticism and Theory.

12 Abiola Irele, "In Praise of Alienation," in *The Surreptitious Speech,* ed. V. Y. Mudimbe (Chicago: University of Chicago Press, 1992), pp. 201–224.

13 René Maran, *Batouala: An African Love Story,* trans. Alexandre Mboukou (Maryland: New Perspectives, 1973), p. 12.

14 Jean Vaillant, *Black, French, and African: A Life of Léopold Sédar Senghor* (Cambridge: Harvard University Press, 1990), p. 37.

15 Léopold Sédar Senghor, *Liberté: Négritude et humanisme* (Paris: Le Seuil, 1964), p. 98.

16 Léon-François Hoffmann, *Le Nègre romantique: Personnage littéraire et obsession collective* (Paris: Payot, 1973). The translation of these documents is my own.

17 Gobineau, *Essai sur l'inégalité des races humaines,* pp. 205–6. Also cited in Hoffmann, *Le Nègre romantique,* p. 184.

18 Hortense J. Spillers, "Mamma's Baby, Papa's Maybe: An American Grammar Book," *Diacritics* (summer 1987): 68–69.

19 Spillers, pp. xx.

20 Edouard Corbière, *Précis sur la traite des nègres,* cited in Hoffmann, *Le Nègre romantique,* p. 189.

21 Cited by the chancellor E. D. Pasquier in his *Histoire de mon temps,* vol. 6 (n.p., 1895), p. 42. Also cited by Hoffmann, *Le Nègre romantique,* p. 161.
22 Césaire, *Notebook,* p. 47.
23 M. L. E. Moreau de Saint-Méry, *Description . . . de la partie française de l'isle Saint-Dominigue* (n.p., 1797; reprint, 1958), p. 59. Also cited in Hoffmann, *Le Nègre romantique,* p. 191.
24 G. d'Eichtal and I. Urbain, *Lettres sur la race noire et la race blanche* (Paulin, 1839), pp. 22–23. Also cited in Hoffmann, *Le Nègre romantique,* pp. 203–4.
25 The functioning of this "contrasexuality" in a francophone novel is the focus of my analysis of Tahar ben Jelloun's *Sand Child* in chapter 6.
26 Aimé Césaire, *La tragédie du Roi Christophe,* in *Œuvres complètes* 2, Act II, sc. 2, pp. 154–55.
27 Interview of South African leader F. W. de Klerk by Ted Koppel, February 14, 1991, which also included this interview.
28 See Edward Said, *Culture and Imperialism* (New York: Random House, 1993).
29 Fanon, The *Wretched of the Earth,* pp. 38–41.
30 Maran, *Batouala: An African Love Story,* p. 11.
31 Césaire, *Discourse on Colonialism,* pp. 19–20.
32 Césaire, *La Tragédie du roi Christophe.*
33 Mariana Bâ, *So Long a Letter,* trans. Modupé Bodé-Thomas (Portsmouth, N.H.: Heinemann, 1989), p. 32 (emphasis added).
34 See "Legal Storytelling" (symposium), *Michigan Law Review,* vol. 87 (1989), 2073.

5 *Postscripts*
Mariama Bâ, Menopause, Epistolarity, and Postcolonialism

1 Mariama Bâ, *Une si longue lettre* (Dakar: Les Nouvelles Editions Africaines, 1980), p. 40.
2 Mariama Bâ, *So Long a Letter,* trans. Modupé Bodé-Thomas (Portsmouth, N.H.: Heinemann, 1989), p. 25.
3 Fanon, *The Wretched of the Earth,* p. 46.
4 Julia Kristeva, "A New Type of Intellectual: The Dissident," in *The Kristeva Reader,* ed. Toril Moi (Oxford: Blackwell, 1986), p. 298.
5 Emily Martin, *The Woman in the Body: A Cultural Analysis of Reproduction* (Boston: Beacon Press, 1987). While this is not the place for a clinical discussion of menopause, I feel it proper to present data that support my descriptions of the menopausal woman. Among the many possible sources, I find this text to be the most direct and comprehensive.
6 Martin, *Woman in the Body,* p. 42.

7 Ibid., p. 43.
8 Ibid., p. 51.
9 Fanon, *The Wretched of the Earth,* p. 43.
10 Ibid., p. 97.
11 The dangerous "follies" of independence are reinforced in *So Long a Letter* through a secondary character, Jacqueline, an Ivorian who, against the wishes of her Protestant parents, married a Senegalese and returned with him to Senegal, where she faces ostracism in a largely Catholic and Muslim society. The rejection pushes her into depression and brings on psychosomatic disorders, fears of insanity, and thoughts of suicide (pp. 41–45). Her case also addresses the demassification of difference among Africans spoken of earlier. The text addresses it directly: coming to Senegal, she found herself in a new world, a world with different reactions, temperament, and mentality from those in which she had grown up. In addition, her husband's relatives—always the relatives—were cool toward her because she refused to adopt the Muslim religion and went instead to the Protestant church every Sunday.

A Black African, she would have been able to fit without difficulty into a Black African society, Senegal and the Ivory Coast both having experienced the same colonial power. But Africa is diverse and divided. The same country can change its character and outlook several times over from north to south or from east to west (p. 42).

12 Edward Said, *The World, the Text and the Critic* (Cambridge: Harvard University Press, 1983), p. 39.
13 See Alice Walker, *The Color Purple* (New York: Harcourt Brace Javanovich, 1982).
14 The term *polygamy* is traditionally applied to tribal societies, but in my view the issue of polygamy is of great pertinence in urban and rural America, where men have multiple relationships and father children with many partners.
15 Jacques Derrida, *La Carte Postale* (Paris: Flammarion, 1980).
16 Carol Gilligan, "Concepts of Self and Morality," in *In a Different Voice* (Cambridge: Harvard University Press, 1982), p. 74.
17 With regard to traditional Muslim societies, see Tahar ben Jelloun, *La plus haute des solitudes: Misère sexuelle et affective des émigrés nord-africains* (Paris: Editions du Seuil, 1977).
18 Gilligan, *In a Different Voice,* pp. 24–63.
19 See Julia Kristeva, *Powers of Horror: An Essay on Abjection* (New York: Columbia University Press, 1982).
20 Gilligan, *In a Different Voice.* Her chapter "Visions of Maturity" (pp. 151–74), in particular, addresses the issues in Bâ's text.
21 See Michael Riffaterre, *Text Production* (New York: Columbia University Press, 1983), p. 12.

22 See Jonathan Culler, *On Deconstruction* (Ithaca, N.Y.: Cornell University Press, 1982), p. 141.
23 See Gilligan, *In a Different Voice,* pp. 16–17.
24 Marcel Griaule, *Conversations with Ogotemmeli: An Introduction to Dogon Religious Ideas* (London: Published for the African Institute by the Oxford University Press, 1965), p. 642.

6 *Moroccan Independence*
Status Inconsistency, Role Conflict, and Consciousness in Tahar ben Jelloun's *The Sand Child*

1 Tahar ben Jelloun, *L'Enfant de sable* (Paris: Editions du Seuil, 1985), pp. 30–31. The page numbers cited in the text are from this edition.
2 Tahar ben Jelloun, *The Sand Child,* trans. Alan Sheridan (New York: Ballantine Books, Harcourt Brace Jovanovich, 1987). The page numbers cited in the text are from this edition.
3 See M. E. Combs-Schilling, *Sacred Performances: Islam, Sexuality, and Sacrifice* (New York: Columbia University Press, 1989).
4 Ibid., p. 290.
5 Ibid., pp. 275–76.
6 Ibid., p. 300.
7 Ibid., pp. 242, 243, 241.
8 Ibid., pp. 300, 304.
9 For an excellent study of narrative in *The Sand Child* that complements my reading, see John D. Erickson, "Veiled Woman and Veiled Narrative," *Boundary 2* 20, no. 1 (spring 1993): 47–64.
10 For a discussion of "latency" of signification, see Riffaterre, *Text Production,* p. 12; and for a discussion of a text's "worldliness," see Said, *The World.*
11 André Breton, "Notes sur la Poésie," in *La Révolution Surréaliste,* No. 12, 15 December 1929.
12 See Edward Said, *Orientalism* (New York: Vintage Books, 1979), p. 190.
13 Jelloun, *La plus haute des solitudes,* p. 57.
14 Said, *Orientalism,* p. 25.
15 Jelloun, *La plus haute des solitudes.*

7 *The Blossoming of the Undefined Self*
Ken Bugul and *Le Baobab fou*

1 Ken Bugul, *Le Baobab fou* (Dakar: Les Nouvelles Éditions Africaines, 1984). The page numbers in the text for the French quotations refer

to this edition. Ken Bugul, *The Abandoned Baobab*, trans. Marjolijn de Jager (Chicago: Lawrence Hill Books, 1991). The page numbers cited for the English text are from this edition.

2 See Irele, "In Praise of Alienation," pp. 201–24. While Irele does speak of "the pathology of alienation" (pp. 202 and 203), he presents a heroic cultural analysis of alienation. In Irele's terms Ken could be described as "the archetype of the divided consciousness, of the African who suffers in his mind the effects of cultural dispossession . . . marked by a cleavage rather than an integration of its two frames of reference" (p. 203). This essay has preoccupied and indeed inspired me as I meditated upon the protagonist Ken Bugul and the notion of cultural schizophrenia. In particular, the following insights by Irele on alienation are useful in understanding Ken Bugul's condition:

> . . . the notion of alienation as the principle of all becoming or, more simply, as the moving power of the historical process. In cultural terms, it implies a willed movement out of the self and a purposive quest for new horizons of life and of experience. (P. 215)
>
> We need a new determination, a new spirit of adventure fired by a modern imagination: a new state of mind that will enable us to come to terms with our state of alienation and to transform it from a passive condition we confusedly endure into an active collective existential project. We need to take charge of our objective alienation by assuming it as an intention so as to endow it with a positive significance. (P. 214)
>
> Our historical alienation in the light of these observations: the striking thing about our present situation is the discrepancy between the idea of tradition still current among us and the emerging structure of reality in which the fortunes of our cultural and moral values are now engaged. (Pp. 209–10)
>
> Strangers in our own world. It is an illusion to imagine that the problem of alienation concerns only intellectuals and the Westernized elite; it is, in fact, a global phenomenon, affecting every single individual—in varying degrees it is true, depending upon the particular circumstance of each, but every individual nonetheless. (P. 207)

3 Césaire, "L'homme de culture," p. 117.

4 Fanon, *Wretched of the Earth*, pp. 54, 77.

5 National Institute of Mental Health, *A National Plan for Schizophrenia Research: Panel Recommendations* (Rockville, Md.: National Institute of Mental Health, 1989), p. 7.

6 Ibid.

7 National Institute of Mental Health, *Schizophrenia: Is There an Answer?* (Rockville, Md.: National Institute of Mental Health, Center for Studies of Schizophrenia, 1981), p. 6.

8 National Institute of Mental Health, *A National Plan,* p. 82.
9 See Wynter, "1492: A New World View," p. 45.
10 National Institute of Mental Health, *Schizophrenia: Is There an Answer?* p. 8.
11 Ibid., p. 9.
12 National Institute of Mental Health, *A National Plan,* p. 7.
13 Ibid., p. 84.
14 Wynter, "1492: A New World View," p. 45.
15 Ibid., p. 47.
16 Bianciotti, *Sans la miséricorde,* p. 42.
17 Michel Serres, *Le Tiers-Instruit* (Paris: François Bourin, 1991), p. 28.

8 *Words Proffered in Pain*

Gérard Etienne, Shame, and the Counterconfession

1 Frederick Douglass, *Frederick Douglass: The Narrative and Selected Writings* ed. by Michael Meyer (New York: Modern Library, 1984), p. 158; emphasis added.
2 Ibid., p. 265.
3 Gérard Etienne, *Le Nègre crucifié, récit* (Montréal: Editions francophones du Canada, 1974). This book will be cited as *Nègre* in the text. All page numbers cited will refer to this edition. Translations are my own.
4 Gérard Etienne, *La Pacotille* (Montreal: L'Hexagone, 1991). All page numbers cited will refer to this edition. Translations are my own.
5 My understanding of torture and the way it functions under repressive regimes is derived primarily from the works of Gérard Etienne. I have found further confirmation in Frantz Fanon, in *The Wretched of the Earth,* pp. 280–89; in "Colonial Wars and Mental Disorders: Series C, Affective Intellectual Modifications and Mental Disorders after Torture," Gilles Deleuze, *Présentation de Sacher-Masoch: Le froid et le cruel* (*Masochism: An Interpretation of Coldness and Cruelty*) (New York: G. Braziller, 1971); in Elaine Scarry, *The Body in Pain: The Making and Unmaking of the World* (New York: Oxford University Press, 1985).
6 Aimé Césaire, *Discourse on Colonialism,* trans. Joan Pinkham (New York: Monthly Press Review, 1972), p. 53. All further page number references to this text will be cited parenthetically after quoted material.
7 Gérard Etienne, *Cri pour ne pas crever de honte* (Montreal: Poésie/Nouvelle Optique, 1982), hereafter referred to as *Cri.*
8 See Henry Campbell Black, *Black's Law Dictionary: Definitions of the Terms and Phrases of American and English Jurisprudence, Ancient and*

Modern, 6th ed. (St. Paul, Minn.: West Publishing Co., 1990). Testament: p. 1027; parole: p. 771.

9 Joseph L. White, *The Psychology of Blacks: An Afro-American Perspective* (Englewood Cliffs, N.J.: Prentice Hall, 1984), p. 189.

10 It would be interesting to trace the fate of this word in Afro-American literary culture, but two examples will suffice. First, one learns in "The fact of Being Black in the Americas" by James W. Ivy (*Présence africaine* 24–25 [1959]) that in the Americas *la pacotille* as a term can have a racial meaning as well as an existential dimension concerning precisely the question of identity and, in effect, the fact of being Black:

> Le célèbre écrivain abolitionniste brésilien Luiz Gama, un *mulâtre* lui-même, joue habilement sur cette croyance dans ses vers satiriques où il attaque les sang-mêlés qui renient leurs origines nègres. Dans un sonnet qui ridiculise les prétentions aristocratiques d'un mulâtre clair, Gama dit que ce dernier ne peut nier ses origines à cause de son "horrible puanteur"—*une vile odeur nauséabonde.* Dans un autre poème, *Pacotilha* (pacotille), Gama montre à un autre mulâtre clair qu'il n'est ni blanc ni noble, en dépit de son cou semblable à celui d'un chien à pedigree, car il ne peut pas "se débarrasser de son odeur"—*nao perde a catinga.* Le plus célèbre poème de Gama, qui fut d'abord intitulé *Quem Sou Eu?* ("Qui suis-je?") fut bientôt communément appelé *Bodarrada,* foule de métis, en raison de la critique mordante qu'il contient à l'adresse des mulâtres de teint clair qui cherchent hypocritement à prouver qu'ils sont blancs.

> [The famous Brazilian abolitionist writer Luiz Gama, a mulatto himself, in his satirical verses attacks mixed bloods who deny their Black origins. In a sonnet which mocks the aristocratic pretensions of a fair-skinned mulatto, Gama says that the latter cannot deny his origins because of his "horrible smell"—a vile and nauseating odor. In another poem, "Pacotilha" (*pacotille*), Gama shows another fair-skinned mulatto that he is neither white nor noble in spite of his neck, which is similar to that of a pedigree dog, for he cannot "rid himself of his smell"—*nao perde a catinga.* The most famous poem by Gama, which was first entitled *Quem Sou Eu* (Who Am I?), was commonly called *Bodarrada,* a crowd of mulattoes, because of the biting criticism it contained concerning fair-skinned mulattoes who hypocritically sought to prove that they were white.]

11 Antonio Gramsci, *Prison Notebooks* (London: Lawrence and Wishart, 1971), p. lxxxix.

12 Todorov Ducrot, *Le Dictionnaire encyclopédique des sciences du langage* (Paris: Éditions du Seuil, 1972). See "récit" in Michel Arrivé, Françoise

Gadet, and Michel Glamiche, *La grammaire d'aujourd'hui.* (Paris: Librairie Flammarion, 1986).

13 Michael Riffaterre, *La production du texte* (Paris: Éditions du Seuil, 1979), pp. 236–48.

14 See Julia Kristeva, *Étrangers à nous-mêmes* (Paris: Fayard, 1988); and Gérard Miller, *Lacan* (Paris: Bordas, 1987), chap. 2, "Cet autre auquel je suis plus attaché qu'à moi."

15 Eileen Julien, *African Novels,* p. 10.

16 Claude Roy, cover notes for Gérard Etienne, *Le Nègre crucifié, récit* (Montreal: Nouvelle Optique 1974).

17 Léon-François Hoffman, *Le Roman Haïtien: Idéologie et Structure* (Sherbrooke, Quebec: Editions Namaan, 1982).

18 On exile see Isabelle Cielens, *Trois fonctions de l'exil dans les œuvres de fiction d'Albert Camus: Initiation, révolte, conflit d'idenité* (Stockholm: Almqvist and Wiksell International, 1985). See also Michael Seidel, *Exile and the Narrative Imagination* (New Haven, Conn.: Yale University Press, 1986).

19 See Jean-Paul Sartre, *Being and Nothingness: An Essay on Phenomenological Ontology,* trans. Hazel Barnes (New York: Philosophical Library, 1956).

> By the mere appearance of the Other, I am in the position of passing judgment on myself as on an object for it is as an object that I appear to the Other. Yet the object which has appeared to the Other is not an empty image in the mind of another. Such an image, in fact, would be imputable wholly to the Other and so could not "touch" me. I could feel irritation or anger before it as before a bad portrait of myself which gives to my expression an ugliness or baseness which I do not have, but I could not be touched to the quick. Shame is by nature *recognition.* I recognize that *I am* as the Other sees me. (P. 222) Now, shame . . . is shame of *self;* it is the *recognition* of the fact that I am indeed that object which the Other is looking at and judging. I can be ashamed only as my freedom escapes me in order to become a given object. (Sartre, *Being and Nothingess,* p. 260)

20 Gérard Etienne, *Dialogue avec mon ombre* (Montreal: Editions francophones du Canada, 1972), p. 122.

21 Quoted in Jean Jonassaint, ed., *Le Pouvoir des mots, les maux du pouvoir* (Montreal: Les Presses de l'Université de Montréal, 1986), p. 70.

22 See Gérard Etienne, "La Femme noire dans le discours littéraire haïtien, *Présence francophone* 18 (spring 1979): 109–26.

23 Gérard Etienne, *Gladys* (Port-au-Prince: Editions Panorama, 1963).

24 Gaston Bachelard, *L'Air et les Songes, Essai sur l'imagination du mouvement* (Paris: José Corti, 1965), p. 64.

25 Gaston Bachelard, *La Poétique de la rêverie* (Paris: PUF, 1965), p. 69.

26 Gérard Etienne, *La Question raciale et raciste dans le Roman québecois* (Paris-Montreal: Balzac-Le Griot, 1995).

27 Gérard Etienne, *L'Injustice! Désinformation et mépris de la loi* (Quebec: Humanitas Circonstances, 1998).

28 Gérard Etienne, *La femme noire dans le discours littéraire haïtien* (Paris-Montreal: Balzac-Le Griot, 1998).

Conclusion

1 See Michael Leiris, "Perséphone," in *La Règle du jeu I: Biffures* (Paris: NRF Gallimard, 1948), pp. 72–127.

2 Césaire, "Chevelure," in *Œuvres complètes,* 1:232.

3 Césaire, "Les Pur-sang," in *Œuvres complètes,* 1:85.

4 Césaire, "Revue culturelle, Introduction, Poètes Nègres Américains," *Tropiques* 2 (July 1941): p. 37.

5 Anne Hébert, *Le Torrent: Nouvelles* (Paris: Editions du Seuil, 1963), 26–27, 28.

6 For a discussion comparing current standards of living in independent French West Africa with those of Martinique, a French department where Césaire has been mayor of Fort-de-France since the late forties, see Lilyan Kesteloot, "En suivant un roi dans son île," *Présence africaine* 151–52 (1995): 17.

7 Césaire, "Présentation," *Tropiques* 1 (April 1941): p. 5.

8 Cited in *Aimé Césaire: Une voix pour l'histoire,* prod. and dir. Euzhan Palcy, California Newsreel, 1994, videocassette.

9 Aimé Césaire, *Une Saison au Congo* (Paris: Editions du Seuil, 1967); translation by Ralph Manheim, *A Season in the Congo* (New York: Grove Press, 1969).

10 Achille Mbembe, "Écrire l'Afrique à partir d'une faille," *Politique Africaine* 51 (October 1993): 86–87.

11 Césaire, "L'Homme de culture et ses responsabilités," p. 119.

12 Césaire, "L'Homme de culture," p. 118.

13 Aimé Césaire, "Culture et Colonisation," *Œuvres complètes* 3:435.

14 "Interview with Aimé Césaire," Charles Rowell, *Callaloo* 12, no. 1 (winter 1989): 55.

15 See Césaire, *Une voix pour l'histoire.*

16 Ibid.

Index

Keith L. Walker is Associate Professor of French and Italian, and Chair of African and African American Studies at Dartmouth College.

Library of Congress Cataloging-in-Publication Data

Walker, Keith.

Countermodernism and francophone literary culture: the game of slipknot / Keith L. Walker.

p. cm.

Includes index.

ISBN 0-8223-2110-6 (cloth : alk. paper). —

ISBN 0-8223-2143-2 (pkb. : alk. paper)

1. French literature—French-speaking countries—History and criticism. 2. Modernism (Literature) 3. Blacks in literature. I. Title.

PQ3897.W35 1999

840.9'112—dc21 98-49702